BROOKLYN ODYSSEY

SASHA NIZGODA

The author and his family celebrate Liba's bat mitzvah in 2023.

FROM LEFT TO RIGHT: *Zalman Newfield, Maya, Liba, Jenny Labendz.*

BROOKLYN ODYSSEY

My Journey out of Hasidism

ZALMAN NEWFIELD

TEMPLE UNIVERSITY PRESS *Philadelphia Rome Tokyo*

TEMPLE UNIVERSITY PRESS
Philadelphia, Pennsylvania 19122
tupress.temple.edu

Published 2026

Library of Congress Cataloging-in-Publication Data

Names: Newfield, Zalman, 1982– author
Title: Brooklyn odyssey : my journey out of Hasidism / Zalman Newfield.
Description: Philadelphia : Temple University Press, 2026. | Includes bibliographical references. | Summary: "This memoir tells of the author's coming of age and disaffection with the demands of the Lubavitch Hasidic Jewish community in which he is raised. He describes the values and self-denial he experiences in his yeshiva education and the secular books and diverse perspectives he encounters that expand his thinking"— Provided by publisher.
Identifiers: LCCN 2025045513 (print) | LCCN 2025045514 (ebook) | ISBN 9781439927618 paperback | ISBN 9781439927625 pdf
Subjects: LCSH: Newfield, Zalman, 1982– | Ex-Orthodox Jews—New York (State)—New York—Biography | Jews—New York (State)—New York—Biography | Habad—New York (State)—New York—Biography | Crown Heights (New York, N.Y.)—Biography | LCGFT: Autobiographies
Classification: LCC F128.9.J5 N48 2026 (print) | LCC F128.9.J5 (ebook) | DDC 305.892/40747092 [B]—dc23/eng/20251114
LC record available at https://lccn.loc.gov/2025045513
LC ebook record available at https://lccn.loc.gov/2025045514

The manufacturer's authorized representative in the EU for product safety is Temple University Rome, Via di San Sebastianello, 16, 00187 Rome RM, Italy (https://rome.temple.edu/).
tempress@temple.edu

♾ The paper used in this publication meets the requirements of the American National Standard for Information Sciences—Permanence of Paper for Printed Library Materials, ANSI Z39.48-1992

Printed in the United States of America

9 8 7 6 5 4 3 2 1

To all the brave souls

who dare to be different

Contents

Author's Note

Every episode in this book actually happened to me. I took great pains to confirm even minor details in this work. To assist me in reconstructing the past, I consulted history books, personal notebooks, school report cards, old pictures, home movies, emails, and the recollections of friends and family. The dialogue in this book is not a transcript of conversations but my honest attempt to re-create what people said based on my memory of them and their personality. When possible, I have shared passages with their subjects and adjusted my text in response to their recollections and feelings. Besides occasionally contracting the time span of events to maintain the narrative flow, the only intentional alterations are the names and other minor narrative details I changed to protect the privacy of others. I do not intend to hurt or offend anyone and sincerely apologize if I have.

BROOKLYN ODYSSEY

—∿∿—

Introduction

The First Generation of the Redemption

I was ready that night to usher in the redemption. I was eleven. I understood full well why thousands of us had gathered at 770 Eastern Parkway in the Crown Heights section of Brooklyn, the central synagogue of Lubavitch Jews around the world. The Gothic Revival red brick building was known to Lubavitchers the world over simply as "770," and they imbued it with mystical symbolism.

That night, our spiritual leader, "the Rebbe," Rabbi Menachem Mendel Schneerson, was finally going to publicly and unequivocally declare that he was indeed the righteous messiah of the Jewish people—the Redeemer whom the biblical prophets had promised to the Israelites; the one whom the devout had prayed for during the Crusades and the Inquisition; the one whom the Jews in the concentration camps had cried out for on their way to the gas chambers.

It was January 31, 1993, the forty-third anniversary (according to the Hebrew calendar) of the Rebbe's assuming leadership of the Chabad Lubavitch community. Everyone in the massive hall was pushing and shoving to see the wood-paneled balcony overlooking the sanctuary where the Rebbe was expected to appear. I stood precariously on a crude metal-and-wood bench amid a sea of thousands of eager Lubavitchers. Their pressure crushed me from all sides.

The men and boys who occupied the main sanctuary wore large black velvet yarmulkes (skullcaps), white dress shirts, and dark pants.

Those above the age of thirteen also wore black fedoras and dark sports jackets, and the married men wore long black silk coats called *kapotas*. As was customary, the men never shaved or trimmed their beards. The girls and women—crowded together on the upper level and peering down into the main sanctuary through dark one-way glass partitions—were modestly dressed, wearing long-sleeved outfits with hemlines covering their knees. The married women wore stylish wigs entirely covering their natural hair. Despite being midwinter, it was hot, very hot, inside.

The swirling overhead fans did nothing to alleviate the stuffiness. Beads of perspiration dripped down my face. Even though I was perched on a bench, I still had to stand on my tiptoes to get a better look. Fortunately, the middle-aged stranger in front of me was so preoccupied by the tumult that he seemed unaware of my gripping his moist shoulders to steady myself.

The crowd repeatedly sang the most popular song in Lubavitch those days, the Hebrew *Yechi* mantra: "Yechi adoneinu moreinu v'rabeinu melech ha'Moshiach l'oylum vo'ed" (Long live our Master, our Teacher, our Rebbe, King Messiah, forever and ever). I had been taught for as long as I could remember—by teachers, camp counselors, and my parents—that our Rebbe was the Moshiach (the messiah). Along with the rest of the community, I believed it with complete faith. I was not deterred in this belief despite the fact that slightly less than a year prior to this gathering, the Rebbe, at ninety, had suffered a severe stroke. From then on, he was unable to speak or move his right side. Although outsiders speculated that the Rebbe would inevitably soon pass away, I knew such talk was ridiculous. The Rebbe would never die. I knew in my heart that any day now the Rebbe would rise up from his sickbed fully healed and poised to lead the Jewish people out of exile and into the era of the redemption.

The Rebbe was born in 1902 in Nikolaev, in the Russian Empire (now Mykolaiv, in Ukraine), to a prominent kabbalist father, Rabbi Levi Yitzchak, and devoted mother, Chana. He spent the 1930s in Berlin and Paris pursuing an engineering education and escaped Nazi-occupied France with his wife and came to America in 1940. Years later he moved into a large private house at 1304 President Street, in Crown Heights. But I no more thought of the Rebbe as "from" Nikolaev as I thought of him as from Paris, Berlin, or President Street. He may have resided in those places, but as far as I was concerned, he was from planet Atzilus, the supernal mystical realm explored in the Zohar. To me, the Rebbe was infallible. Every word he uttered was true, and everything he did was perfect—by definition.

It was established fact, accepted without question by Lubavitchers, that the Rebbe performed miracles. He blessed barren women to have children; he foretold the future; he healed the sick. In fact, my mother told me that I myself was a "miracle baby." A week past my due date, in January 1982, I was delivered by emergency caesarian section. This was necessary due to the prolapse of the umbilical cord. "You survived because the Rebbe gave you a *brachah* [blessing]." I believed her. I owed my life to the Rebbe.

The men and boys standing on my bench and on the other benches throughout the sanctuary began jumping up and down and clapping their hands while chanting *Yechi*. It was as if the thousands of souls in the packed sanctuary had fused into a single organism that was surging up and down with each repetition of the mantra. I also jumped and chanted. The bench, whose metal frame was custom-welded for this sanctuary, began to buckle under the weight of the crowd. I was terrified. I recalled that three months earlier, my classmate Levi Farkash had been injured when a bench like this collapsed and dropped the men standing on it right onto little Levi, who required surgery on his injured leg and a stay in the hospital.

I had seen the Rebbe several times since his stroke, always on the balcony for precious, fleeting moments. Seated in a wheelchair, he still had the penetrating deep blue eyes and distinguished white beard, but his expression was strangely blank. Gone was the vibrant magnetic charisma that could energize his followers to stand for hours attuned to his every word.

I knew he could no longer lift his arms to inspire the crowd to jump and sing and clap with abandon. The man I saw those few times since his stroke had little in common with the Rebbe I remembered. In four decades of leadership, he had taken the remnants of a Hasidic sect founded in the late eighteenth century by Rabbi Schneur Zalman, which for more than a century was based in the town of Lyubavichi, Russia, and revived it in America. Where, I wanted to know, was the Rebbe who had inspired his followers to travel the world erecting thousands of Jewish outposts, called "Chabad Houses," from Brooklyn to Melbourne, from London to Hong Kong, and from Buenos Aires to Cape Town?

The "Rebbe beepers," small black devices that were modified by a local store to alert Lubavitchers any time the Rebbe was about to make a public appearance, had started sounding their alarm hours earlier. No one in my family owned a Rebbe beeper, but we didn't need one to alert us to tonight's gathering. It was announced days in advance that the Rebbe would be making a special appearance in honor of the anniversary of the day he accepted the leadership of Lubavitch forty-three years earlier. Now everyone waited impatiently for the Rebbe to appear.

I was taught that when the messiah arrived, there would be a great banquet where we would feast on the *levyasan* (the Leviathan, a massive sea creature), along with *shor habor* (an enormous wild bull). I could almost taste these delicacies in my mouth. The Rebbe assured us that we had already finished *putsin der kneplach*, polishing the buttons on our uniforms to greet Moshiach. We could already hear *ickvisa d'mishicha*, the footsteps of the messiah.

For years the Rebbe dropped public hints about the identity of the messiah, but they were ambiguous and open to conflicting interpretations. Possibly the most explicit such hint was given in August 1989 in a talk in which he referenced a passage from the Talmud (Sanhedrin 98b) where one sage claims that the messiah's name will be "Menachem," which was the Rebbe's own first name. The Rebbe declared, "We have Menachem, which refers to the righteous messiah." Those straining to absorb the Rebbe's every word were left to wonder: Was the Rebbe referring to himself, or was he merely restating the line from the Talmud? The Rebbe's wording was maddeningly vague. Most Lubavitchers interpreted this and similar hints to mean that the Rebbe was saying that he himself was the messiah.

Although Lubavitchers spoke a great deal about the coming of the messianic age and about the fact that the Rebbe was the messiah, they said much less about the nature of the end time itself. I was taught, however, based on ancient Jewish sources, that once the redemption began, all Jews and all synagogues from around the globe would be miraculously lifted up on glorious clouds and transported to the Land of Israel; that the streets would be paved with diamonds and precious jewels; that the gentiles would become our servants; and that all the Jews who had died throughout history would be resurrected and reunited with their families. I also learned that the Third Temple would descend from Heaven and the ancient rituals of animal sacrifices described in the Bible would be reinstated.

Lubavitchers had taken some concrete steps to prepare for the messiah's arrival. Inspired by the example of the ancient Israelite women who gladly parted with their gold jewelry (Exodus 35:22) to help build the Tabernacle in the desert, my mother, along with other Lubavitch women, donated gold necklaces, bracelets, and pendants to be melted down and refashioned into vessels for use in the Third Temple. After all, new holy vessels would soon be needed.

Finally, after standing for what felt like hours, the gold curtains parted to reveal the Rebbe. I expected the Rebbe to spring up from his wheelchair, raise both fists in the air and thunder in a booming voice of a man half his age that he was our righteous Redeemer. Instead of rising up, he sat, hunched over, sunken into himself. He sat there, mute and motionless, surrounded by several aides. To me he seemed crushed by the weight of the Jewish exile from Zion, as well as the numerous personal tragedies he had endured, the latest one being the passing in 1988 of his beloved wife, Chaya Mushka, possibly the only other human being who truly understood him as a person. Undeterred, we continued chanting *Yechi* with ever more enthusiasm and determination, as if the strength of our singing could tip God's hand and force the redemption. The Rebbe remained on the balcony for eight excruciating minutes. Then the curtains swung shut again. That was it.

What on earth is going on? Why didn't the Rebbe reveal himself to us? Were we not worthy of the messianic redemption yet? Is the Rebbe not the Moshiach?

Standing in 770 waiting for the Rebbe to reveal himself, we were like the ancient Israelites standing at the foot of Mount Sinai, united, one person with one heart. It was a unity given urgency by the promise of the coming redemption. But it was also an urgency animated by all we stood to lose if we should doubt. I heard how neighbors spoke about Shimon Margolis, the son of a prominent Lubavitch rabbi, who cut off his beard, grew long hair, and went to college. "He's a *frayak*! A bum!" They spoke with dripping disdain, as if he were a leper, diseased and contagious. Every time I heard this type of gossip, a cold shiver went through me. *If I mess up, if I stop being as Lubavitch as my friends, they will cut me off and spit me out. I would lose everything: my family, my certainty, my place in the world, my redemption.*

I

In the Tent of Torah

I was terrified of not knowing the words. "*Bireishis—in der unhoyb* . . ." My second-grade classmates and I repeated the words that our teacher, Rabbi Piekarski, chanted. Rabbi Piekarski was a tall man with an inordinately long beard, which made him appear even taller. When he spoke, I could smell on his breath the pickled herring he had eaten for lunch.

For as long as I could remember, I was taught that every word in the Bible was literally true: that God created the universe in six days, that Adam walked the earth for nine hundred and thirty years, and that Jonah really lived in the belly of a whale for three days and nights. On that cool September day, my class was just starting the adventure of learning to read the Torah verses ourselves. We were beginning in the beginning with the first lines of Genesis, translating each Hebrew word into Yiddish. My knowledge of both languages was shaky.

Rabbi Piekarski's voice boomed. "Remember, *kinderlach* [children], I'm walking around the room to make sure your fingers are on the line in *Chumash* [Torah] that we're reading."

I sat in my chair pressing my finger into the words, my green eyes staring at the page, hoping my teacher wouldn't check up on me. My short brown hair, a number 3 on the barber's electric clipper, Lubavitch-style, held my black velvet yarmulke properly in place, but my usual smile was absent. My ears, which were too big for my head (my older sister Miriam's friends called me "monkey," which mortified me) felt red-hot as I concentrated on the day's recitation.

I was terrified of not knowing the answers when Rabbi Stein, our principal, tested us a few weeks later. He must have weighed four hundred pounds and would get angry if students didn't know their studies. Once, when a classmate had the effrontery to tell him that he "forgot" the answer, the good Rabbi fumed.

"Did you forget to put your pants on this morning? No. So how did you forget the answer?"

That day in Rabbi Piekarski's class, I was also busy thinking about what time my mother would return from grocery shopping in Borough Park. I wanted her to be home when I got there. That way I could see if she bought us doughnuts from The Doughnut Man, vanilla-glazed with chocolate drizzle on top.

I mostly earned As and Bs on my report cards, but I wasn't the type of student for whom learning came naturally. I needed to work hard with tutors after school for hours to keep up with my class. Years later my *yeshiva* (Jewish school) teachers would comment in report cards:

"Nothing stands in the way of the will."

"Zalman has a strong will to be a good student."

"Zalman is making progress and as it says, 'If you work hard you will succeed.' He should go from strength to strength."

My effort evidently stood out over my adeptness at study—an effort fueled by a fear of being found without the answers.

My class continued chanting: "Bara eloykim—hut gut bashafyn."

At home and among friends we spoke Yinglish, a Hasidic patois consisting mostly of English with choice words and phrases from Yiddish, Hebrew, and Aramaic thrown in, like a cholent that is mostly beans and potatoes with a few cubes of beef added for flavor. The language of instruction in my school, Oholei Torah (the Tents of Torah), was Yiddish, and the curriculum included only religious subjects: Bible, Talmud, Hasidic philosophy. No English, mathematics, or social studies.

The ponderous building that housed Oholei Torah at 667 Eastern Parkway was adorned with enormous stained-glass windows and a stained-glass dome and included an ornate social hall and a brownish marble staircase, all vestiges of its glorious past when it housed the Brooklyn Jewish Center. The center was a legendary progressive American Jewish cultural institution from its opening in 1920 until its decline in the 1960s. Albert Einstein had spoken there; Mark Rothko had taught art classes there; Richard Tucker had sung there; and Columbia University had even offered extension courses there. In the 1970s, as it experienced a decline due to white flight, the center rented space to Lubavitch to run their school, and in 1985 the center sold the building to Lubavitch.

Now, five years later, the school taught us to read Hebrew, Yiddish, and Aramaic, but not a minute of the day was devoted to the English alphabet or grammar. The Lubavitchers tried to construct a wall of virtue around the Jewish section of Crown Heights, demarcated by Eastern Parkway in the north, Lefferts Avenue in the south, Utica Avenue in the east, and Nostrand Avenue in the west. In those days, only a handful of Lubavitchers in Crown Heights lived beyond these boundaries. Lubavitchers created a pure space dedicated to keeping out the pernicious influences of the "goyish," or non-Jewish, world.

There were no American flags in my school, and no one pledged allegiance to America each morning. To do so would be totally *treif* (unkosher) and *meshugah* (crazy). Instead, each morning during prayers we proclaimed, "It is our obligation to praise the Master of everything for not making us like the other nations of the world, for they bow down before vanity and nothingness, but we give thanks to the King of kings, the Holy One, blessed be He." I never gave this prayer a second thought. Just as I never questioned the propriety of the morning prayer thanking God for not making me a woman. These are just some of the prayers we recite each morning to get the day off to a good start.

With the school day over, I slung my backpack holding my precious Trapper Keeper binder over my shoulder and skipped along Eastern Parkway's wide, tree-lined boulevard. I was on a mission to buy nash from Shlomie's, the candy store around the corner from my house. I was a good kid, but no one is perfect. To support my sugar rush, the night before I had executed a deft maneuver while hiding in the kitchen closet. With the aid of a large screwdriver from my father's tool collection in the basement, I popped open the flimsy lock on a metal charity box and pocketed its contents, which amounted to a whopping $9. The charity was intended to assist Jewish refugees from the Soviet Union to resettle in America.

Mommy fills the house with treats, but I enjoy buying my own nash and eating it by myself, away from my sisters' pleas and my brother Yossi's threats to share with him. Not that Yossi ever shares any of his nash with me! Plus, I'm not worried about God punishing me for stealing the money. Why should I be? Everyone does some kind of shtick to get what they want. My friend Lipa goes into the bodega around the corner and makes off with packs of Topps baseball cards. I take a few dollars from charity to buy candies. Same thing. And besides, God's too busy punishing yeshiva students for real sins like eating a slice of pizza without first making a blessing on it.

I crossed the four lanes of traffic and the two service lanes of Eastern Parkway. I could have walked straight down Brooklyn Avenue, but this route would have forced me to confront the massive Tudor Gothic–style, age-blackened brick Episcopal Church of St. Mark, with its bright red windows and spire topped with a crucifix. My teachers had instructed me to spit on the ground and walk across the street when I passed a church. Personally, I was terrified every time I passed St. Mark's. Adding to my fear were the golem stories written by Arnold Fine and illustrated by Howard S. Speilman serialized in the children's section of the *Jewish Press* that my father would read to me each week.

An anthropomorphic being created out of clay by Rabbi Judah Loew, the golem protected the Jews of sixteenth-century Prague. Each week I learned how the golem, in the nick of time, subverted the devious plot of Father Thaddeus to concoct a blood libel against the Jews. Every time I passed St. Mark's, I shuddered. I imagined seeing Father Thaddeus in its cavernous basement scheming sinister tricks to plague the Jews.

So instead I stayed on Eastern Parkway. Then I stood in front of 770. I felt as if I knew its every nook and cranny like I knew my own body. There were small stained-glass windows located twenty feet above the front door of 770 depicting rustic Chinese scenes.

The windows displayed two Asian women standing attired in traditional-looking garb, a male figure in Chinese dress sitting in a lotus position, a teapot, and a Chinese junk with multiple-gaffed sails, and several characters of Chinese script. I'm stumped as to why, over the past eight decades, no zealous Lubavitcher possessing a screwdriver took it upon himself to deface these "goyish" images from the iconic façade of the Lubavitch world headquarters. These small stained-glass panels may be the only physical reminder of the former non-Orthodox life of the building.

As I turned right onto Kingston Avenue, the commercial heart of Jewish Crown Heights, I wove my way through the crowd of commuters exiting from the Kingston Avenue subway station. On the corner of Kingston and Union I saw the tiny storefront of the World Lubavitch

Communications Center, known to Lubavitchers as WLCC, the organization that broadcasts live the weekday public talks of the Rebbe and sells audiocassettes and VHS recordings of those talks. According to legend, the soul of the Baal Shem Tov, the founder of the Hasidic movement in eighteenth-century Eastern Europe, ascended to Heaven in a temporary spell and met with the messiah. He asked the messiah when he would arrive. The messiah responded, "When the wellsprings of your teachings [Hasidic thought] are dispersed throughout the world." The unassuming storefront of WLCC was actively assisting with the dispersion of the wellsprings and thereby hastening the messiah's arrival.

As I continued my journey to reach Shlomie's along the uneven pavement of Kingston, swarms of girls from Bais Rivkah sporting their school uniforms of modest light-blue blouses and navy-blue skirts scurried around me. The sound of the girls giggling competed with the honking from motorists angered by double-parked cars. Once I turned left on Crown Street, my street, the racket from the cars diminished.

After walking a block and a half I hurried past the massive dilapidated old hospital building on Crown between Albany and Troy. The hospital might have been beautiful when it was built years ago, but now its façade was defaced with graffiti, its oversize windows smashed, and anything movable long since been carried off.

As I treaded warily alongside this dumping ground, a young Black man in an undershirt and shorts approached me walking a ferocious-looking pit bull on a glistening chain.

The hound growled at me. I jumped back in fright. "Got a problem?" the owner asked.

I had learned in yeshiva that if a dog barks, we should recite the verse from the Bible (Exodus 11:7) that promises Israelites that no dog will bark at them during their exodus from Egypt. Reciting this verse was supposed to silence the creature because dogs are by nature in awe of the soul of a Jew. However, if the dog continues to bark after the verse is recited, this indicates that the person reciting the verse is spiritually deficient. In that case, the dog fails to recognize the presence of a Jew. Given the spiritual deficiencies of my soul, not least because I had pilfered $9 from charity the night before, I decided not to take my chances with reciting the verse. I dashed across Troy Avenue instead and kept running until I was safely inside Shlomie's.

Shlomie Goldman, the owner of the store, was a rotund man with a stout head that looked like a massive orb affixed to an even more massive spherical base. As I entered the poorly lit store, Shlomie greeted me with, "Boychick, do you have cash? No more credit for anyone. I'm not running a *tzedakah* [charity] here."

I perused the half-empty shelves and selected a package of button candies and a big bag of Golden Fluff Potato Stix, all the while trying not to trip on the two gray cats leisurely prowling about their domain. Shlomie packed my goodies into a shopping bag and I made my exit.

I took a circuitous route home to give me time to eat all my treasures. I arrived home only after all was consumed and the evidence discarded in an overstuffed garbage can on the street.

As I walked up the cracked cement steps, I glanced at the front yard where my father toiled to grow irises, tulips, and daffodils. Privet hedges surrounded the small square space like a *gartl* (a long, thin black silk prayer sash) that adorns the midsection of a Hasidic man at synagogue, and the branches of the weeping cherry tree in the corner provided a kind of prayer shawl over the garden.

My house, a two-story red brick structure attached on one side, had a backyard with a rickety swing set and many more of my father's plants. There was a red climbing rose bush hugging the sagging fence. The house was built in the 1920s. By the time I arrived on the scene, the house was showing its age. The steam radiators throughout the house sputtered and wheezed all winter; the cluttered basement leaked (but only when it rained); and the once beautiful wood parquet flooring was coming loose. But it was the only home I knew, and I loved it.

As a child I didn't appreciate it fully, but I was part of a tribe within a tribe in Crown Heights. I was a Lubavitcher who was the child of *baal teshuvahs* ("returnees" to Orthodoxy). With its mix of openness to non-Orthodox Jews and strict adherence to the Hasidic lifestyle, Lubavitch attracted thousands of newcomers to its ranks, my parents among them. My parents had been raised Jewish but non-Orthodox and joined the community as young adults.

Although only 10–20 percent of my classmates' parents were *baal teshuvahs*, because of my parents' circle of friends in the community, all of the kids I played with outside of school were the children of *baal teshuvahs*. So it seemed perfectly natural to me at the time that my parents had joined the community from the outside. Aside from the party line that *baal teshuvahs* possessed a high spiritual status because of the many sacrifices they endured to transform their life and join Lubavitch, I didn't hear any community discussion about what the process of becoming a *baal teshuvah* entailed or about the lifestyles these newcomers left behind, my parents included.

Maybe they felt that they could never really explain their previous life in that faraway place called secular America. There was no vocabulary in Lubavitch to describe such things as sweet sixteens, high school crushes, and so on. Best never to allude to such matters.

I never felt prejudice against me personally because my parents were *baal teshuvahs*. I only realized years later that such a prejudice does exist among old-guard Lubavitch families when my older siblings tried to find a marriage partner and my parents' status as *baal teshuvahs* was considered a strike against them.

Nonetheless, it was always obvious who were the *baal teshuvahs* in the community. They tended to read Hebrew and speak Yiddish with a pronounced American accent that set them apart from the rest of the community, whose speech was colored with an Eastern European inflection. The children of *baal teshuvahs* also stood out because they lacked the extensive networks of cousins within the community enjoyed by their classmates.

Many of the Lubavitchers in Crown Heights arrived in America after World War II as survivors of the Holocaust or of decades of Soviet oppression against religious Jews. They did not view America as a *goldene medina* (golden land) of opportunity but as a *treif* country and were wary of its secularizing influences. In contrast, all except for one of my great-grandparents came to America in the early 1900s and joined the wave of Jewish "greenhorns" who were eager to become citizens and fully Americanize. They were proudly Jewish but had no desire to maintain all the religious rituals from the old country.

My mother was raised in Queens and my father in Flatbush, in typical American Jewish homes, where major Jewish holidays were observed, but not strictly, and both sides of the family were connected to left-wing political circles. As a teenager, my father's mother, Ruth Chellin, was a member of the Socialist Youth League, and her sister, Anne, was a member of the Young Communist League. My great-aunt even met the legendary Mexican artist Diego Rivera, a staunch communist, who painted her portrait and inscribed it, "To Comrade Anne." A framed copy of it now hangs in my home office. On my mother's side of the family, my great-grandmother Mildred Byer, née Sachnovsky, was friends with the communist journalist John Reed and the communist poet and novelist Maxwell Bodenheim.

My mother, the daughter of the psychologist and sexologist Samuel Janus and the schoolteacher Esther (Byer) Janus, started her affiliation with Lubavitch while attending Queens College. Samuel was no stranger to religious rebellion. He had rejected the pieties of his Orthodox mother, Miriam Feiga Yanushewitz, née Rothenberg, who was born in Poland and only arrived in America as a forty-year-old in 1929 along with a determination to maintain the religious standards of the old country. Samuel was the only one of his siblings to graduate from college, and he was horrified that his daughter, who showed so much promise in the secular world, had turned her back on it and chose to join a fringe religious group.

All of my grandfather's reasoning and cajoling was for naught. My mother had fallen in love with Lubavitch and could imagine no other way of life for herself. In her last semester at college two years before her marriage, she took a course with a visiting professor, Betty Friedan, entitled "The Sociology of Sex Roles" and argued in class against the professor's assertion that the Bible and Jewish law were sexist.

Friedan had claimed that the Bible was sexist because it doesn't include a single female prophetic figure and that Jewish law is reactionary because it requires women to wait helplessly for men to arrive home from synagogue and chant the blessings of the Sabbath kiddush ritual. Based on ammunition provided to her by Lubavitchers during her regular visits to Crown Heights, my mother countered that there are seven prophetesses in the Bible, such as Sarah, Miriam, and Deborah, and that according to Jewish law, if men are absent, women are permitted to chant the kiddush blessings all by themselves.

It seems fitting that my mother, who was shortly to embrace with both hands the role of full-time Lubavitch housewife and caregiver to a growing tribe of children, would clash with the author of *The Feminine Mystique*. In that groundbreaking work of the second wave of American feminism, Friedan had proclaimed: "We can no longer ignore that voice within women that says: 'I want something more than my husband and my children and my home.'"

There was another aspect of my mother's upbringing that played a role in her choice of a strictly religious lifestyle. Only once I became an adult did I realize that my mother was the product of a broken home. Her parents were divorced when she was in elementary school, and her mother struggled with her own demons. My beloved grandmother was incapable of keeping house. As a consequence, in elementary school, my mother would end up making lunches for herself and her brother, who was two years her junior.

When my mother visited Crown Heights for Shabbos as a college student, she saw the "Norman Rockwell" version of Lubavitch families and fell in love with them. They looked like everything her home was not. Instead of a few kids and a dog, these families boasted eight to ten kids all sitting around the Shabbos table smiling at their parents and dutifully answering questions about the weekly Torah portion, their innocence intact. Even the parents were sheltered from the destructive and radical trends plaguing secular American society, including sexual violence, extreme political ideologies, and feminist thought that claimed that men and women were exactly the same in their makeup and roles. Blithely resistant to the cosmic order, secular Americans were doomed to a meaningless, chaotic existence. At least, it seemed that way to my mother.

The Lubavitchers knew in their hearts that men and women possessed different souls and were created by the Almighty to perform different tasks. Their daily lives are absorbed with the performance of countless *mitzvos* (commandments), each imbued with deep meaning. This tableau of Hasidic life was only part of the picture, but it was the part that was visible to my mother at the time.

My father, the son of Joseph Newfield, an accountant who soon retired due to ill health, and Ruth (née Chellin), a math teacher in a Brooklyn public school, was a quiet child. He didn't receive much attention from his mother, who was preoccupied with working full time, maintaining the home, and taking care of her ailing husband. My father became adept at solo activities such as reading *Compton's Pictured Encyclopedia* and growing radishes and carrots in his parents' backyard.

My father was socially awkward in elementary school. He spent six years with the same group of classmates and never managed to learn the names of most of them. He felt left out from the clique of popular students.

My father's time as an undergraduate at Columbia University, beginning in 1968, overlapped with major social agitation on campus. Yet the Age of Aquarius left him cold. In that era's division of the world into the freaks and the squares, my father was solidly entrenched in the latter camp. In my father's sophomore year, he was annoyed to discover all the dust bins in his dorm gradually disappeared. It turned out an industrious undergraduate commandeered them all, filled them with rich alluvial Manhattan soil from South Field, and, with the help of a bank of florescent lamps, began growing pot in his fifth-floor dorm room in John Jay Hall. Needless to say, although my father had years of horticultural experience, he neither was asked for nor offered his botanic wisdom to the pot-growing operation. He was at Columbia, but not of it.

I have an easier time understanding why the Lubavitch lifestyle appealed to my mother than to my father. Given my father's aversion to the freaks at Columbia, it's hard for me to understand what attracted him to the Lubavitch tribe, with their long beards, dangling *tzitzis* (side fringes), and incessant talk of making a dwelling place for the *shechina* (divine presence) down here on Earth.

My father was often asked by curious non-Orthodox Shabbos guests at our home, "How did you land in Crown Heights?"

He would always respond with a version of the following: "On my second day at Harvard Medical School I met the local Lubavitch rabbi, Dovid Wichnin, who invited me to his home for Shabbos." The rabbi didn't speak to my father the whole Shabbos, but on Saturday night, after a day of communal prayers, meals, and song, he turned to my father and said, "I want you to stay with us every Shabbos." My father went on to stay with the Wichnin family every Shabbos for the next four years. By the time he graduated medical school, my father's clean-shaven face was sporting a bushy black beard and he had joined the Lubavitch "team."

My father never said the word *team*. He never used a sports metaphor in his life, just as he never played a sports game. Ever. He made it seem like it was an inevitable metamorphosis, like the forces governing the transformation of a baby flamingo's gray and white feathers into pink. He was a loner who read C. W. Ceram's *Gods, Graves, and Scholars* in second grade and was content to putter around in the garden by himself for years. It seems he finally felt the urge to join a group and be part of something larger than himself.

By the time my parents met in 1977, they were both fully committed to the Lubavitch way of life. To symbolize their new religious status, they had independently shifted from using their English names, Beth Robin and Stanley Austin, to using their Hebrew ones, Basha Rayzl and Shlomo Asher, in all areas of their life.

Because my parents were totally committed to Lubavitch and the Rebbe, when they had doubts about whether they should proceed with their wedding plans, like all good Lubavitchers, they wrote to the Rebbe for his counsel. He responded with six Hebrew words: "Nachon hashidduch v'tov. Azkir al hatzion" (The matrimonial match is good and correct. I will pray for you at the resting place of the previous Rebbe, Yosef Yitzchak Schneersohn). On the strength of those six Hebrew words, all doubt was cast aside, and they went forward with the union. My parents' lives, as individuals and as a married couple, were devoted to the Rebbe's dictates and guidance.

Although my parents wholeheartedly threw their lot in with Lubavitch, they hadn't had much formal education on its extensive school of thought and its two-century history and culture. My father spent several weeks at the men's yeshiva for *baal teshuvahs* in the Catskills during college and medical school vacations and also a few days at its Crown Heights location. My mother made multiple trips to the Lubavitch women's seminary in Minnesota and spent a year in a similar institution in Crown Heights. That was the extent of their formal Lubavitch instruction.

So my parents were in effect learning on the job, trying to educate themselves on how to be Lubavitchers while simultaneously trying to raise their children in a Hasidic atmosphere. My father had mountains of audiocassettes in his home office that contained lectures by Lubavitch rabbis on topics ranging from Jewish medical ethics to parenting according to the Torah. He was so busy taking care of his patients and his family that he seldom ever touched these cassettes.

The main source of Lubavitch knowledge my parents received once married was from the occasional public talks by local rabbis they would manage to attend. The bottom line was that the total knowledge my parents acquired was a fraction of what their daughters would receive through their attendance in Lubavitch formal schooling from kindergarten through seminary, and even less compared with what their sons would receive through their decades of intensive yeshiva training.

Notwithstanding her limited Lubavitch knowledge, my mother, whom we called "Mommy," was completely committed to its program. While in college, she had ambitions to follow in the path of her father and become a psychologist, but by the time she joined Lubavitch, she had put all that aside and had one main ambition: to raise a large family of healthy and happy children who would grow up to be devout Lubavitchers. She didn't pursue any personal interests or hobbies, unless you count shopping for food and clothing for a full house.

As a young mother, she spoke quickly, drove her red Ford Crown Victoria station wagon even more quickly, and was able to size up a person in a matter of minutes. And she was usually right. She wore a short brown *sheitel* (wig) and often had at least one kid in her arms. She was extremely devoted to every detail of her children's lives. She stayed up till 2 A.M. to curl ribbons on birthday bags for my first-grade classmates. And it was to her that I came running when I woke up crying in the middle of the night with my legs aching from growing pains. She would rub my legs, administer Tylenol, and have me repeat after her, "Hashem shik meer a refua sheleyma" (God send me a complete recovery). That combination of affection, science, and faith always worked to make me feel better.

One of the key ways my mother expressed love was through her culinary creations. She was a Lubavitch Julia Child who whipped up mouth-watering meals throughout the year, but especially for Jewish holidays. The heavenly aromas of the holiday dishes are embedded in my mind. On the eve of Yom Kippur, we had salmon steaks and fried *kreplach* (meat dumplings); for Sukkos, we had stuffed peppers and stuffed zucchini, roast duckling in orange jam, and Silver Tip beef; for Chanukah, we had potato latkes and homemade doughnuts; and for Purim, we had pepper steak stew and stir-fried vegetables. She never accepted the conventional belief that Passover food, with all its restrictions, was tasteless and endlessly experimented with shepherd's pie recipes and schnitzel covered in crushed almonds or walnuts.

My mother produced all these dishes even before she democratized her kitchen and allowed my sisters to assist her. (The boys were never allowed in the kitchen except during Passover, when we were conscripted to peel mountains of potatoes and apples for her cooking.) Given the countless demands on her time and energy from her budding crew, each dish she created was a testament to her love for us and her desire to create beautiful holiday memories.

My father, whom we call Tatty—Yiddish for "Daddy"—had short dark-brown hair that has since grayed, and he wore thick glasses that pressed into the arch of his nose. He was quiet, and when he spoke, he spoke slowly. His best friends were the tulips, daffodils, and hyacinths he tended to in our front- and back-yard gardens and those of our neighbors. He was forever pointing out to me trees, bushes, and flowers.

He was not a typical Lubavitcher. He worked outside the community as a dermatologist and treated mostly non-Jewish patients. At the time, no Lubavitchers who were born in the community became physicians. And although he had a long beard, wore a black fedora, and enthusiastically retold miracle stories of the Rebbe, as any Lubavitcher would, he appreciated secular culture and knowledge.

My father grew up listening to opera—in grade school, he even performed in the Metropolitan Opera Boy's Chorus—and walked around our house singing snippets from Puccini's La Bohème, Turandot, and Tosca. He woke us on Saturday mornings to go to shul by singing Irving Berlin's "Oh! How I Hate to Get Up in the Morning." He subscribed to the *New York Times*, *Smithsonian*, *National Geographic*, *Columbia College Today*, *Harvard Magazine*, and three archeology magazines. Only years later, once I was out of the house, did he exchange the Berlin song for one of his own creation, "Early in the Morning the Chasidim Wake Up Yawning, tralala la la la la la," and cut down on the secular subscriptions and added to the mix the *Algemeiner Journal* and other ultra-Orthodox periodicals.

My father occasionally took us kids to the Brooklyn Museum and the Metropolitan Museum of Art but hurried us along when we encountered nudes or paintings of Jesus. Once, while visiting friends in Pittsburgh for Passover, he took us to a nineteenth-century millenarian Christian village that had been turned into a museum. What could go wrong? The beginning of the tour was just fine. We inspected the giant barrels they used to make beer and their collection of stuffed rare birds. Then we entered the huge dining hall—the tour guide said that when it was built it was the largest room in the United States without supporting pillars. On the wall was painted a huge mural of Jesus feeding the masses. He yanked me out of there so fast my yarmulke almost fell off my head.

My parents, like all Lubavitchers, took the biblical commandment to be fruitful and multiply literally. Each child born brings down a new soul into the world, hastening the messianic redemption. Within a span of eighteen years, my parents had nine children. They had five daughters, Miriam Feiga (whom we called Miriam), Chana Sara, Rivkah Yocheved (Rivky), Ester Bracha (Esty), and Chaya Mushka (Chaya), and four sons, Chaim Yosef Moshe (Yossi), me, Shimon Eliezer (Shimmy), and Menachem Mendel (Mendy).

It is common for boys in Lubavitch to be named after the rebbes of Lubavitch and girls to be named after the rebbetzins (the wives of the rebbes). I was named Schneur Zalman in honor of the first Lubavitcher rebbe, whose *yahrzeit* (anniversary of his passing) was celebrated three days before my birth, on the twenty-fourth day of the Hebrew month of Teves. But there is a deeper meaning to a name. Lubavitchers believe a name represents the essence of a thing. Thus, when the Bible recounts that Adam gave names to all the creatures of the Earth, he wasn't simply giving them a linguistic label by which to be referred but was actually revealing their essence. Time would tell the inner nature of my essence.

As we grew up, my siblings and I were exposed to aspects of the outside environment through our non-Orthodox relatives. Our parents encouraged loving relationships with them but also sought to protect us from their worldly influence. Uncle Jeff, a Shakespeare and American Civil War enthusiast, took us to ballgames at Shea and Yankee stadiums. Similarly, my mother's father, whom we called Pops, relished telling me about Murder Incorporated and Jewish gangsters, and when he did, he always spoke about it as if he were part of it somehow, as if he were a personal acquaintance of Bugsy Siegel and Meyer Lansky. And my father's mother, Bubby Ruth, a veteran public school math teacher, always encouraged us to read secular books on a broad range of subjects.

For Thanksgiving, we would visit Aunt Marta, an artist, world traveler, and collector of Mexican and Asian antiques, in her Southampton hotel. We couldn't join the other guests for the traditional turkey. Instead, we brought our own kosher meals, including brisket sandwiches and roast potatoes from Mermelstein's. When we arrived, my mother would rush to hide the crucifixes, ceramic pigs, and Buddha statues that adorned our rooms, stashing them in a closet until we left, just as our matriarch Rebecca hid the idols of her father, Laban.

After World War II, Crown Heights became a center of Hasidic life in America. Thousands of Hasidim from numerous sects made this two-square-mile neighborhood of Brooklyn their home. Some Hasidim, such as Bobov and Skulen, were joined by their rebbes—their spiritual leaders. The Hasidim established more than forty synagogues, along with yeshivas, *mikvahs* (ritual baths), charities, Judaica shops and bookstores, kosher restaurants, and other Jewish-owned businesses.

But by the end of the 1960s, as large numbers of Black Caribbean Americans moved into the neighborhood, most of the Jews, including the Hasidim, fled. This exodus was part of a larger pattern of "white flight" of white ethnics in Brooklyn and other parts of the country in the face of the arrival of Black residents. The Lubavitcher Rebbe was determined to keep his followers in place. The Rebbe declared, "Kan tziva hashem es habracha" (Crown Heights is the place where God commands his blessing). With God's blessings, Crown Heights would remain a neighborhood with a strong Jewish community. On April 10, 1969, the Rebbe proclaimed that Jewish law prohibited Jews in the neighborhood from selling their homes to non-Jews (presumably to Black homebuyers). He declared it forbidden to weaken the Jewish community and threaten the survival of the synagogues and other Jewish institutions in the area.

The Rebbe didn't content himself with theological and Jewish legal pronouncements. He also actively supported a practical initiative, an organization called Chevra, to raise funds to purchase houses and apartment buildings and make them available to Jewish residents, thus stemming the tide of white flight. In 1971, the Rebbe announced that anyone who purchased a share in the Chevra program, which cost $500, would receive a $1 bill from him that was imbued with immense blessings for physical and spiritual well-being.

The Chevra program was successful in selling many shares to Lubavitchers all around the world and in buying up many Crown Heights homes and apartments for the Lubavitch community. In 1976, my father, who was not living in New York at the time, bought a share without knowing that he would end up buying our family home through Chevra in 1979. To this day, my father treasures the laminated $1 bill he received from the Rebbe along with his Chevra certificate.

The white flight from Crown Heights contributed to the Lubavitch community's sense that it was embattled and surrounded by enemies. Many outsiders are aware of the racial tensions that flared up in Crown Heights in 1991 when Yosef Lifsh, a young Israeli Lubavitcher, driving his car as part of the motorcade of the Lubavitcher Rebbe, accidentally struck and killed Gavin Cato, the seven-year-old son of Guyanese immigrants. In retaliation, on the following day a group of Black teens stabbed and killed Yankel Rosenbaum, a twenty-nine-year-old rabbinical student. Rioting continued for three days without sufficient police intervention. Several Jews were injured; stores were looted; and homes and cars were damaged. When platoons of cops finally did arrive and take up positions throughout the neighborhood, I felt safer. The cops were here, I felt at the time, to protect *us* from *them*.

But racial tensions had been simmering for decades, fed by a steady diet of mutual disregard and negative stereotypes, as well as competition between the two communities over scarce government funding and public housing. The city government claimed that it did not have sufficient funds to provide the necessary police protection to residents.

In 1964, in response to the rise in street crime, Rabbi Samuel Schrage established the Maccabees, a community patrol consisting mostly of young Jewish men to alert the police when a violent incident occurred and help the victims. The police and municipal government provided funding for the patrol to purchase police equipment such as two-way radios. The Maccabees had a dispatcher, and residents in a crisis could call for emergency assistance.

Schrage was criticized by some local Jewish residents who viewed the patrol as vigilantes. He considered disbanding it, but the Rebbe encouraged him to expand the patrol. At its height, the patrol boasted five hundred members. Leaders of the Black community, who were critical of the patrol, referred to the Maccabees as "Jew police." The Maccabees disbanded in 1971, but the group reemerged in the late 1970s under the name of Shmira (the Guardians) and is still in existence.

As a kid growing up in 1980s Crown Heights, I would occasionally hear the one-word alert "Chaptsim!" (Catch him!) It was a kind of distress call in Yiddish, a Bat-Signal to alert Lubavitchers to spring into action and surround an outsider for alleged wrongdoing.

There was a yawning gulf between the Lubavitch community of Crown Heights and their non-Jewish, and mostly Afro-Caribbean, neighbors. I routinely watched Black families in suits and dresses, holding Bibles, going off to church on Sundays. In the summertime, young Rastafari men with dreadlocks carried large boom boxes and played reggae music late into the night. On hot days, young Black girls in tank tops and shorts, their hair made up in braids, played double Dutch jump rope and licked large blue-and-red popsicles and young Black boys turned on the fire hydrants and cooled off in the jetting water.

I observed all of this but never interacted with any of it, as if I were living behind a clear glass wall. I didn't know the first or last name of any of my Black neighbors, and doubtless they didn't know mine. We lived, attended school, worshipped, and played in two completely disconnected worlds that just happened to occupy the same crowded city blocks.

Apart from the basketball courts at Lefferts Park, where my older brother Yossi occasionally joined mixed pick-up games with Lubavitchers and Black Caribbeans, there was no place in Crown Heights where the two communities met in respectful cordiality.

Not only did most Lubavitchers not interact with their Black neighbors, but there was intense negativity aimed at them. It was common to refer to them as *shvartzes*, a derogatory Yiddish word for Black people. I regularly heard, "Hey! That's the *shvartza* that stole my cousin's bike." I also frequently heard hateful "jokes" at school.

One sabbath during the height of the racial tension in 1991, I slept over at my friend Avigdor Schwartz's home. At the Friday night meal, while munching on homemade multigrain challah and hummus, Avigdor's parents discussed the "increase the peace" project created by the maverick Lubavitcher David Lazerson, which sought to bring Lubavitch and Black teens together for basketball games. "Is he *meshugah*? Our decent boys playing with those *vilder chayas*!"

How can these sweet people, who always host me for Shabbos sleepovers and go out of their way not to embarrass me when I wet the bed, say such mean things about our Black neighbors? Aren't we all created by God in His image? I realized that even the "nice" Lubavitchers thought of their Black neighbors as dirt. It was obvious that for Lubavitchers the commandment "Ve-ahavta le-re'acha ka-mocha" (To love your fellow as yourself) didn't apply to loving Black people.

Although I never had a meaningful interaction with any of my Black neighbors, when I was ten or eleven I did have a brief friendship with Michael Jones, a non-Jewish Black visitor who was staying with an aunt living a few doors down. He was my age but a few inches taller than me. I'm not sure how the friendship was sparked, but I remember hanging out with him and chatting about playing baseball. He offered me several bent Topps baseball cards and his well-worn batting glove. I accepted the cards but declined the glove.

A few days into our friendship, I was hanging out with him when a Lubavitch neighbor of mine, Yecheskel, invited me to come to his backyard. I came and brought my friend Michael. As soon as we were in his backyard, Yecheskel's father came outside, called his son over, and whispered something. Yecheskel came over to me and said, "My father says *you* can stay but he can't," and pointed to Michael. I was confused by Yecheskel's father's demand. We had just arrived. Michael didn't have any time to misbehave or do anything to upset Yecheskel's father. I decided to leave Yecheskel's backyard with Michael. I still don't know why I did that. I certainly didn't have a well-developed theory about racial prejudice. It just seemed wrong to exclude someone from our play.

Lest I give the impression that I was somehow uniquely sensitive to racial injustice at age ten, I must admit I was not. Around that time, my nonreligious Aunt Marta, with her dangling and jangling Tibetan necklaces, hauled an armful of drawing books, colored pencils, and toy soldiers from her Upper West Side apartment to my house. She had the soul of a Buddhist monk and the spirit of a Wall Street tycoon, was invested in real estate in Manhattan and Key West, and regularly trekked through India and the Far East. She wanted me to use her supplies to start a business on my street. My first response was, "The *shvartzes* are gonna steal them!"

I remember a fourth-grade substitute teacher named Nuchum Shapiro bragging to my class that he and a few buddies had beaten up a Black man accused of stealing from a Jewish home. Nuchum claimed that he pounded the alleged thief in the face with such force that blood spurted from the man's mouth into Nuchum's, requiring that he rush to Hatzalah, the Jewish ambulance service, to "disinfect" his mouth. I'm not sure if the story was fabricated to impress us, but my whole class was riveted by it, and no one seemed to question the morality of meting out such street "justice."

Without realizing it, I had absorbed into my consciousness the foul taint of racial animus. Every Passover during the Shefoch Chamascha ritual, I would open the front door, lit candle in hand, and call for God to pour out his wrath on nonbelievers. "Pour out Your wrath upon the nations who do not know You": This angry plea was introduced in the Middle Ages in response to the cruelty of the First Crusade in 1095. When we recited the prayer at the seder, a time I was assured the gates of Heaven are especially open to sincere requests, I regret it seemed to my young mind righteous to think of our Black neighbors who stole our bikes and broke into my family's car.

The fact that Lubavitchers stayed in Crown Heights when most other Jewish residents fled is still a puzzle to me. My Lubavitch friend Mordecai Goldberg has a theory. According to Mordecai, the Rebbe wanted to stay in Crown Heights to prevent assimilation. As Mordecai saw it, the Rebbe strategized that seeing the economic hardship and social distress that their Black neighbors suffered would cause Lubavitchers to remain committed to their insular form of Judaism. "This took away the temptation for Lubavitchers to be like their neighbors."

The Rebbe's insistence on staying in Crown Heights does seem to echo the prayers of his predecessor a century and a half earlier, the first Lubavitcher Rebbe and founder of the Lubavitch movement, Schneur Zalman of Liadi. During the Napoleonic Wars he beseeched God to intercede in favor of Czar Alexander to preserve the piety of the Jews. Under Napoleon, he reasoned, the material condition of the Jews would improve, and they might forget about God. Under the czar, they would suffer more, but then they would need to depend on God and maintain their religious commitment.

On the cold night of December 31, 1897, Brooklyn surrendered the status as an independent city it had enjoyed for more than two hundred years and became a mere borough of the modern City of New York. As far as the Lubavitch residents of Crown Heights were concerned, not only was Brooklyn still an independent city, but Crown Heights was an independent universe. The norms that held true in other locales simply didn't apply here. In far-off places (such as America), young people chose careers for themselves. But for Lubavitchers, there was only a single profession that was ever discussed: to become an emissary (*shliach*) of the Lubavitcher Rebbe and help strengthen Jewish communal life in far-flung regions of the world. It's not that the word *career* was a dirty word so much as an unheard of one. We were all supposed to become *shluchim*.

Historically, in Eastern Europe religious Jews made a living through a variety of vocations. Hints of this past are still retained in common Jewish surnames based on Yiddish words for particular lines of work, such as Kramer (*kremer*, shopkeeper), Druker (*druker*, printer), and Schreiber (*shrayber*, writer). Some of my nonreligious relatives would ask, "So you're gonna become a doctor like your Daddy?" I always felt like they were crazy. I couldn't even read English. How in the world was I going to get through college, let alone medical school?

In Lubavitch, it was assumed that young people would become *shluchim*, even though that often didn't happen, and many members would eventually go into a business of one sort or another. It was not as if Lubavitch society so disdained wealth that people used gold to make chamber pots, as the subjects of Thomas More's *Utopia* did. Still, Lubavitchers did seem oddly unconcerned about careers and making a living.

The Rebbe and other community leaders must have known that many, if not most, Lubavitchers would not end up as *shluchim*, but they didn't seem to make any preparations for these people to be successful in business or other secular professions. It is possible that many Lubavitchers accepted the Rebbe's rejection of secular studies and the related rejection of secular careers because they truly believed that the messiah would arrive any day and obviate such mundane concerns. Once the messiah arrived, the streets would be paved with precious stones.

Given the intense Lubavitch focus on Jewish outreach and *shluchim*, Crown Heights itself had a contradictory quality for the community. On the one hand, it was the heart of the Lubavitch solar system because that is where the Rebbe, the sun, was located. On the other hand, Crown Heights was also only a staging ground for the Rebbe's army to launch its outreach invasion of the rest of the world. Of course, *shluchim* would occasionally return to see the Rebbe, just as soldiers return to central headquarters to receive new orders. But the ultimate objective of any army is to take to the field of battle and not to remain closeted in its barracks.

Although growing up I had heard stories of wealthy Jews in Europe before the Holocaust who were honored with the best seats in the synagogue near the eastern wall of the sanctuary, I had never thought about class distinctions among Lubavitchers. Born into a family that regularly dined on baby lamb chops and pepper steak, I had assumed that all my classmates did the same.

Only in my twenties did I first learn of Lubavitch parents who couldn't afford to pay for their kids to go to sleepaway summer camps, as I did, and that some of my elementary school classmates and their families lived in government-funded Section 8 housing. Rabbis, religious schoolteachers, and small shop owners, all without high school diplomas, often found it hard to make a living. My father only recently shared with me how the administrators at Oholei Torah, my elementary school, would greet him with a smile when he came to pay tuition each September. By paying the full tuition for his children, my father was in effect sponsoring several other kids who were less fortunate.

As is so common for children raised in comfort, I had no conception of my actual economic status. My mother was never swathed in mink, her hands were never weighed down by diamonds, and my family never took lavish Passover vacations to Israel or Florida, as was the case with some others in Crown Heights. My parents drove the same car for nineteen years. They never remodeled their kitchen, even though they lived in the house for forty years. Nonetheless, my family was extremely comfortable and much better off than most of our Lubavitch neighbors.

2

Long Live the King

"The Rebbe, *nasi doyreinu* [the patriarch of our generation], needs us to demand from *Hashem* [God] that he make a *neis* [a miracle]," roared Rabbi Hirsch.

It was an overcast morning at the end of March 1994, a little more than a year since I had stood on the bench in 770 waiting for the Rebbe to reveal himself as the messiah. Now I stood with my fifteen classmates surrounded by bare trees in the public park adjacent to Beth Israel Medical Center in Manhattan. Beth Israel is a foreboding thirteen-story tan brick building. When it opened in 1929, it was the tallest hospital in the world. Inside, the Rebbe, the spiritual leader of our community, was lying in a hospital bed, surrounded by doctors and nurses, being treated after his second stroke in as many years.

Once news spread of the Rebbe's critical condition, Lubavitchers across the world dropped everything and raced to New York to be near the Rebbe and to pray for him. They were like children running to the deathbed of their beloved father, except that instead of expecting and preparing for his demise, the Lubavitchers were convinced that the Rebbe, at ninety-two, paralyzed on his right side and in intensive care, would miraculously recover and—this time, at long last—reveal himself to be the messiah.

My sixth-grade teacher, Rabbi Hirsch, a rail-thin man with boundless nervous energy in his mid-thirties, would normally spend each morning in class struggling to explain to us the Hasidic views on the nature of God, all the while fussily drinking tea through a handful of sugar cubes strategically placed between his teeth in the old European style. But that morning, outside the hospital, he was as serious as death. Pounding the air with his tightly clenched fist, he continued, "The Rebbe already told us that we need to do everything we can to bring Moshiach [the messiah]. It is now our job to demand for the Rebbe to get better so he can come back to us and take us out of *gulus* [exile]."

Turning to face the imposing hospital, Rabbi Hirsch declared: "The Rebbe is right in there waiting for our *tefiloys* [prayers]. We are going to say the Rebbe's *kapitl* [the chapter of Psalms corresponding to his age]. I'll say a *posuk* [verse] at a time, and everyone repeat after me."

Removing a *gartl* from his pocket, Rabbi Hirsch quickly tied it around his waist—a movement he did as automatically as he tied his shoelaces—and then began: "Mizmor shir l'yoym hashabbos" (A psalm, a song, for the Sabbath day).

Rabbi Hirsch recited each verse, and my class thundered it in response, as if the louder our voices, the surer God would be to answer our supplications. When he reached the verse, "Tzaddik k'tamar yifrach" (The righteous shall flourish like the palm tree; he shall grow like a cedar in Lebanon), I saw Rabbi Hirsch's eyes overflow with tears.

The Rebbe was *unzer futter*, our father, with whom we each felt a personal bond. Our teachers taught us that as Lubavitchers, we were the luckiest people on Earth. It was our Rebbe who was directly connected to God, and through him we strengthened our connection to the Almighty. And it was our Rebbe who was the messiah, and every commandment we performed brought the messianic redemption one step closer. As the popular Lubavitch children's song put it, "Every *mitzvah* that we do so carefully / adds a brick to the *mikdash hashlishi*," the Third Temple, to be built in Jerusalem in the messianic era.

Our teachers taught us that all humans, even non-Jews, received spiritual sustenance from God through the Rebbe, and all humans would be redeemed in the messianic era. But it was our good fortune to have a personal relationship with the Rebbe. We got to pray with him every day, to study his teachings in school, and ask him for blessings any time we needed. We were living on the inside, while everyone else was clueless.

When I was a teenager, I heard stories of how the Rebbe enjoyed the practical humor of his secretary, Rabbi Moshe Leib Rudshtein, who once arranged a row of wind-up toy soldiers to march into the Rebbe's office. He also once brought the Rebbe a very short pencil that was almost used up, and when the Rebbe said that it was too small, Rudshtein produced an oversize pencil and handed it to the Rebbe. The Rebbe laughed. But the Rebbe also had a deadly serious side that could burst forth, especially when non-Lubavitchers were absent, like a father who lashes out only when the neighbors and outsiders are away. After all, the Rebbe had as his mission nothing less than to bring about the messianic redemption, fulfilling the cosmic purpose of creation. When you're on a mission to save the world, there's not a lot of room for laughs.

Photos and paintings of the Rebbe adorned walls, key chains, clocks, and charity boxes wherever Lubavitchers lived. His piercing blue eyes, full white beard, black fedora, and silk coat were with us wherever we went. To use the language of the medieval liturgist whose prayer describes the face of the high priest on Yom Kippur after entering the Holy of Holies, the Rebbe's visage radiated "like the brightest star that shines in the eastern sky."

Images of the Rebbe were considered sacred and were usually treated with reverence. In fact, there is a well-known story of a Lubavitcher who, once out of anger, threw a shoe at a picture of the Rebbe. Several months later, this Lubavitcher, having forgotten all about the incident, went to receive a blessing from the Rebbe. When his turn came, the Rebbe put a hand on his own cheek and said, "It still hurts where you threw the shoe." The Lubavitcher turned pale. This story may be apocryphal, but its continued circulation among Lubavitchers highlights their attachment to images of the Rebbe not as mere keepsakes but as sacred objects.

I was not a relative of the Rebbe's, and I didn't hail from a *gezhe* family—one whose Lubavitch roots trace back a hundred years, like the Posners, Raskins, Gurarys, and Marazovs. My siblings and I didn't have special private visits with the Rebbe's wife where she served cookies to the children in her modest home. Still, I felt that I had a unique relationship with the Rebbe, the kind that every devotee has with a popular charismatic leader. The Rebbe had top billing in the internal narrative of my life.

Although the Hasidic movement—marked, among other features, by its introduction of the personage of the rebbe, the Hasidic master—was less than three hundred years old, Lubavitchers see biblical precedence for their devotion to the Rebbe in the verse (Exodus 14:31) "And they believed in the Lord, and in His servant Moses." The Rebbe was the Moses of our generation, and we were as faithful to our leader as the ancient Israelites were to theirs.

We began studying the Rebbe's teachings in elementary school, poring over his discourses on key passages in the Bible and the Talmud and learning from him that bringing the messiah is the primary mission of our generation. We memorized and were tested on the important dates in the life of the Rebbe and his family, such as birthdays and anniversaries. We wrote letters to the Rebbe requesting blessings. We sang songs about our love for the Rebbe and our devotion to him. One of the most popular Hebrew songs, "The Rebbe," which we sang in his presence many times, ends: "Al yedei ha-ramatkal ha-gadol mi-kulam, nitgaber al ha-olam" (Through the commander-in-chief, the greatest one of all, we will triumph over the world).

The Rebbe held public gatherings, *farbrengens*, on Saturday afternoons and on holidays in his synagogue at 770 Eastern Parkway in Crown Heights. Due to the Orthodox practice of eschewing all electronics on the Sabbath, the Rebbe spoke on Saturdays without a microphone. The large audience strained to hear his words, which were in Yiddish. He would sit on a royal-red upholstered chair at a long dais, consisting of multiple old wooden tables lined up together and covered in a clean, plain white tablecloth. Twenty or thirty Lubavitch dignitaries and elders filled the three rows behind him, while in the room in front of him and on bleachers on each side stood legions of his faithful.

One Shabbos afternoon while the Rebbe was speaking, a few friends and I managed to sneak away from the children's program upstairs to forage in the main sanctuary for the small white paper bags full of candies that were thrown at grooms during the Torah reading service earlier in the day. As my skinny five-year-old body slithered among the forest of black pants, I suddenly found myself under the Rebbe's dais, staring straight at his well-worn, plain black shoes. I wasn't alone. Under the table were huddled a handful of men, young and old. They were there because that was an ideal place in the large synagogue to hear what the Rebbe was saying. I just wanted candy. But I had arrived at the feet of the Nasi Hador—the Patriarch of the Generation himself. To my dismay, the huddled men quietly but firmly shooed me away.

Our fascination with and veneration of the Rebbe knew no bounds. An enterprising Lubavitch snoop managed to take a series of black-and-white pictures of the Rebbe in his private study through a window. In the grainy pictures the Rebbe can clearly be seen wearing his black kapota but without his signature fedora, his large yarmulka positioned on his prominent head. In one picture, the Rebbe is standing reading a religious book; in another, he is seated at his desk taking notes while pressing his moustache with his other hand. Lubavitchers expressed disgust at this gross violation of the Rebbe's privacy but also viewed and shared these photos widely. The temptation to observe the Rebbe when he thought he was alone and to imagine what he was thinking in those rare moments of solitude was just too great.

I shared the veneration of the Rebbe that all Lubavitchers felt, and I had no doubt that the Rebbe could and did perform miracles. I imagined that he had X-ray vision and could see all our hidden thoughts when we walked past him. But I didn't like attending the *farbrengens*. As a young child with only a hazy grasp of Yiddish and Hebrew, it was impossible for me to follow the hours-long lectures, which crisscrossed dense topics in Hasidic philosophy, Talmud, and Jewish law. I would sit tying and releasing slip knots with the strings of my *tzitzis*.

One Chanukah when I was seven and the Rebbe was holding a *farbrengen* for children at 770, I arrived late. When I entered 770, I realized that I had missed the customary recitation of the twelve Torah verses and rabbinic maxims that preceded all Lubavitch children's programs and events, and which I loathed. Excellent. I also missed the lighting of the six-foot gold-colored menorah located in the front of the sanctuary. This menorah was distinct because of its V-shaped branches, which follow Maimonides's description of the great menorah of the ancient Temple, rather than the rounded, U-shaped branches famously depicted on the Arch of Titus in Rome.

My luck, the Rebbe was in middle of delivering his hour-long talk to the rows of gathered children. Although I didn't understand most of what the Rebbe was saying, I had learned to detect when the Rebbe was wrapping up. The Rebbe would always end each talk by praying for the speedy arrival of the messiah. The Rebbe would then quote the biblical verse (Exodus 10:9) where Moses insists to Pharaoh that the Israelites must leave Egypt to worship God in the wilderness. When Pharaoh inquires who exactly will be going on this mission, Moses declares, "Bini'areinu u'vizkeinaynu neileich, be-vaneinu u-bivnoseinu" (With our young and with our old shall we go, with our sons and with our daughters). As soon as I heard that phrase, I knew the end was nigh and, like my ancestors in the Bible, I would shortly be released from my confinement.

Far more special to me than these public gatherings were the brief moments when I had the opportunity to stand directly before the Rebbe, looking at him eye to eye. These meetings took place on Sundays when the Rebbe's followers would line up to file past him and have a personal interaction. The Rebbe would stand for hours giving each person a dollar bill to contribute to *tzedakah* (charity), which at that moment became a prized keepsake for its new owner, and a blessing. It was customary to redeem—that is, exchange—the dollars touched by the Rebbe's holy hand for ordinary currency that we would later deposit in a charity box of our choosing.

In order not to prolong the Sunday receiving line, Lubavitchers who lived in Crown Heights ordinarily only "went for dollars" on their birthdays or particularly special occasions. On my eighth birthday, I decided to try to prolong the encounter ever so slightly. Usually, I would just tell the Rebbe that my birthday was on such-and-such a day of the coming week. This time, standing in a line around the corner leading into 770, I practiced the phrase I had hit upon: "Ich vil a brachah az ich zol davenen un lernen besser" (I want a blessing so I can pray and learn better). I didn't particularly look forward to praying and learning better, but I did look forward to an extra moment with the Rebbe. I recited it over and over again in a whisper, lest I falter in front of the Rebbe. I had to be ready to say it quickly and clearly, so as not to be prematurely pushed along by the assistants standing nearby, whose job it was to keep the congested line moving.

As the line snaked its way from outside 770 through the front entrance, I shuffled into the narrow and crowded foyer, which was dominated by the figure of the Rebbe, who stood, slightly hunched over, behind a large table with a green upholstered cover, on which he leaned one arm. Rabbi Leibel Groner, the Rebbe's secretary, stood on the other side of the table and prepared rows of dollar bills for the Rebbe to retrieve and hand the visitors. When I was standing right in front of the Rebbe, I looked up and meekly delivered my line. It's possible the Rebbe detected the insincerity of my request—I was sincere about stealing a fraction more of his attention, just not about the praying and learning—or maybe in the tumult he simply couldn't hear my little voice. Either way, the Rebbe gazed right at me, handed me a dollar, and wished me the usual "brachah v'hatzlachah" (blessing and success).

When I was in fifth grade, in 1993, the holiday of Lag Ba-Omer fell on a Sunday in May, which meant there would be a Lag Ba-Omer parade in Crown Heights, a massive production with thousands of Jewish children from all across the New York metropolitan area and beyond. This was a year after the Rebbe suffered his first stroke and was already gravely ill, but it was also my only opportunity to be in my school's marching band. Our band had no horns, trumpets, or flutes. We only had as much band practice as could be crammed into two weeks, and we needed to be realistic.

There were three options: snare drums, bass drums, and cymbals. Given my limited musical abilities, I was chosen to play the cymbals. I was terrified. If the Rebbe came out of his sick room and watched our performance, as he used to do when he was well, it would be like playing for royalty.

We practiced for hours marching up and down the uneven soccer field, trying to avoid the rocks and ditches. The guys holding the snares would pound out *bududum, bududum, bududum, bududum, buddudum*. Then came my big moment. I would grasp the wooden handles and smash one giant brass cymbal against the other and—crash. My hands shook from the vibrations.

The plan was for us to march along Eastern Parkway, stop in front of the large stage intended for the Rebbe, dramatically turn to face him, and recite three times in unison, "Yechi adoneinu moreinu v'rabbeinu" (Long live our Master, our Teacher, our Rebbe). Then the band leader would blow his whistle. We would salute the Rebbe, play our number, and march on.

The night before our performance, I tossed and turned for hours. The thought of me and a handful of other boys standing alone in front of the Rebbe saluting him filled me with terror. The morning of the big day, I dressed in our band uniform: fire engine red shirt with a white "X" on the front and two gold buttons, along with white pants with a gold stripe down the outside of the legs. We also had white gloves and a red hat with gold trimming and a blue plume attached to the crown.

The morning of the parade, we still didn't know whether the Rebbe would be coming out. Moments before we were to march, right after a slew of floats depicting various biblical stories and before the clown car act, the bandleader told us, "The Rebbe is not coming out. We will do the whole thing as if the Rebbe is there." *Shucks! Now I'll never have a chance to perform in front of the Rebbe!*

Under a blazing sun, we marched in three rows from the corner of Brooklyn Avenue down Eastern Parkway. The organizers tried to arrange separate men's and women's sections, but in the hubbub of the parade, the divided areas morphed into a disorganized mass. The street was jammed with crowds of children wearing T-shirts of various colors and insignias representing their schools. Many of the children held signs attached to wooded sticks proclaiming, "We Want Moshiach [the messiah] Now!"

As we marched, I looked straight ahead to avoid getting distracted and flustered. My stomach was doing summersaults, and beads of sweat dripped down my forehead. We marched and played our song to the cheers of the crowd. When we arrived at the stage, we turned to where the Rebbe would have stood. With my gloved left hand I held both cymbals, and with my right hand I saluted.

Our community would become accustomed to practicing and performing as if the Rebbe was there.

Nine months after the parade, my classmates and I were standing outside the hospital praying for a miracle. The Rebbe was the center of Lubavitch life, its pulsating heart, and the idea that the Rebbe could die was unimaginable to me, as well as to his myriad followers.

Three months after our hospital prayer session, on the early morning of June 13, 1994, my father came into my room and shook me awake. Outside it was still dark. He just stood there. I could see his eyes were red and his lips were quivering. "Th . . . th . . . the . . ." He tried to speak, but his mouth refused to form any words.

I looked at him in terror: "What?"

A moment later he forced out of his mouth two words, "the Rebbe," and left the room crying.

That was all he said, but it was enough to convey to me that what we all feared, what we believed could never, ever happen, had happened. My family was then living in Morristown, New Jersey, and our house was very quiet. Yossi, who was going to yeshiva that year in Crown Heights, was already there and was the one who called to report the shocking news. The rest of the family silently made the hour trip from Morristown to Crown Heights. What would confront us when we arrived? I couldn't imagine. It was like trying to imagine what it would look like after a massive nuclear explosion.

I learned later that the Rebbe had died the night before and that after the *chevra kadisha* (the volunteers designated to ritually prepare bodies for burial) had discharged their duties, the Rebbe was wrapped in a prayer shawl and placed on the floor in his office in the upstairs of 770, surrounded by twelve tall memorial candles. Thousands of Lubavitchers, my brother Yossi included, filed past the Rebbe in a vigil to pay their respects.

When we got into Crown Heights, I walked to Eastern Parkway and positioned myself adjacent to the walkway in front of 770. I stood only yards away from the stained-glass windows of the Rebbe's office, decorated, as always, with the Asian figures of two standing women and a man seated in the lotus position.

These silent sentinels had seen decades of Lubavitch euphoria on display at 770. They saw Lubavitchers by the thousands assemble to receive dollars each Sunday from the Rebbe's hand and honey cake from the Rebbe on the eve of each Yom Kippur. They saw the Rebbe stand outside in the night air to join his Hasidim in blessing the new moon each month. These incongruous figures even saw the exuberant crowds at the Lag Ba-Omer parades pass by the Rebbe in noisy holiday spirit. But nothing could have prepared them for the scene that presented itself on that day.

It was one of total chaos. A crowd of some thirty thousand Lubavitchers and other mourners had gathered. Thousands of people pressed together. Many Lubavitchers had made a tear in the lapel of their jackets or blouses, the traditional Jewish sign of mourning for the death of a loved one. Grown men openly wailed like young children. A few men danced slowly in a circle and sang Hasidic melodies. A few women shook colorful tambourines. These fervent mourners believed that the "apparent" death of the Rebbe was somehow actually just another step, a last divine test, before the Rebbe would return as the messiah. Many in attendance were so profoundly dazed that they stood transfixed in a stupor.

It had been a clear day, but the heavens opened, and it began to pour at 4 P.M. when the Rebbe's coffin was taken to the cemetery, as if even God was joining in the mourning with his Lubavitch children. Although many Lubavitchers carried umbrellas, many more seemed oblivious to the rain. I, myself, had no protection from the elements.

Then the front door of 770 swung open and the Rebbe's simple pine coffin covered with his black kapota emerged, held aloft by some dozen Lubavitch men who were buffeted by the pressing crowd. As the coffin journeyed the short distance along the brick path to the sidewalk and the fifty paces to the waiting van, the coffin seemed to float above the heads of the Lubavitchers like a small box drifting along a choppy sea.

As the pallbearers continued to force their way through the anarchic crowd to the hearse, thousands of onlookers lunged forward to touch the box. I reached out to touch it, too, but the force of the crowd almost knocked me off my feet. The tidal wave slapped me back into my place. It seemed to mock me. *Who do you think you are? You think you deserve to have your puny hand touch the container that holds the most elevated being that ever lived? You think your mumbling of a few chapters of Psalms when the Rebbe was lying in the hospital was enough of a demonstration of your devotion to him?*

Because of the wave of Lubavitchers pressing against them, the pallbearers struggled to lower the coffin enough to slide it inside the police van that was being used as a hearse. At one point, the coffin was pitched at a precarious angle as it was buffeted by the crowd. It seemed that the physics of the crowd resisted the process of laying the Rebbe to rest.

With the coffin in the hearse, hundreds of men surged around the vehicle, trapping it. A phalanx of police officers pushed them back to allow the hearse to move forward. Still, dozens of Lubavitchers pressed against the hearse, impeding its progress. The driver did his best to inch his way along. This was too slow for one husky police officer, who pounded the hood of the van to get it moving, like an impatient horseman whipping a steed to urge it onward.

Inexplicably, the back door of the hearse remained open, and just before the vehicle picked up speed, a nimble Lubavitcher in his twenties jumped in beside the coffin, unable to resist the last opportunity for a private audience with the Rebbe.

Once the hearse departed, there was pandemonium to get into cars and race to the cemetery for the burial. Five-seater cars were packed with eight to ten passengers. Lubavitchers struggled to get into cars that were already speeding away.

My family drove to the cemetery, but we gave up hope of reaching the actual gravesite given the crush of thousands of Lubavitchers struggling to get close to it. We stayed outside the chain-link fence surrounding the cemetery and watched in disbelief. A radio reporter approached my father with a microphone and asked for his reaction. All my father could say was, "We came so close." He was referring to the redemption. "We came so close. We came so close."

I probably cried sometime during that day, but I don't have any memory of it. All I remember is feeling like I was drowning in a sea of chaos and confusion. I was confused because I'd been told by my teachers that the Rebbe wouldn't die—that the Rebbe couldn't die. And I felt overwhelmed by the sheer spectacle of the funeral, as well as its implications.

I'd been told that we were the last generation of exile and the first generation of the redemption. I'd been told that the Rebbe was the messiah. I'd been told that if we just prayed hard enough and demanded forcefully enough, the Rebbe would reveal himself to be the messiah. I'd been told the Rebbe could not die, but on that rainy June afternoon, we buried our beloved Rebbe in a grave in the Old Montefiore Cemetery in Springfield Gardens, New York.

I felt like screaming at the top of my lungs. How could the Rebbe die? There are basic facts about the operation of the universe. The Earth orbits the sun; every action has an equal and opposite reaction; and the Rebbe is the messiah and will usher in the final redemption. What does it mean if one of these axioms of the universe is revealed to be false?

The Rebbe had no children, and there were no obvious successors, so the status of the Rebbe remained unresolved for years after. Among Lubavitchers, the Rebbe's passing was almost always referred to simply by the date of its occurrence, Gimmel Tamuz, the third day of the Hebrew month of Tammuz, as if adding any more specific details about the event would have been too painful. In the months and years that followed the Rebbe's passing, the split that was already simmering in Lubavitch over the messiah issue sprouted into full poisonous bloom.

Lubavitch split into two camps, which were known as the messianists and the anti-messianists. The messianists, many of whom came from the ranks of the *baal teshuvahs* who joined the community from the outside, maintained that it was essential to continue to declare publicly that the Rebbe was the messiah. The anti-messianists, many of whom came from the old-guard Lubavitch families and the Lubavitch emissaries around the world, keenly attuned to public perception, were adamant that, to protect the public image of the Rebbe and Lubavitch, all public statements regarding the Rebbe's messianic status must cease immediately.

Astute non-Lubavitch observers noted that the disagreement between these two camps seemed to be about tactics, what to tell the outside world, rather than religious substance, what Lubavitchers themselves privately believed about the Rebbe still being the messiah after his death. Predictably, the anti-messianists strongly rejected this view. The messianists were happy with the narrative that deep down all Lubavitchers still accepted the Rebbe as the messiah.

The rift within Lubavitch caused great turmoil. Families threatened to break apart over it. Some Lubavitchers on opposite sides of the divide wouldn't marry into each other's families. Some parents withdrew their children from the established Lubavitch schools and summer camps and started rival programs because they disagreed with these institutions' positions on the messianism issue.

My parents didn't speak about the exact status of the Rebbe after his passing. So one Shabbos afternoon a few months after the Rebbe died, I asked my father whether he thought the Rebbe was still the messiah. My father started to prevaricate, "Well, it's hard to say," and I cut him off.

"Rabbi Hirsch told my class that there was no doubt about it. The Rebbe was still the messiah and would be returning to us very soon."

"I see," my father said. My father wasn't a Torah scholar, and he seemed to take the position that if my teacher was saying this, it must be the prevailing Lubavitch attitude. This would be one more thing he would have to take on board as a good Lubavitcher. And like a good Lubavitcher, once he accepted this view, he seemed to stick with it unquestioningly for years to come.

One of the battle fronts among the Lubavitch factions was language. Would the Rebbe be referred to simply as "the Rebbe" or would the clause "King Messiah" be added to his title. The battle also included fierce disagreement over reciting or printing the *Yechi*, the Hebrew mantra: "Long live our Master, our Teacher, our Rebbe, King Moshiach, forever and ever." A large banner with the mantra hung in the main sanctuary at 770, where it was routinely ripped down, only to be replaced the next day by a new one.

There was also intense disagreement over whether to add in printed material the three Hebrew letters *zayin*, *yud*, *aleph*, following the Rebbe's name. These letters were an acronym for "May his merit protect us." The acronym is used exclusively once a person has passed away, and the messianists felt that this phrase was a betrayal of the Rebbe's status as messiah.

Several years after the Rebbe's passing, while the battle still raged, the anti-messianist officials who held legal rights over the building of 770 erected a plaque in its red granite façade to commemorate the renovations of the building. The plaque included the Rebbe's name, followed by the contested acronym. The messianists could not let such a public affront to their beliefs stand. A zealot chiseled away the offending letters, leaving an ugly gash in the inscription.

Many Jews from across the Jewish spectrum were concerned that the Lubavitch belief in the Rebbe as the messiah even after his death sounded disturbingly similar to the Christian belief in the second coming of Jesus—which Jews have rejected for two millennia. This connection wasn't lost on Christian missionaries proselytizing to Jews. They put up a massive billboard in California; they purchased an advertisement in the *New York Times*; they printed T-shirts. All featured an iconic picture of the Rebbe with the caption: "Right idea: wrong person!"

Some Lubavitchers claimed that the Rebbe had never actually died and only appeared to the naked eye to have passed away. Other Lubavitchers believed that the Rebbe had in fact died but would be returning shortly, either as the messiah or simply as our spiritual leader.

The idea that the Rebbe might still be alive after his apparent death or that he would come back to life did not seem as outlandish to Lubavitchers as it may seem to others. We knew all along that it was possible to transcend the limits of the corporeal body, as well as the partition between the realm of the living and the realm of the dead.

It was in this atmosphere of messianic fervor, disillusionment, and confusion that I was about to become a *bar mitzvah*, a Jewish adult, and a foot soldier of the Rebbe.

3

The Light at the End of the Holland Tunnel

"You should not allow your emotions to lead you into temptations," Rabbi Minsky intoned.

Is it even possible for the mind to be in total control of all emotions and urges? my pubescent self thought. If such mastery over physical urges were possible, is it healthy? Would it make me a better person if I didn't pursue any of my physical urges?

Jews don *tefillin* in fulfillment of a verse in Deuteronomy (11:18) to remember the exodus from Egypt: "Therefore shall ye lay up these My words in your heart and in your soul; and ye shall bind them for a sign upon your hand, and they shall be for frontlets between your eyes."

Although the exact meaning of this crucial verse is ambiguous, and some Jews in antiquity understood it to be metaphorical, for at least two thousand years Jews have been binding prayer objects containing pieces of parchment with verses from the Bible on their arms and heads to fulfill God's wishes. I was now joining their ranks.

"You put the *tefillin* on your arm, near your heart, and on your head to symbolize that the mind should always control the heart." Rabbi Minsky, a thickset man with unusually strong hands and equally strong breath, told this to our class as he stroked his long brown beard and we munched on chocolate glazed donuts and sipped Coca-Cola. The little party was in honor of the first time I put on *tefillin* before my bar mitzvah.

Everything Rabbi Minsky said had special validity in my mind because he was more than a rabbi. He was a member of Hatzalah, the local volunteer Jewish emergency medical service. He was a Hasidic superhero who raced, with his two large black attaché cases, to comfort the injured and save lives. When I got a bee sting, Rabbi Minsky instantly had an ice pack for me. When a classmate broke his finger playing basketball, Rabbi Minsky produced a splint and set the finger. And when one of the grandfathers in the community was having trouble breathing, Rabbi Minsky pulled out an oxygen tank and averted a catastrophe.

From that day on, I took out my navy-blue velvet *tefillin* bag, inscribed with my full Hebrew name, Schneur Zalman Newfield; it even noted that I am a Cohen, a descendent of Moses's brother Aaron, and a member of the priestly caste. Below it is embroidered in silver thread a floral arrangement tied with a bow. I would unzip the bag and remove the phylacteries, the two leather boxes with their long black leather straps wrapped around the boxes' sides. When I held them, one in each hand, it felt as if I was cradling two baby birds that intended to fly off and carry my prayers heavenward.

Each morning, I carefully tightened the strap of my arm *tefillin* so it wouldn't become loose and slide down. Then I put on the head *tefillin*, pushing the rear knot down onto the base of my skull and centering the box in the front at my hairline. The straps of the head *tefillin* pushed my hair up like the top of a mushroom, and the knot at the base of the arm box dug into the tender skin near my armpit, pinching it. The straps left marks on my arm for hours, like a needle mark after giving blood—a bodily reminder of the act performed.

On each side of the box that is placed on the head there juts out the Hebrew letter *shin*, which is painted shiny black. The *shin* represents one of the names of God, Shaddai. The straps on my *tefillin* are the thick kind rather than the thin kind. Though my father had a house full of children to feed and was always looking for ways to save money, he paid an extra $150 for the thicker straps because they were less likely to rip apart after decades of use.

Putting on *tefillin* and praying became as much a part of my morning routine as brushing my teeth and showering, and I believed it was more effective than the latter activities at preserving my health. By the time I started putting on *tefillin*, at thirteen, I knew all the prayers by heart, so the prayer book in my hands was a stage prop, something to hold while swaying, rather than as a source of the words.

Still, my emotions and temptations were not entirely in check.

When I was ten, my parents temporarily relocated our family to Morristown, New Jersey, to escape the escalation in racial tension in Crown Heights. My parents asked the Rebbe for a blessing to move to Morristown. The Rebbe gave his blessing, so we moved. Three years later, my family moved back to the house in Crown Heights, which we had rented out in the meantime, because things had quieted down somewhat racially and because the small Lubavitch school in Morristown didn't go up to the high school grades that my older siblings and I were fast approaching.

In Morristown, my family lived at 79 Mills Street, in a three-story house located on a huge field. There was so much grass and so many trees I couldn't believe it was all ours. Coming from Brooklyn, it felt as if we had taken up residence in Central Park. The house on Mills Street was so large and had so many crawl spaces and extra secret compartments that another family could have been living there without us knowing it. Through diligent exploration, I discovered all kinds of treasures in the house left behind by the previous non-Jewish tenants, including a stash of faded Christmas cards from the 1940s and a small suitcase full of used tickets from old football games, some dating from as early as the late 1920s.

The center of Lubavitch life in Morristown was the eighty-two-acre leafy campus on Sussex Avenue that housed two yeshivas for adult men—one for those born in the community and another for those joining it from the outside—a boys' and a girls' elementary school, and a community synagogue. It also boasted a baseball field, a basketball court, a soccer field, and enough trees to build Noah's ark.

From its purchase in 1930 until its sale in 1971 to Lubavitch, the campus was owned by the Sisters of the Good Shepherd. The main building on the campus, a squat, four-story brown brick structure, had stone arches above the second-floor windows, and beneath the arches had been stone crucifixes. When Lubavitch bought the campus, they chiseled out the crucifixes, but their outline remained, a palimpsest of sorts, a reminder in masonry of the building's former faith.

As my bar mitzvah approached, I felt nervous. Not only would I need to deliver a five-page speech in Yiddish from memory to the 250 guests gathered at my celebration, but once I turned thirteen, according to Jewish law, I would be considered responsible for my own sins. All my deeds (and misdeeds) would go on my permanent record. If I forgot to pray one morning, boom, it would be on the cosmic record. If I failed to make a blessing before eating a slice of pizza, boom, it was on the record. If I got into a fight with a classmate, boom, on the record.

I was taught that hell existed for people who committed sins, and I completely believed in it. I believed everything I was taught at that time. I remember when I was eight or nine and enjoying a sleepover at my friend Baruch Brisky's house, I asked his mother about the resurrection of the dead in the messianic era. "Are people really gonna wake up and come out of the ground?"

My question wasn't motivated by disbelief. On the contrary, I totally believed what I had been told; I just failed to imagine the mechanics of how it would work. Mrs. Brisky assured me, "It is 100 percent going to happen when Moshiach [the messiah] comes," but she didn't provide any additional clarification of the mechanics.

Now that I was becoming *bar mitzvah* and responsible for everything I did, I could end up in hell for my sins. I knew that Jewish hell is not forever. It only lasts, at most, twelve months, just enough time for the impurities that have attached themselves to the soul to be washed away. Somehow knowing that hell was time limited didn't make it any less horrifying.

One of my favorite parts of living in Morristown was the mile-long hike to shul from our house up Sussex Avenue that I made with my father every Shabbos morning. I loved those walks because my father would hold my hand and play a game with me where we sent each other secret signals through hand squeezes. The squeezes didn't actually represent any content, but to me they were our special language. He squeezed five times; I squeezed back five times. I squeezed three times; he squeezed me back three times. The rest of the world was oblivious to our communications, as if we were undercover agents. I think he made up the game so that he got to hold my hand. The secret was that I also wanted to hold his hand.

My father is a quiet person who usually keeps his thoughts to himself. But sometimes on these walks, he would talk to me. I was often accused by teachers of talking too much. Some even ridiculed me for it based on the Talmud's (Kiddushin 49b) association of loquaciousness with womanhood. But I never seemed to know what to say to my father. So I just listened as he told me about books he read and topics that interested him. He told me about the tragic life of Richard Feynman and about his involvement in the Manhattan Project at Los Alamos, New Mexico, to make the first atom bomb. He told me about how the U.S. military recruited Navajo Indians during World War II to transmit coded messages in their native language to aid the Allied war effort. And he told me about how Jonas Salk discovered the first polio vaccine and how he tested it on his own family. During these talks I mostly listened and didn't say much.

I inherited my father's curiosity, and it manifested in a desire to connect with those around me. While living in Morristown, I developed a penchant for befriending strangers, especially people who were troubled or alone. I befriended a disturbed fifty-something-year-old named Moshe who dreamed of inventing a supersafe talking car. Some classmates claimed he used to work for NASA and was unhinged by an acid explosion in a lab. Others claimed he was a *lamid vuvnik*, one of the thirty-six hidden righteous men who maintain the world. Either way, he didn't have a lot of people to talk to at lunch at the yeshiva, and I was willing to listen to his grand plans. "If I could pull this off," he would say between bites of his tuna fish sandwich, "there would never be another car accident."

I also befriended a lonely workman in his thirties named Dovid, who had black hair and a bushy black beard. He fixed some broken closets in the house we were renting, and my parents were pleased, so they asked him to build a wooden table cover for our dining room table to accommodate our growing family. He constructed a wonderfully strong pine plywood cover with a frame that fit snugly over the table, thereby enlarging it to nine feet in length. We hung out together, and one day he drove me in his beat-up 1978 blue Ford van to a storage unit he rented. I was a bit nervous about what I might discover inside. He unlocked the door, and I saw rows and rows of shelves filled with appliances and power tools and a few lawnmowers and weed whackers resting on the floor. He told me, "I just drive around town and pick up broken stuff people leave on the sidewalk. I bring them here and fix them up. All these things now work."

After six months, Dovid vanished. It was as if he was never there. A year later, on a Friday night after shul, I heard one adult in the community tell another that Dovid suffered from schizophrenia and was admitted to Greystone Psychiatric Hospital and that he had died that week in the hospital. I walked away shaking. Looking back, it seems as if he was fixing those broken things to fix some brokenness in himself. He had no children. There is no plaque in his honor hanging in a synagogue. But he built my parent's dining room table cover that they still use every Shabbos. And every time I eat on it, I remember that gentle soul.

After three years living in Morristown, my parents decided to move back to Crown Heights. Since I enjoyed my teachers in Morristown, I stayed on for a year as a boarder with a Lubavitch family, the Cohens, and visited my family on the weekends. I had gone to sleep away camp for three summers already and would see my family on the weekends, so I didn't mind living away from home.

One Friday afternoon, as I made my way from the subway station to my house along a crowded Kingston Avenue, I stopped at the corner of President Street. A Russian Jewish man with a wild beard and a sailor's cap had a stall there where he sold books and tchotchkes, and I wanted to take a look. As I stood there, I noticed a fellow bystander. He looked like he was in his seventies; had a prominent red nose and liver stains on his face and arms; and was schlepping a large upright duffle bag with wheels.

Maybe I asked him whether he needed help with the bag. Not sure. All I remember is that by the time I walked with him the nine blocks to his apartment building, I knew enough to know I would be seeing him again. His name was Larry Weeks, and he was a professional juggler. He served in World War II traveling to Army bases performing as part of Irving Berlin's United Service Organizations (USO) show *This Is the Army*. As a child he saw the escape artist Harry Houdini perform, and for years he had been a collector and dealer of magic and juggling supplies. He was also a collector and dealer of Houdini memorabilia and was at that moment the only person in the world to own a copy of the 1919 Houdini film *The Grim Game*.

A few months before I met Larry, Rabbi Minsky, my teacher, had notified my parents that "Zalman is interested in magic, juggling, martial arts, old coins and stamps, painting, and first aid. He is interested in everything but learning Torah." This was an accurate assessment, and now here was a guy who knew all about juggling and magic. My heart sang.

Larry, a nonreligious Jew who happened to reside in Crown Heights, lived on Brooklyn Avenue in an old building that, like him, was past its prime. The elevator had long stopped working; the paint in the hallways was peeling; and a musty smell permeated the building. He rented two apartments right next to each other. One was supposed to be for his supplies, and the other was intended as a home for him and his dog, Charlie. In fact, both apartments were jammed floor to ceiling with books, magazines, and supplies related to magic, juggling, and clowning. We agreed that I would help him organize his stuff, and he would teach me how to juggle.

I organized some boxes and took some bags of garbage to the dumpster. Larry insisted, "You know this is really great stuff, it's just falling apart because I've had it for years." Then Larry started my juggling classes using tennis balls full of sand. "You know, I used to get paid fifty bucks per class to teach juggling; now you're getting it for free." We stood in the hallway of his apartment building. "You know, I developed this technique of teaching juggling myself." First he demonstrated with one ball. "You throw it from one hand to the other. You make an arch." I practiced a few times.

"Not bad. Now put one ball in each hand and try to throw one up in the air and before it lands in the second hand, throw the other ball under it to the first hand." Because of the sand, they felt a lot heavier than I expected. I tried it but kept dropping both balls, and they would go rolling down the empty hall.

"OK. You see what you need to do. Now go home and practice. Come back next week."

I came back the following Friday and moved more boxes. Then he said, "Come into my office," and walked me out of his apartment and into the hallway. "Now, let me see what you can do." I showed him that I was able to throw both balls without dropping them. "Good job, Zelman." For some reason, he always called me Zelman. I tried to correct him but then realized it was both hopeless and unimportant. He had seen Houdini with his own eyes.

"OK, Zelman, now I'm going to teach you how to throw all three balls. Watch me."

He threw up one ball, then the next, but by the time he threw up the third, he had lost control and all three balls came crashing down. "Dammit, my arthritis is acting up. I'm going tomorrow to the VA

[Veterans Affairs hospital] for my dialysis; maybe they can help with the arthritis. Just . . . just wait a minute."

He tried again, and this time it went flawlessly, like it was as easy for him to juggle as it was for others to scratch their elbow. "You saw what I did? You put two balls in the right hand, one in front of the other. You throw the first. Then you throw the one in the left hand. Then you throw the second one in the right hand. That's juggling, baby."

He handed me all three balls. I set them up as he instructed. I threw the first, then the second, then the third. Then all three fell to the ground. I tried several more times. Charlie was pawing at the apartment door, so Larry took him out. Charlie walked around and got in the way. "Stay. Good dog," Larry said and patted his head. "You know, Charlie was in the circus and can still perform."

"I didn't know that," I said as I looked over the slow-moving creature. Maybe he was a fox terrier. He seemed as if he was crawling toward the end of life, and now Larry was about to put him to work just to impress me. "It's OK. I believe you."

"No, no, watch this." He took a small dog treat out of his pocket and ordered, "Dance." Then he lifted his hands in the air, and sure enough the dog stood up on his hind legs and put his front paws in Larry's hands. Larry smiled widely and held him there for a few seconds.

"Wow. That's great." I really was impressed that the dog could do anything.

"No, no." Larry waved his hands. "There's more."

He tried to get Charlie to weave in-between his legs as he walked down the hall, but the dog couldn't keep track. He kept getting lost. Then he just stopped trying and lay down.

"It's OK. He did the other trick," I said.

"Charlie used to be able to do all of this in his sleep."

With months of practice my juggling improved, and hanging out with Larry intensified my interest in magic. He would sometimes perform tricks, which he then agreed to teach. He taught me how to appear to make a handkerchief dance without moving it and how to make a coin go through a solid handkerchief. After allowing me to practice a bit, he removed from a shelf a thick volume on magic tricks by the legendary Harry Blackstone Sr. and read a passage out loud. The crux of it was that an amateur manages to master the mechanics of a trick, but a true performer makes the effect look effortless. I kept practicing and expanding the number of tricks I could perform.

I considered whether magic tricks were likely to go on my record of sins. Throughout this time, I thought of magic as a harmless pastime, if one that distracted me from learning Torah. I knew it was "goyish," but on the scale of heretical things, it was harmless. A year later, when I moved to Chicago to attend a Lubavitch high school, I met a Lubavitcher who was a former magician, and he discouraged me from doing magic. "The truth is," this guy told me, "magic is a kind of cheating. You're being dishonest with the audience, and *halacha* [Jewish law] prohibits it." I was sorry to hear this, but I wasn't ready to give up something I enjoyed so much and had worked at for so long.

Then, a few months later, while walking with Berel Teibenfeld, one of my teachers and my personal mentor, on Michigan Avenue near the Chicago Water Tower, he tried to persuade me to stop doing magic. Berel had a pleasant face and a hairline that was in full retreat. "I once knew a *bocher* [yeshiva student]," Berel said in his thick British accent. "He got involved in magic and ended up performing in bars, and he stopped being *frum* [Orthodox]. I'm not saying that will happen to you, but magic could cause trouble."

"I hear you, Berel. I'll have to think about it."

The following week, I sat at a *farbrengen* in the basement of the Chicago yeshiva, and Rabbi Lefkowitz, the dean of the school, thundered, "In the times of the Frierdiker Rebbe [the Rebbe's father-in-law and predecessor] *tmimmim* [students in Lubavitch yeshivas] were *moyser nefesh* [sacrificed their lives] for the Rebbe. They literally went to the gulags to fulfill the Rebbe's wishes. What are you willing to give up for our Rebbe? What are you willing to give up to be *mekusher* [connected] to the Rebbe?"

As I sat there, I decided my sacrifice would be giving up magic. I thought it was worth it to be close to the Rebbe.

Most of the loners I befriended in my time exploring Morristown were kind and sensitive individuals who only wanted to talk to someone who would listen. One person I befriended was of a completely different sort. He went by the name Uriel Ben David.

Uriel Ben David was in his early forties and stood over six feet tall; he had a pockmarked face and thinning blond hair. Uriel worked for the yeshiva at odd jobs, especially spackling and painting the yeshiva walls. He had a temper and often blew up at kids who touched his paint equipment. "You're *mazikim* [little demons]" was a common refrain of his.

One sunny day, he gave me a Marlboro cigarette to smoke, and we struck up a conversation. Later that day, I went to his room to hang out. In the middle of talking, he casually reached into a rectangular cardboard box under his bed full of pornography, picked up a magazine of pictures of naked women, and dropped it into my lap. He said, "Here. You can check it out if you're interested." I looked through the *Playboy* wide-eyed.

I wasn't even allowed to speak to girls, and now I was staring at pictures of naked women. It felt awkward to look at the magazine in the presence of Uriel, but I had never heard of the concept of "stranger danger" or the idea that there are people who sexually abused children.

The only time up to that point I ever heard a glancing reference to child molestation was, of all places, in a mikvah. I heard two adults talking. One whispered the name of a Lubavitcher. The other one said, "*Yemach shemo* [May his name be erased], he ran away to Israel to avoid the American courts." I asked my father what they were talking about, and he mumbled something about "a bad person who hurt children." But I had no idea what "hurt" meant.

Uriel smoked Marlboro Reds, and the walls of his cramped and cluttered bedroom on the Morristown yeshiva campus reeked of his cigarettes. I remember the brand because he told me, "Marlboro is connected to the Ku Klux Klan. It's obvious. Just look at the wrapper." He pointed to three decorations that, when turned over, looked like the letter *K*. He also showed me that in the word *Marlboro* on the wrapper, the top of the *M* is shorter than the tops of the *L* and the *B*, so if you put your finger over the name and leave only the tops of those three letters showing, and you turn it over, it looks like a person watching another being hanged.

One evening about a month later, when we were alone, he sat at his computer in his bedroom holding a lit cigarette and told me, "It's perfectly natural to want to look at pictures of naked women." As he spoke, he jerked the cigarette and streams of smoke followed his hand. "You're almost thirteen; it's natural to want to be with girls." Then, maybe to emphasize this point, or to allay my fears that he was sexually interested in me, he added, "I drive to Newark to pick up Black women for sex. It's perfectly natural." I was stunned and said nothing.

Uriel handed me a *Penthouse* magazine. I took it and was mesmerized. He encouraged me to touch myself in front of him. "Don't worry. It's perfectly normal. Even Rabbi Gershovitz [the head rabbi of the adult yeshiva in Morristown] does it. I promise." I felt extremely uncomfortable and didn't know what to do. I ignored him and he didn't push the point. I continued staring at the pictures of scantily clad women performing gravity-defying feats.

A few minutes went by and then I heard a gentle knock on the door. I froze. Another knock. Uriel motioned for me to stand behind his closet door on the left side of his room. With me tucked out of sight, Uriel sauntered up to his room door and opened it a crack. "What can I do for you, Sir," he said in a flat voice, expressing no emotion. Looking around my hiding spot I eyed a wooden broomstick with a pink dildo-type sleeve stuck to the top of it. I had no clue what it was used for.

"We're having problems with the mainframe of the computer we use to produce the yeshiva's pamphlet of *chidushim* [Torah insights]. It keeps on crashing. What should we do about it?"

I realized immediately that the twenty-year-old yeshiva student with the computer trouble was Gavriel Mishulovin, my bar mitzvah teacher. My heart raced. Uriel was a computer whiz, and people came to him with computer questions.

Uriel growled. "It's always something with that computer. OK. I'll check it out in half an hour."

With that, Uriel closed the door. I was relieved that Gavriel left without discovering me, but the experience left me shaken. Not only was I worried about being caught looking at pornography and getting into trouble, but I also wondered what Gavriel would think about what I was doing. *Did good Lubavitch boys like Gavriel do the kinds of things that Uriel claimed were "perfectly normal"?*

Two weeks after I hung out with Uriel in his room, I biked through a wooded trail and returned to the yeshiva soaked in sweat. Uriel spotted me and rushed over. He wore his white painter's cap and paint-speckled jeans. "Hey, Zalman, do you want to go with me to the mikvah [the ritual bath, which also housed the yeshiva showers]?"

"No, thanks. I'm good." I wasn't sure exactly what he wanted from me, but the thought of us naked together made me want to puke.

"Are you sure?" He looked at me with a face that was both kind and insistent at the same time.

"Yep. I'm all good. I'm just going to get a cup of water." I slowly walked my bike in the opposite direction from Uriel. After that day, I never went to Uriel's bedroom again or spent any more time with him alone.

Uriel wrote and published a weekly Torah newsletter on brightly colored paper and deposited them in the community synagogue and the two yeshivas on campus. Although he occasionally wrote slightly wacky opinions—such as that Esau and not his brother Jacob was the real victim in the biblical story—Uriel's true designs were hidden from the adults in the community. Uriel would include in the newsletters cartoon characters and would take pictures of young boys in the community and digitally place their heads on the cartoon bodies. I was devastated to learn years later that once Uriel had these boys in his room to take the pictures, he arranged to take nude pictures and videos of them, as well. Tragically, he also molested some of them.

He never molested me or took pictures of me, but I was embarrassed about the pornography. I put *tefillin* on every day and was instructed to control my bodily urges—and did not tell my parents.

Although my father never had any kind of "sex talk" with me, Refael Cohen, the father of the family I was boarding with in Morristown, took it upon himself to educate me on Judaism's attitude toward the body. Cohen had an unsmiling face with an angular nose. He was not a typical Lubavitcher. His day job was as a software engineer, but he was an ascetic and woke up each morning at 4 o'clock to study in the yeshiva for a few hours. He would make the mile-long trek to the yeshiva to study even in rainstorms or blizzards.

One night before I went to bed, he told me, "Now that you are *bar mitzvah*, it is crucial that you know that the *aveyra* [sin] of *moitzi zera livatalah* [wasting one's seed] is very grave. Many *mikubbalim* [kabbalists] write about how such bodily impurities pollute the *nishama* [soul] and make it harder for us to feel the *shechina* [divine presence] around us."

I felt like bugs were crawling up my arms and legs and desperately wanted him to stop talking about this. I looked away. He wouldn't give up. "I know this is an uncomfortable topic, but it's very important. There are ways to avoid this grave problem. One should avoid thinking thoughts by day that can lead to emissions at night. Also, one is forbidden from sleeping on one's stomach so as not to stimulate the *ayver* [limb] and lead to unfortunate results."

I figured he had exhausted himself and was done with the topic, but I was wrong. "One more point, Zalman: It is clearly forbidden for a person to touch the *ayver* [limb] at any time, even when urinating. One must direct the organ indirectly. Do you understand?" I had no idea what he was talking about but desperately wanted him to stop, so I nodded my head as if I comprehended.

That summer, I attended the yeshiva program in Morristown, designed for boys who were bar mitzvah age. We slept in the dorms for the older boys, who were away at other summer camps employed as counselors and learning teachers. One of the highlights of the summer program was a two-day camping trip. I was assigned to a tent with three other boys from Crown Heights, only one of whom I was close to.

Before we set out on the camping trip, we talked among our tentmates about doing "stuff" to each other. I don't remember who instigated this discussion, but I don't think it was me. All I remember is that on the first night of the trip I touched the rear end of one of the boys in the tent. For like a second. That was it. I don't think the boy whom I touched touched me. The other two boys in the tent touched each other, as well, but I'm not sure precisely what they did. I didn't give the incident much thought.

A week later, back at our home base in Morristown, I was pulled out of my bed after lights out, KGB-style, and marched off to a meeting with five staff members. My heart was pounding. My main interrogator, a wiry bloodhound of a man in his twenties with large glasses, paced around the room while pummeling me with questions: "What happened in your tent at the overnight? Don't try to lie to us! We already know everything!"

I stared at my interrogator, fighting back tears. My lips quivered. *What did they know, and who gave me up? Why did they think this was all my fault? I did almost nothing!*

"You better tell us the truth!" My interrogator pounded his fist on the table. "Where did you learn such *ekeldiker zachin* [disgusting things]?"

I couldn't contain myself and burst out crying. My whole body was shaking. Through my tears I blurted out, "Uriel Ben David . . . showed . . . me . . . pictures . . ."

As soon as I said that, the room became quiet. All the staff started whispering to one another. After a moment, my interrogator turned to me and said, "Everything is going to be OK, Zalman. You can go back to your room now."

It turned out that a few weeks earlier, a brave teen who knew what Uriel was doing told his parents, who informed the police. The police arrested Uriel and confiscated his computer. They used a decryption program to crack the sophisticated password on the computer and found a stash of incriminating pictures and videos. The police also discovered that Uriel wasn't actually Jewish; that his real name was Peter King, and he was a fugitive of the Federal Bureau of Investigation hiding out in our yeshiva. Now the rabbis at the yeshiva were assisting the police effort to collect testimonies from Uriel's victims.

My interrogators notified Rabbi Hirsch, who was liaising with the police; he contacted my parents and informed them about my involvement with Uriel. Rabbi Hirsch assumed that since I was involved with Uriel, I had also been molested, and he wanted me to talk to the police investigator.

I was walking into the banquet for the last night of camp when my mother phoned. She called on the public pay phone located in a small room right off the hallway where all the campers were now passing to enter the banquet. "Zalman . . . Zalman . . ." Her voice was halting. "I know what Uriel did to you and the other boys." Now she was crying. "I spoke to Rabbi Hirsch and to the detective running the investigation." Blood rushed to my face, and my throat went dry. She blew her nose loudly. "I wish you would have told me what was happening; I could have been there for you."

I didn't say a word. I was stuck in place, the large black plastic handset pressed against my ear.

"I'm so sorry. I'm so sorry this happened. We will do . . . We will . . . whatever we can to help you deal with this."

My eyes teared up. I could hardly talk. I hung up the phone and went to the banquet.

A week later, in a tearful and excruciatingly awkward conversation in my parents' kitchen, I would explain to my mother and father that I was not molested by Uriel. At first, they thought I was hiding the truth and encouraged me to be totally honest. My mother implored, "Don't worry. We are not angry with you. We just need to know what really happened." When I persisted with my story, they finally accepted it as the truth.

With the help of the testimony of several courageous victims, Uriel was sent to prison.

I'm not sure exactly what the impact of my exposure to Uriel has been on my life. Over the next few years, I ended up having several brief sexual encounters with Lubavitch boys my age. None of us knew what we were doing. We spoke constantly about girls, but because of the gender segregation in the community, those girls were outside our lives. We felt desperate to do something. Did Uriel's exposing me to pornography at a young age make me aware of sexual desire earlier than it would have happened on its own? Did my stirring sexual desire at that age mean that it would be expressed with boys rather than girls? Did it make me more suspicious of outsiders? Of insiders? I'm not sure of the answers to these questions.

Looking back, my heart is full of love for my parents. They responded to the news with compassion and sensitivity and total support. Many other parents can't be counted on to respond that way. Their love for me, I knew, as for all their children, would never falter, and they would move heaven and earth to protect us from harm.

I was lucky not to need much protection from the abuse in Morristown, since I had been spared all but a few creepy interactions. But it wasn't long after this that a tsunami of pain headed straight toward my family, and despite all the efforts to protect us, none of us would remain unscathed.

4

Dearest Shimmy

"Zalman, your dad's on the pay phone," a friend informed me. I was startled. My father never called during the day. I strode up the darkened stairs of my yeshiva in West Rogers Park, Chicago's main ultra-Orthodox Jewish neighborhood.

I reached the pay phone on the wall. "Hi, Tatty, what's going on?" I said.

"I have some serious news. It's about your brother. Shimmy had a large lump on his neck, and we had it tested. It's not good. I took him out of class today, and we're at the hospital now. *Im yirts' Hashem* [God willing], everything will be OK."

"What do you mean it's not good? What is it?"

"It's leukemia."

I could feel my hands shaking. "Is that cancer?"

"It's a cancer of the blood."

I hung up and felt woozy. My legs couldn't bear my weight. I went into the yeshiva office nearby and sat down. A classmate standing around realized something was wrong and called over Berel Teibenfeld, who was one of my teachers and my personal mentor.

"Zalman, is everything all right?"

I swallowed hard, fighting back tears. "My father just called to say that my brother Shimmy has cancer. He's only eleven."

"That's terrible. I'm so sorry to hear that."

"I just know he's going to die," I confessed as I stared at the brown floor tiles.

"*Chas vasholom* [God forbid]. Don't say that. There are many cures and treatments, and with *Hashem*'s [God's] help things will turn out right."

Hot tears poured down my fifteen-year-old cheeks. Berel came over and hugged me tight. As he had done on several other occasions when I cried at *farbrengens*, devotional gatherings, he then tucked my head into the crook of his neck and leaned his ear on mine, my tears moistened his hairy neck. I felt so safe and loved in his embrace.

I don't know whether my mind ran to Shimmy dying because all the people who I ever heard of who had cancer had died—I didn't know any kids who had it—or whether I was already then a natural pessimist.

Shimmy was diagnosed on Thanksgiving in 1997. Given how many doctors and nurses were off, it was a thankless day to be admitted. At the time, I was beginning my first year attending the yeshiva in Chicago. It was common for teenage boys to board away from home for school to experience more immersive learning among peers and teachers, without the distractions of family and home life.

Of my eight siblings, I was closest to my younger brother Shimmy, whose full name was Shimon Eliezer, but everyone called him by his nickname. In grade school, I would get into brawls with Yossi, my older brother by two years, that often ended with me being pinned on the ground with his elbow in my back. Yossi seemed to hold the fact of my birth against me. Although the fisticuffs were behind us, we hadn't yet found common interests to bond over. My only other brother was Mendy, who was still in diapers.

As for the girls, I loved my sisters dearly and enjoyed hearing about the book reports they were writing for school. (They were forever pumping out book reports. It seemed like there were too many to count, like the conveyer belt that produced too many chocolates for Lucille Ball to handle in the chocolate factory scene in *I Love Lucy*.) But given how separate the schooling and socializing of girls and boys in Lubavitch were, we were hardly buddies.

I was accustomed to protecting Shimmy. When we lived in Morristown, the kids at school would tease him for speaking fast and for his thick Brooklyn accent. He would refer to his parents as "mudda" and "fadda," and H_2O as "wooda." I did what I could to shield him from their insults. But now I felt as powerless as a one-legged frog.

The thought of Shimmy as a frail and weak cancer patient was unfathomable. He was a head shorter than many of his classmates, but he was a firecracker. He was a total showman and always positioned himself at the center of the action. He loved the attention. At my bar mitzvah, Shimmy, age nine, decked out in a black suit with a tuxedo shirt and bowtie, joined me on top of a wooden table that my friends lifted high in the air and spun around and around as they danced.

Shimmy initially crouched on the table, too scared to stand up. Then he stood up cautiously and I held his hands, but he immediately waved both hands downward and screamed at the top of his lungs, "I'm gonna fall! I'm gonna fall! Don't drop me!" As soon as the table was lowered to the ground, he jumped off clapping his hands and smiling broadly as though he had just climbed Everest. He shouted, "Yay! We made it! Anytime!"

In the coming months, in addition to consulting with oncologists and submitting to their treatments, my family tried to boost Shimmy's recovery through spiritual means. My siblings and I would read a chapter of Psalms each day for Shimmy, and my sisters arranged for their classmates to give coins to charity in his honor. We were beseeching God's mercy by every means at our disposal.

Back in Brooklyn for Chanukah, I went to visit Shimmy in the hospital. Ordinarily, my mother stayed with him in the hospital, but she was off that night, and my father was with him instead. Shimmy now had an IV pole that he dragged around the ward like an extra limb. He zoomed down the wide halls, dangling IV lines trailing behind. He seemed in a good mood. His doctors were still cautiously optimistic.

After Shimmy lay down on his hospital bed, my father and I put on our fedoras and sat on gray chairs to pray *maariv* (the evening service). I opened my *siddur* (prayer book) and read the first line: "V'hu rachum yichaper ovoyn" (He is compassionate. He forgives iniquity and does not destroy). Tears welled in my eyes.

I glanced over at Shimmy, his body riddled with cancer, his arm hooked up to IVs. *Was this an instance of God's compassion? What sins could Shimmy possibly have committed to warrant such savage abuse?*

With our prayers finished and Shimmy asleep, my father confided, "The doctors say Shimmy will probably need a bone marrow transplant."

"What is that?"

"They will give Shimmy strong radiation to completely wipe out the cancer from his blood. Then they take bone marrow from a donor and put it in Shimmy's body. If all goes well, his body will accept it and use it to make new blood."

"That sounds good."

"Yes," he said slowly, chewing on the inside of his right cheek. "There are two problems, though. They need to find a match, and the donor bone marrow needs to accept Shimmy's body."

"What could happen if the donor marrow doesn't accept his body?"

"*Chas v'shalom* [God forbid] if the new bone marrow is not a good match, it will attack Shimmy's body, a condition known as graft-versus-host disease. That is extremely dangerous."

The next day, my whole family, including fifteen-month-old baby Chaya, went to the office of a pediatric hematologist at New York University to give blood to test whether we were potential donors. The tests showed that none of us were. If Shimmy was going to get a bone marrow transplant, it would have to be from a nonrelative, which carries much higher risks for the recipient.

Once I returned to Chicago, my father would call and update me on his condition. Shimmy was receiving an intense regimen of chemotherapy, and his beautiful light-brown hair had fallen out due to his treatment. One night, my father explained the difficulties of Shimmy's treatment.

"The problem is that all the medicines Shimmy gets are really poison. If they help attack the cancer, they damage his kidneys. If he takes something for the kidneys, it damages his heart."

"So what do they do?"

"The whole thing is a balancing act. The hope is that they are able to get rid of the cancer before the other major organs are totally destroyed."

My father was a dermatologist. The closest he came to cancer professionally was diagnosing melanoma. Leukemia was totally beyond his training and expertise, but he was doing the best he could to get educated about Shimmy's condition and treatments.

Eventually, the treatments succeeded in ridding Shimmy's body of cancer so that he was in remission. But the doctors explained that this probably wouldn't last and that he would need to have a bone marrow transplant to keep him cancer-free.

That summer, since he was in remission, in addition to attending Camp Simcha, an Orthodox summer camp designed for children with terminal illnesses, he joined me for a Shabbos at Camp Gan Yisroel, in upstate New York. The Shabbos he visited, the camp had another guest, a wealthy middle-aged banker. The banker, who wasn't Orthodox but was connected to Lubavitch, spoke to Shimmy and was moved by his charm. The banker—who took a lackadaisical approach to shaving his facial growth and wore black dress shoes with no socks—bought the whole camp ice cream sandwiches to do something special for Shimmy. None of the campers ever knew that their surprise treats were the result of a skinny twelve-year-old who had just completed months of mortal combat with cancer.

Once we said our goodbyes to summer and dragonflies, I went back to yeshiva in the Windy City but returned home for Yom Kippur. On the eve of the holiday, I was standing in the living room when my father entered clad in his *kittel* (a white linen robe) and fedora. We had both already submerged in the mikvah, the ritual bath, and knelt on all fours and submitted to mock whipping with a leather belt of thirty-nine "lashes" in remembrance of those administered in Jerusalem in ancient times. All these rituals were part of our preparation for Yom Kippur.

My father placed his hands on my forehead to give me the traditional priestly benediction from the book of Numbers. He recited, "Yivarechicha adoynoy v'yishmirecha" (May God bless you and keep you. May God cause the divine light to shine upon you and be gracious to you. May God turn toward you, and grant you peace). He held my head in his soft hands and gently kissed my forehead. I walked into the dining room.

My father turned to bless Shimmy. Shimmy's hair had grown back over the summer and my father placed his hands on Shimmy's full head of hair. My father was silent. I could see his shoulders shaking slightly and his eyes tightly closed. Then, in a quivering voice he began, "Yivarechicha adoynoy v'yishmirecha" (May God bless you and keep you. May God cause the divine light to shine upon you and be gracious to you). My father's head shook up and down, and he started to cry. He paused. Then, in a lower voice, he continued with the last verse of the blessing, "Yisa adoynoy ponov eylecha, v'yosaym l'cha shalom" (May God turn toward you and grant you peace). As I watched from the dining room, tears of hopefulness tinged with trepidation ran down my cheeks.

From the moment Shimmy was diagnosed, I never had a conversation with my parents about whether I should stay in Brooklyn to be close to him. My parents tried to shield their children from the chaos and pain of his treatments. So after the holiday, I returned to Chicago.

By early October, malevolent lumps again had appeared on Shimmy's neck. The cancer was back. He again went on chemo. When, through a mutual friend, the banker heard about it, he bought Shimmy two bulging shopping bags full of lollipops the size of Frisbees and candy canes as long as my arm. One of these confections could have kept the average kid busy for days. It was ridiculous—totally out of proportion—but they completely matched Shimmy's outsize personality. Unfortunately, at that point the side effects of the chemo were so severe that he couldn't stand the thought of candy. Just as our prayers failed to keep the cancer away, the lollipops failed to comfort him.

When Shimmy reentered the hospital, my mother joined him, overcoming her natural dislike of doctors and hospitals to oversee every detail of his care. She knew the name of every doctor and nurse and kept a journal of every medicine that was ordered for him and its proper dosage. More than once, her vigilance prevented the wrong medicine or dosage from being administered.

Even when sick in the hospital, Shimmy's spirit was unbeaten. A charity for pediatric cancer patients gave him a small video camera, and he would make videos of his daily life. Avraham Fried, a celebrity singer in the ultra-Orthodox music world whom Shimmy had befriended at Camp Simcha, came to visit one night. Shimmy recorded their encounter.

Fried, a slim thirty-nine-year-old with a long, pointy beard, entered Shimmy's room. He had on a forest-green vest and a dark sports jacket, his black hair brushed to the side. After chitchatting for a minute, Fried said, "I came to wish you a *refuah shelama* [complete recovery], Shimmy. Chanukah just ended. May Chanukah give us light and *refuas* [cures] and *yeshuas* [salvation] and, of course, the ultimate light [the messiah]."

Without skipping a beat, Shimmy, like a perfect Lubavitcher, added, "The ultimate *geula* [redemption]!"

Shimmy was wearing blue scrubs, an undershirt, his *tzitzis*, an open green flannel shirt, and brown Birkenstocks and on his completely bald head rested a large yarmulke. His voice was much weaker than usual, but he was completely in control. He sounded like a young Steven Spielberg directing a set. He instructed, "How about you stand up against the door and I'll videotape you singing."

Avraham Fried was almost forty, had been performing around the world for nearly two decades, and had already produced twenty-two albums, but Shimmy wasn't the least bit intimidated. Fried graciously complied with Shimmy's request. He stationed himself at the wall, which was decorated by my mother with a large picture collage and the message "We love you Shimmy," as well as a large picture of the Rebbe. Fried sang a few bars from his newly released song, "Modah Ani," based on the prayer thanking God for giving new life each morning. Shimmy observed, "It sounds different when you sing it on tape because of all the music."

Fried joked with him, "Different or better?"

Shimmy, ever the gentleman, held back from criticizing Fried's unadorned voice and responded, "Just different."

Then Fried sat down on a blue recliner right next to the maroon recliner on which Shimmy was seated as my mother took over camera duties. He and Fried sang together Fried's hit song released the year before, "Chazak," based on a verse from the Bible (Isaiah 41:6), "Ish es re'eihu ya'azoru ule'achiv yomar: chazak" (Everyone helps his neighbor and says to his brother, "Be strong!").

The main refrain of the song, repeated dozens of times, is the Hebrew word *chazak* (Be strong), a message perfectly attuned to Shimmy's need at the moment. As they sang, Shimmy snapped his fingers, and Fried tapped his knee to the catchy beat. In the middle of the duet, the director cuts in with advice to Fried: "We have to sing a little louder to make sure it picks it up."

A week after Avraham Fried's visit, I made a trip to see Shimmy in the hospital. As his condition had worsened, he had gotten so thin he seemed to be sinking into himself. His physical body, the vessel for his soul that anchors it to this world, was disappearing.

After the Rebbe's passing, Lubavitchers continued to turn to him in moments of despair. Instead of calling the Rebbe's secretary or writing a letter to the Rebbe's office, followers would write letters and read them at his gravesite in the Old Montefiore Cemetery in Springfield Gardens, New York, after which they would tear them up and place the scraps in the enclosure around his grave. Shimmy wanted to write a letter to the Rebbe to ask for a blessing, but his hands were too weak to hold the pencil. He was too ill even to petition the Rebbe to be healed. He dictated, and I wrote it out in Yiddish.

On the car ride home from the hospital, my father told me in a measured voice, "Unfortunately, Shimmy has not responded to his latest treatment as the doctors had hoped. We will go ahead with the bone marrow transplant."

Three weeks later, the hospital found a match through a global donor database. While I was back in Chicago, Shimmy was subjected to intense radiation to eradicate the cancer and destroy his bone marrow to prepare his body for the donor's marrow. The donor's marrow was given to him through an IV, which looked like an ordinary blood transfusion.

My whole family waited anxiously to see how Shimmy's body would respond to the bone marrow. My father called two weeks after the transplant to say that Shimmy had developed graft-versus-host disease and that I should say more *Tehilim*, more Psalms.

I sat on a raggedy couch in the common area of my dormitory. My whole body tensed up. I clenched my fist.

Shit! How can Shimmy die so young? He hasn't even had his bar mitzvah! How could God allow my kid brother to die?! Was God too busy keeping track of all the impure thoughts yeshiva students had throughout the day? How could I have abandoned Shimmy and gone back to yeshiva in Chicago? Was I too preoccupied with my own yeshiva studies that I never even protested to my parents about staying in Brooklyn to be close to Shimmy? Or did I just assume that God, my shepherd, wouldn't let such an innocent sheep from his flock die so young?

On February 23, 1998, my father called as I was preparing for bed and said, "Zalman, it's very serious. Shimmy is in a coma. You have to come back home right away."

My mind raced. My heart pounded out of my chest. Could this really be happening?

"Zalman, I spoke to your principal. He told me that there is a van leaving Chicago tonight going to Crown Heights. You should go on the van."

I was too overwhelmed by the news to grasp the logistics.

"What about a van?"

He patiently repeated himself, and added, "Jeff will pick you up from Crown Heights and bring you to the hospital."

When I hung up, Rabbi Klein, one of the teachers in my yeshiva, called. "I heard about your brother Shimmy. I just want to tell you that it says in the *Gemara* [the Talmud] that even when the knife is at the throat, there is still time for *Hashem* [God] to intervene. The whole yeshiva will be *davening* [praying] for him."

The first few hours of the drive, I rested my chin on my fist and stared out the window into the unending blackness of the night, which perfectly mirrored my state of mind. Eventually, I must have fallen asleep, because the next thing I knew we were bumping along Brooklyn streets approaching Crown Heights. Jeff and Kathryn, my uncle and aunt, picked me up, as planned.

Once I got settled in their gray Lincoln Town Car, Jeff warned me, "It's bad." But I really had no way to prepare myself since I had no idea what "bad" looked like. When I entered Shimmy's room in the intensive care unit, the bedside monitors beeped persistently, reporting his vital signs, and an antiseptic smell pervaded. I saw my twelve-year-old brother's motionless body on a bed, his face obscured by an oxygen mask, with electrodes and wires sprouting out from under numerous blankets like a sinister strange garden. His bald head and shriveled body were covered in paper-thin greenish-yellowish-brownish skin, the result of multiple rounds of chemotherapy and the failed bone marrow transplant.

Shimmy looked nothing like the fashion-conscious heckler with a high-pitched voice and full head of brown hair who repeatedly interrupted my magic show by shouting, "I know how to do that trick! I know how to do that trick!" As gusts of wind battered the few remaining leaves on the trees outside on that unforgiving February day, I watched as the last measure of life force seeped out of my brother.

My family and I stood around the bed with our prayer books pressed into our hands. Hot tears rushed down my cheeks that I tried to hide. I thought, as one of the older sons, that I had to "be strong" for my parents and younger sisters, but they were all crying uncontrollably, so I joined in.

I read Psalms Chapter 20, which is what devout Orthodox Jews recite when they need God's help and protection. I read the words that the faithful believe King David composed thousands of years ago when he was in mortal danger: "May the Lord answer you when you are in distress; may the name of the God of Jacob protect you." I was not convinced that God would come through and heal my dying brother, but like the smug proverb goes, "There are no atheists in a foxhole." And for good reason. With death closing in, all possible avenues of relief are maddeningly pursued. I would have prayed to the Egyptian medicine goddess Isis, or to Apollo, or to the Norse god Eir—if only I knew how.

Possessed, I kept racing through the recitation of the Psalms, as if reading them fast enough would prevent my mind from mocking my superstitious mumblings. "May he give you the desire of your heart and make all your plans succeed." But my mind was already flooded with the terrifying, nauseating thought that, regardless of what I said or did, Shimmy would never raise himself up from that bed.

After about an hour, my mother arranged for my older sister, Miriam, to take my younger siblings home. Miriam had just flown in a few days earlier from Melbourne, Australia, where she was studying for the year in a Lubavitch girls seminary, and she was a comforting presence for the scared younger children. Yossi and I stayed with my parents at Shimmy's bedside. A few hours later, the machines started beeping wildly, and all the lines on the vitals monitor went flat. Without saying a word, a nurse entered the room and shut off the monitor.

As tears poured out, my father, my mother, Yossi, and I recited together the prescribed verses Lubavitchers say when a person passes away.

We recited once: "Shema Yisrael Adonai Eloheinu Adonai Echod" (Hear O Israel, the Lord, Our God is One).

Then we recited three times: "Boruch shaym kevoyd malchuso l'oylum voed" (Blessed be the name of the glory of His kingdom forever and ever).

Then we recited seven times: "Adoynoy hu haeloyhim" (God is the Lord).

This prescribed liturgical recitation gave my mind something to grasp onto and prevented me from shrieking like a madman out of raw unbridled anguish.

My father went over to the bed and unhooked all the tubes attached to Shimmy by himself, because Orthodox law states that once a Jew is deceased, he is not supposed to be touched by a non-Jew. A plain white sheet was placed over Shimmy. He departed this Earth eight months shy of his bar mitzvah.

Bereft of the sound of Shimmy's breathing and the monitor's beeping, an eerie silence descended on the room as my family waited for an employee of the funeral home to wheel my brother away.

When Shimmy was seven or eight, he had walked around our house pointing at various vases, paintings, and bowls, declaring, "When Mommy and Tatty die, I want to take this, and this, and this to my house." At the time, none of us could ever have imagined that in a few short years we would be burying him and dividing up among his siblings the fancy presents, including amateur sets of magic tricks and many sports caps, that he received while in the hospital.

Shimmy's death was like an explosion that disorients and dulls the senses of those close to it. At the funeral home and at the shiva I was only dimly aware that others were around me. It was like seeing through a fog. I could make out the shape of people, but it was hard to discern their exact features. It was all a blur. People kept being kind to me and expressing sympathy, but this was totally discordant with my own feelings. I was mad as hell. *How could my little brother die?*

I had seen my parents sitting shiva for my mother's mother, Bubby Esther, when I was about eight years old. I remember my mother sitting on a box low on the ground and my father organizing a prayer quorum so the kaddish prayer for the dead could be recited. But nothing prepared me for Shimmy's death. I felt like my insides were on fire and no substance existed that could douse the blaze.

Is the Torah really an "eytz hayim," a tree of life to those who embrace it? It certainly wasn't for Shimmy. How could God in His lofty abode allow Shimmy to die? Shimmy's oncologists also failed to keep him alive, but I never put my faith in them. I hadn't prayed to them three times a day beseeching them to spare my kid brother. I hadn't spent hours reciting psalms, hoping that my prayers would find favor in their eyes and they would annul the decree of Shimmy's death. I hadn't praised, glorified, exalted, extolled, honored, lauded, and acclaimed their names. It was not doctors but God whom my community had assured me—from the day I learned his diagnosis to the day he died—could save him, would save him. All those heaps of prayers—what a waste. Fuck God and His mysterious ways.

After the funeral, Lubavitchers tried to comfort me by telling me that Shimmy's passing was all part of God's plan. One would-be comforter recounted the story of the Baal Shem Tov, the eighteenth-century Polish mystic and founder of the Hasidic movement who, after being pressured by a barren woman, gave her a blessing to conceive. She bore a child who then died after three months. When the woman complained to the Baal Shem, he told her, "The soul of your child was perfect, but it had never nursed from a Jewish mother. It was sent back to earth to fulfill this one goal. Once this was accomplished, the soul returned to Heaven."

I hated this rationale for suffering—that we never knew what the soul needed to complete to enter heaven—and it didn't make me feel the slightest comfort or diminish my anguish. It made me think that God was indifferent to our suffering. That he was not a loving father.

For only a pathologically twisted father would give his children priceless treasures just to cruelly snatch them away.

For years, it remained impossible to imagine our family life without Shimmy. Every time our family gathered for a meal and every time we took family group pictures without him it hurt and felt strange. How can we possibly begin the Passover seder when our cleverest and most vivacious member has yet to take his seat?

At the time, I did not realize the impact of Shimmy's death on my own faith. It was like the aftershocks of a great earthquake whose wreckage took years to become discernible. At the time, I did not associate his passing with any general rejection of belief in God. I was angry at God *because* I believed he existed and loved us and took care of us. It would make no sense to be angry at an entity that does not exist or one that is unable or unwilling to protect us. Only years later would I realize how much Shimmy's death undercut my general belief in God's very existence.

Nowadays when I think of Shimmy, there is so much I wish I could share with him. Although I reject psychics' claims to communicate with the dead, I understand the profound urge to speak to loved ones who have passed. He was intrigued by a high-quality set of black walkie-talkies that had a range of two blocks. I want to tell him about the invention of the internet and how I can send an email to a friend in Australia, and the friend can receive it in an instant. I want to tell Shimmy about the life I now live. And I want to tell him that, although my heart has toughened and I no longer burst into tears when I think or speak of him, I love him as passionately as the day I last laid eyes on him lying motionless in that hospital bed.

5

Loyal Soldier

"Do you believe everything in the Bible?" I cross-examined the elder pastor on the Christian ministry hotline. "Yes, of course," he said, "but it must be properly interpreted." It was 9:30 at night. I was in yeshiva in Chicago's West Rogers Park and desperate for a distraction.

The summer before, the director of my camp showed all the teen campers a video of Immanuel Schochet, the brilliant and acerbic European-born Lubavitch rabbi with a thick Swiss accent, poke holes in Christian theological claims using the Christian Bible. I decided that night, at the ripe age of fifteen, to try my hand. My first shot was, "How can Christians say that Jesus is about peace and love when Jesus himself says in Matthew that he didn't come to bring peace to the world, but to bring the sword?"

At that point, I hadn't laid eyes on a single page of the Christian Bible. I just memorized what Rabbi Schochet said and repeated it. The pastor tried to explain, "When Jesus says that he came to bring the sword, he doesn't mean to make war; he means to separate the faithful from the temptations of the world."

I hardly let him finish before I fired my next salvo: "How can Christians say that the 'suffering servant' discussed in Isaiah refers to Jesus when Isaiah says that the suffering servant will be called Immanuel and nowhere in the Christian Bible does it ever refer to Jesus as Immanuel?"

"Well, you see, Immanuel means 'God is with us,' and Jesus as God . . ."

Speaking into the white cordless phone, I paced the cramped communal space in our basement dorm. The barrage continued. "How can Christians revere Paul when in First Corinthians he says that to the Jews he comes as a Jew and to the Gentiles he comes as a Gentile. Isn't Paul being a hypocrite?"

The pastor tried to explain, but he must have realized that my inquiries lacked sincerity. Before we hung up, I asked him to send me a large box of literature to share with my friends. I gave him the address of the yeshiva and planned to throw away whatever he sent, thereby diminishing the arsenal of the enemy. Four days later, an envelope arrived with one measly pamphlet with a pale-blue cover. It was in English but had a Hebrew title, *Kenafayim Al Tzion* (*Wings over Zion*). I threw it in the garbage, but I did not feel the rush of excitement that I had imagined vanquishing Christianity would bring me. I never called again.

A part of me wanted to learn about Christianity for "professional" reasons, to be able to argue and win against missionaries I encountered while doing Lubavitch outreach. But a part of me was genuinely curious about this enemy faith. Were all their ideas and beliefs as ludicrously childish and nonsensical as I was told? Did they also have a complex system of interpretation of their Bible the way Judaism had?

West Rogers Park is three and a half miles square. For the two years I studied in Chicago, I hardly ever ventured beyond this enclave. West Rogers is a quiet multiethnic and multiracial middle-class neighborhood dotted by many modest two-story dwellings with manicured front lawns. The yeshiva is only ten miles west of the city of Chicago, but a world away. Inside the walls of the yeshiva, the famous curse against the Cubs allegedly issued by the disgruntled Billy Goat Tavern owner William Sianis in 1945 was unknown, and no one was waiting for the players at Wrigley Field to win a World Series. In fact, within the world of the yeshiva, the Cubs didn't exist at all; neither did the Art Institute of Chicago or the Steppenwolf Theatre Company.

The dictum of Heraclitus, the ancient Greek philosopher, that says that one cannot step into the same river twice seemed to be contradicted by the sameness of each day and each year of my yeshiva studies. The monotony and length of each day's schedule was exhausting. What's more, in his Monastic Rule, Saint Benedict warned, "Idleness is the enemy of the soul." The Lubavitch yeshiva system clearly agreed. Our days were ordered to exclude any time for impure thoughts or deeds. Our class periods started at 7:30 A.M. and ended at 8:30 P.M.

Each day commenced with an hour study of Hasidic philosophy, followed by morning prayers and breakfast, followed by two hours of Talmud, afternoon prayers, lunch, and recess. After recess, came another two hours of Talmud and an hour of Jewish law, followed by evening prayers, dinner, and another hour of Hasidic philosophy. For most of these study periods, instead of listening to a teacher lecture, we learned with a study partner, a *chavrusa*, trying to figure out the meaning of the texts on our own and consulting a teacher only when we got stuck.

Since the yeshiva had no sports facility, we spent recess playing touch football at a nearby public park. When Rabbi Lefkowitz, the principal of the school, learned about this leisure activity, he was furious and prohibited us from going to the park. He had the mind of a Talmud scholar and the temperament of a drill sergeant. He was fond of quoting the Kotzker Rebbe who said, "Shlufin shluft men nuch a hundred un tzvantzic," which roughly translates as, "You'll sleep when you're dead."

Instead of watching his students playing in the park, Rabbi Lefkowitz arranged for a basketball hoop to be mounted on the back wall of the yeshiva. We played basketball every recess after that. Then Rabbi Lefkowitz started preaching at *farbrengens*—religious gatherings—that playing basketball was a waste of time. "You could be learning Torah instead, and it's very *grub* [coarse] for yeshiva *bocherim* [students] to play sports."

Rabbi Lefkowitz viewed his pupils as *hekdesh*, an object that was consecrated to the ancient temple in Jerusalem and designated to be used only in holy service. No other purposes were acceptable, no matter how positive those other purposes were. Plus, he didn't think sports were positive to begin with. Sports were a distraction from the study of Torah and potentially led to a focus on the physical body, something that could only lead to vice. Under Rabbi Lefkowitz's austere guidance, we stopped playing, and the hoop remained untouched, a symbol of our commitment to piety.

There were many other restrictions at the Chicago yeshiva. The administration required us to wear plain white dress shirts, dark pants, and, when praying or when outside of the yeshiva, a sports jacket and black fedora. When Tommy Hilfiger came out with white shirts decorated with white buttons adorned with a streak of color on the back of each button, a scandal erupted. The rabbis outlawed them.

Another rule forbade all contact between our yeshiva students and the girls at the Lubavitch high school. The principals of the two schools agreed that we boys were forbidden to walk on Devon Avenue, where their school was located, and the girls were banned from California Avenue, near where our school was located. It was not exactly fair, since Devon was the commercial center of the community and boasted many Jewish businesses, including Rosenbloom's Judaic store; Mi Tzu Yon, a Chinese restaurant; a pizza shop; and a bakery, but we still had Tel-Aviv Pizza, so we made it work. Most of the students in the yeshiva came from communities where teenage boys commonly did not interact with teenage girls, so these rules were familiar.

But one student, Moti Abramowitz, soft-spoken and slight of build, was from Johannesburg, South Africa, where things were not as strict. Every Saturday afternoon, Yitzi Fagin, our teacher, who was only in his mid-twenties, chaperoned us for the mile hike from our yeshiva to B'nei Ruven, the local Lubavitch community synagogue on North Whipple Avenue, for afternoon prayers. One week, as we marched along in a neat row like soldiers on maneuvers, an Orthodox teenage girl came walking in our direction wearing a long skirt and a long-sleeve shirt. As she passed, Moti looked at her and said, "Good Shabbos."

In unison, all fourteen students and our teacher gawked at Abramowitz. Yitzi, barely able to contain his outrage, barked, "Moti, why did you do that?"

"Do what?"

"Why did you talk to a girl?"

"I didn't talk to a girl. I wished her a good Shabbos. Is that not allowed?"

"No, it's not allowed."

"That's nuts. In Jo'burg we wish everyone good Shabbos."

"Not here."

That wasn't the end of Moti's girl troubles, such as they were. In early December, he managed to meet a girl named Tova from the Lubavitch high school at Kol Tuv Kosher Foods and (dodging fellow shoppers and potential informers) slipped her a note arranging a tryst the next Tuesday night in an alley. Moti told me about the planned rendezvous and asked whether I would escort him to the spot. I agreed. When Tuesday night arrived, he switched his white shirt for a green Gap sweatshirt and spritzed on enough cologne to fill Lake Michigan. We made our way down a dark alley littered with broken glass and arrived at the designated meeting spot. Tova hadn't arrived yet. Moti told me to leave.

I walked back to the dorm clutching my winter coat for warmth. I appreciated the appeal of talking to girls, but the thought of acting so bold as to try to meet one never entered my timid heart.

The next day, Rabbi Lefkowitz called me over. His expression was harsh, and he was breathing heavily, like an enraged bull. "Zalman, sit down." I complied. He paced the floor of his office. "Zalman, I'm going to ask you a question, and I need you to be completely honest. I can handle a *bocher* [yeshiva student] not learning. I can handle *chutzpah* [impudence]. I can handle anything, but not this. You understand?"

"Yes," I said, although I had no clue what he was referring to.

He strode up and confronted me. "There was a *bocher* who went last night and met someone he was not allowed to meet. Do you know anything about this? Were you involved in this *parsha* [business] in any way?"

As he spoke, he pointed his index finger at me like a dagger. "I don't have to spell out your punishment for lying. *Dai chakima b'rimiza* [A wise person understands with a hint]." I had never heard someone quote a rabbinic maxim with such menace.

"I have no idea what you're talking about," I brazenly lied. Rabbi Lefkowitz scrutinized my countenance intensely, as if he could detect who was a deviant simply by examining a person's appearance, as the Italian criminologist Cesare Lombroso had once believed.

I felt terrible about lying. The rabbi and his wife had been very kind to me—his wife made me an eggless chocolate cake each week because I was allergic to the bakery cakes—but this was no time for scruples. I could tell that if I answered in the affirmative, I would be sent packing.

Sure enough, the next day Abramowitz was on a plane back to Johannesburg. Moti's assignation was innocent by secular American standards, but for violating a cardinal (and carnal) yeshiva rule, he was shipped back home. I would stay in Chicago for another year and a half.

Why doesn't Rabbi Lefkowitz show Moti some Ahavas Yisroel, some love for a fellow Jew, and allow him to stay in his yeshiva, even if Moti messed up? My teachers are always saying that Hasidim love one another and must be devoted to one another, but then Rabbi Lefkowitz just goes and kicks Moti out of yeshiva. Now that Moti has been kicked out, what will happen to him? It's obvious that if I don't follow all the rules I'll get kicked out too. But why are the rabbis so strict about the rules? If I get kicked out of this yeshiva, what other yeshiva would want to accept me? Where will I end up? Will my parents still support me if I'm not going to yeshiva? Will they still love me?

We weren't free from the rules even when we were asleep in bed. As Rabbi Lefkowitz recalled one night at a *farbrengen*, "The Frierdiker Rebbe [the Rebbe's predecessor] would check if the yarmulkes fell off the heads of the *tmimim* [yeshiva students] when they were sleeping. Those whose yarmulkes fell off were immediately expelled."

Rabbi Lefkowitz stuck his thumbs into the small pockets in the front of his black vest, which he wore like a uniform, and continued. "You can ask, but it's not the *tumim*'s fault, they were asleep?" He hit his hand on the table vigorously. "The point is, if they had true *yiras shamayim* [fear of Heaven], the instant their yarmulke fell off, they would immediately wake up and put it back on." The message was clear. There was not a moment that we were off duty. We were responsible for our actions (or inactions) even while slumbering.

(Years later I learned that this story of the Frierdiker Rebbe probably never happened. Yet at the time, it made a deep impression on me and caused me to be extremely conscious of the location of my yarmulke while I slept.)

Some rules needed to be obeyed strictly and others were honored more in the breach than in the observance. One rule that fell into the latter category was the Rebbe's directive that his followers who were younger than forty drink no more than three *l'chaims* (shots) at *farbrengens.* Having no illusions about the drinking habits of his followers, the Rebbe specified that the three shots together should be less than a *revi'us*, a rabbinic measurement approximately equal to four ounces.

But the Rebbe's prescriptions were for naught. My friends and I circumvented the rule with Talmudic sophistry of our own.

"The Rebbe meant three *l'chaims* an hour."

"The Rebbe meant three *l'chaims* in a row."

"The Rebbe meant three *l'chaims* at each *farbrengen.* It's been two hours; this is now a new *farbrengen.*"

There was no discussion by the students or the rabbis of alcohol addiction, just as there was no talk of sex education. These things didn't exist, at least not for teenagers.

At our weekly *farbrengens*, we sometimes drank whiskey (Crown Royal), but we usually drank vodka—more often than not, Smirnoff. We drank it straight, and we drank it out of seven-ounce plastic cups. I followed the lead of those around me and often swigged a quarter of a cup at a time. There was a religious competition for who could drink the most. Of course, we knew that only goyim get *shicker* (drunk). Hasidim get *freilech* (happy). I had never seen this kind of intense drinking at home; my father still had half a bottle of Smirnoff vodka left from his wedding.

The purpose of the alcohol at *farbrengens* was not simply for thrills. As Rabbi Katz, one of my teachers with a reputation for Talmudic brilliance, elucidated: "Usually our head separates us from our heart. It prevents us from getting emotionally excited about *ruchniasdike* [spiritual] things. So at a *farbrengen* we take some *mashke* [alcohol] to put the head to sleep so the heart could feel what it always wants to feel."

At another *farbrengen*, our teacher, Berel Teibenfeld, stood up and announced to the assembled innocent students whose faces were just beginning to sprout beards: "Your job is not to be *tzaddikim* [saints], but to be *beinonim*." A *beinoni*, a person who is of an intermediate spiritual status, occupies a central position in Lubavitch thought. Such a person has physical desires but doesn't allow them to control the "garments" of the soul: his thought, speech, or action. "A *tzaddik* is like a perfect painting. It's beautiful but boring. A *beinoni*'s life is messy, but he is constantly striving to overcome his animal instincts and unite with Godliness."

Berel took a shot of vodka from a plastic cup and continued. "Think of it this way. *Malachim* [angels] are always in a state of spiritual perfection serving the *eybeshter* [Almighty]. They have no egos, no slip-ups. So why did *Hashem* [God] bother creating humans? Because He takes *hana'a* [pleasure] from those who strive, who work on themselves. I know it's hard," he said as he repositioned his glasses on his ample nose, "but just remember: The Boss doesn't make mistakes. If you were given the challenge, it is because you can handle it."

In Lubavitch culture, and especially in yeshiva, we took seriously the words from Psalms (63:2): "My soul thirsts for You; my flesh longs for You, in an arid and thirsty land, without water." But this land was not completely arid; there was plenty of alcohol to go around.

For all the chutzpah and bravado of Lubavitch male culture, there was also deep tenderness. It was common for us to cry openly at *farbrengens* out of despair over our spiritual imperfections. As the poet Adrienne Rich observed, "There must be those among whom we can sit down and weep and still be counted as warriors." My yeshiva was just such a place.

Maybe no one associates Hasidim with warriors, and possibly that is as it should be. But no one lost any social standing for crying at *farbrengens*. In fact, piety was one of the currencies in yeshiva, and those who cried gained in that currency. Personally, I found it cathartic after downing a few cups of vodka to cry my eyes out and have a friend put an arm around my neck and promise me, "Morgen vet zayn gor andrish" (Tomorrow will be much better).

I entered the Chicago yeshiva two years after the Rebbe's passing in 1994. I, like all Lubavitchers, had been fed a steady diet of miracle stories of the Rebbe, and this didn't stop after the Rebbe passed away. If anything, it intensified. After the Rebbe's passing, it was believed that he was more "present" to the faithful than ever, since he was no longer limited by a mortal body and its physical needs, such as food and sleep.

Before I went to Chicago, I didn't know the yeshiva was fervently anti-messianic and opposed to all mention of the messianic status of the Lubavitcher Rebbe. Not only did they forbid the singing of the messianic mantra *Yechi* or the hanging of *Yechi* banners on the walls, but Rabbi Lefkowitz outlawed all yarmulkes with writing on them. He said such yarmulkes were "babyish" and not suitable for yeshiva students, but everyone knew his target was yarmulkes with *Yechi* written on them.

Rabbi Lefkowitz also derided the messianic bibliomancy practice of consulting the *Igros Kodesh*, the published volumes of the Rebbe's epistles. Someone in need of the Rebbe's advice would write a letter and place it randomly into a volume of the *Igros*. He would then open the volume and read the Rebbe's epistle that was printed on the page he chose, searching for some connection between his question and the printed answer of the Rebbe.

Lubavitchers who performed this ritual were convinced that the Rebbe was still speaking to them and guiding them. All that was required was for them to wrestle the words on the page into some kind of answer to their query. Sometimes the connection was less than obvious. Rabbi Lefkowitz would scoff, "A woman wants to know who to marry so she writes to the *Igros*. The Rebbe's letter is about setting up a yeshiva in Australia. She decides it means she must marry an Australian. This is not *Hasidis*; this is voodoo."

Although I grew up in Crown Heights, the Lubavitch heartland, I was somehow ignorant of the finer points of disagreement between the messianist and anti-messianist factions. This got me into trouble. Every month we had one Shabbos off to visit Lubavitch rabbis in the area. I usually visited Rabbi Kalmanson in Munster, Indiana, who, unknown to me, was a fervent messianist. He read passages to me from a book by an Israeli rabbi, Shalom Dov Wolpo, titled, *Hanisoyon Ha'acharon* (The Last Test). Based on Wolpo's teachings, Kalmanson explained, "The Rebbe isn't really dead; he's only hiding in order to test us, the last test, to see if we are truly committed to the *ge'ula* [redemption]. If we pass this test, the Rebbe will finally be *nisgaleh* [revealed] as the Moshiach [the messiah]."

Rabbi Kalmanson also taught me a song about our relationship to the Rebbe after Gimmel Tamuz, the Hebrew date of the day the Rebbe passed away. The song went like this: "Gimmel Tamuz didn't change a thing. The Rebbe's still our *nossi* [prince], our leader, and our king. Though we may not see him, he is always there, and with this thought in mind, we have nothing to fear."

I thought the song meant that, even after the Rebbe passed away, we were still connected to him, and I was moved by this message. I failed to grasp that the song really meant that nothing changed because the Rebbe, in fact, had never died, and he was still the messiah. Blithely unaware of its messianic overtones, I sang the song at a *farbrengen* at yeshiva in front of Rabbi Lefkowitz. He'd had a few *l'chaims* by then, but his reflexes were perfect, like a seasoned gunslinger at a saloon. As soon as I uttered the first line of lyrics, he swung around, extended his arm, and whack. He slapped me right across the face. He didn't mean to hurt me, but the slap stung and stunned me. To take away the bite, he pulled me over and hugged me tightly.

After a year of studying in Chicago, I was no longer a messianist. Not only did I abandon the *Yechi*, but my feelings toward the mantra changed drastically. I realized the depths of the change the following fall while praying back in Crown Heights at 770 on Yom Kippur. I started off in the main sanctuary on the first floor, which catered to a largely messianist crowd. Right before the Kol Nidre service began, I heard the packed assemblage sing *Yechi*. The mantra seemed pathetic to me; the Rebbe had been dead for three years, and there was no sign of him coming back. To me it felt like the Rebbe's dignity was being assaulted. I burst out crying and ran upstairs to the much smaller group praying in the Rebbe's private office, a stronghold of the anti-messianists. It felt comforting to be with "my people," again.

Notwithstanding the tumult of weekly *farbrengens* and head-spinning shots of vodka, I studied more in Chicago than at any other time in my young adult life. In the early mornings, we studied, for example, a Hasidic tractate written by the third Lubavitcher Rebbe, the Tzemach Tzedek, called *Derech Mitzvosecha* (The Path of Your Commandments). The Tzemach Tzedek, who lived in the nineteenth century, explained, based on the teachings of the sixteenth-century mystic Chaim Vital, that the one God could have different manifestations, just as a beam of light passing through glass of different colors emerges in different hues.

Yitzi Fagin had the burden of giving us a lecture on the Tzemach Tzedek's work three mornings a week starting at 7:30. He was not a morning person. He fortified himself by guzzling endless cups of black coffee as he lectured. This "solution" seemed only to enhance the impression that his bulging eyeballs were about to pop out of his head.

After breakfast each morning we studied the Talmudic tractate *Baba Metzia*, about the laws of lost and found objects. The law seems simple at the start of the tractate: If two people each claim to be the finder of a certain lost garment and to have sole custody over it, they each swear in court that they have the right to no less than half of it, and they split it. For months we followed the Talmud down a seemingly endless maze of analyses of this law and extrapolations from it. It took me painfully long to realize that no one really cares about a lost shawl. The Talmud uses individual cases such as this one to develop and test legal, moral, and social principles.

The Talmud (Bava Batra 23b) describes a case in which a dove is found and a determination needs to be made regarding its ownership. The law is that if it is found within fifty cubits of a dovecote, it belongs to the owner of the dovecote. But if it is found more than fifty cubits from a dovecote, the finder gets to keep it. The Talmud relates that Rabbi Yirmeya asked: What if one leg of the dove is within fifty cubits of the dovecote and the other leg is beyond fifty cubits? For this far-fetched question Rabbi Yirmeya was thrown out of the study hall. I felt that those other rabbis were hypocrites. They were all obscurantist nit-pickers and should have welcomed one of their own.

I found the study of Talmud in yeshiva extremely difficult. It wasn't just that the text of the actual Talmud, a 1,500-year-old anthology made up of thirty-seven tractates and written in a mix of Aramaic and Hebrew, had no vowels or punctuation marks. (I know that ancient Greek and classical Latin writing commonly had no spaces between words—which the Talmud does contain—so it could be worse, but it's still pretty hard.)

In addition, standard printed editions of the Talmud's many volumes include commentaries running along each wide margin of the page. Our study did not confine itself to the ancient text at the center in medium-sized block print. We had to grapple with Rashi and Toysfos, the medieval Franco-German commentaries printed in a smaller script font ("Rashi script") on each side of it.

To read just the commentary of Rashi wouldn't have been so bad. But Toysfos would come along and contradict Rashi's explanations. Then we turned to the back of the volume, where more medieval commentaries were printed. We read the Rosh, the Maharsha, the Maharam Shif, the Ran, and the Ramban, who proffered yet more, and often contradictory, explanations and interpretations. I struggled to keep straight the interpretations and families of interpretations, let alone the simple meaning of the original Aramaic words of the Talmud.

The difficulties of understanding the Aramaic of the Talmud were compounded by the fact that our teacher, Rabbi Fogel, forbade us from using practically the only available Talmudic dictionary, known as Jastrow. Its author, Marcus Jastrow, was a nineteenth-century Polish American reformist rabbi. The work of such rabbis was not to enter our hallowed halls, in dictionary form or otherwise. Still, one of my fellow students managed to get hold of the thick blue book with tiny broken typeface and was looking up a difficult word one afternoon in the study hall when Rabbi Fogel suddenly appeared. He ran over to the student's table and thundered, his thin, bony hands shaking, "Jastrow was an *apikores* [a heretic]. You should never use his book. It's full of *kefira* [heresy]."

The Talmud's discussions about sex and the female body challenged us yet further. In elementary school, the teachers just skipped such references, and we knew we were missing the juicy bits. Once when the teacher told us we were skipping a passage, a few of us read it together after class and learned that it was a discussion of how many pubic hairs a female must have to be considered an adult. (The answer is two.) In high school, we were expected to read these passages. We read about the "natural" form of sex, *k'darkoy*, and the "unnatural" form, *shelo k'darkoy*, but the Talmud never explicitly states what constitutes each form.

In my last year of yeshiva, at twenty, we read a passage about a man who fell off a roof, landed on a woman, and accidentally had intercourse (Bava Kamma 27a). My friends and I couldn't stop laughing. "You heard about the *nebech* [poor guy] who fell off the roof? What *mazal* [luck]," I said.

Usually, my study partner and I would discuss the meaning of the text we were reading, but I worried about seeming overly interested, naïve, or ignorant about the topic. So I kept my confusion to myself. I just read the passage in Aramaic, intoning as though I fully understood it, and continued on.

Although Lubavitch homes have many religious books and the yeshiva's curriculum included numerous volumes from the "revealed Torah" (the Talmud and Jewish law) and the "concealed Torah" (Hasidic thought), there was one book that stood above all the rest. This was the *Tanya*, the "Bible of Hasidic thought."

The *Tanya* was written by the first Lubavitcher Rebbe, Rabbi Schneur Zalman of Liadi, in the Russian Empire (present-day Lyady, in Belarus) and initially published in 1796. We had formal classes on the *Tanya* and studied it daily on our own. My copy of the *Tanya* was worn by constant use. No single book is quoted among Lubavitchers as often as the *Tanya*. The *Tanya* is both a foundational theological text and a self-improvement manual.

The central theme of the *Tanya* is that each person possesses two souls—one Godly and one animal—and that these two souls vie for hegemony over the "city," composed of the individual's thought, speech, and action. The purpose of life is to tame one's beastly aspect, one's animal soul. All desires that are not expressly for God and the Torah are sinful. Even eating a piece of chocolate cake is sinful if one does so just for pleasure rather than as a means of gaining energy to serve God and through that service elevate the cake to a higher spiritual dimension.

I observed that the educational method of Lubavitch yeshivas tended to emphasize rote learning rather than focus on originality or the deeper meaning of the texts we studied. To learn Torah was a commandment. We were connecting our minds with the mind of God, and we were helping to bring the messiah. End of story. The teachers never tried to come up with original interpretations and never sought them from us.

Like the Christian monks in the Middle Ages who spent their lives in scriptoria copying ancient Latin texts motivated by religious discipline rather than a love of the texts themselves, Lubavitchers spend years in yeshiva studying texts out of a theological commitment to the practice rather than because of an appreciation of the words found between the covers before them. The monks helped preserve the texts by copying them while the Lubavitchers help preserve knowledge of classical Jewish sources by studying them. In both cases, if someone falls in love with the text before them or hits upon an original take on it, it is a fortuitous coincidence.

In the Chicago yeshiva, although some students struggled academically to various degrees—myself included—once Moti Abramowitz was expelled, everyone seemed to be "with the program" ideologically. The one exception was Yeruchem Silver, a tall and lanky guy from Toronto who had the benefit of a full secular education before coming to the Chicago yeshiva. He was extremely studious and had no trouble deciphering the meaning of the texts on the curriculum. He was a gentle soul who was plagued with theological questions.

One day during our lunch break I spotted him sitting with Berel Teibenfeld at a table in the empty wood-paneled study hall pouring out his heart. "According to the Rebbe Rashab [the fifth Lubavitcher Rebbe], in *Kuntres Umaayin* [a Hasidic text written in 1903], the highest human pleasure is intellectual delight. But the Rebbe Rashab quickly adds that a person should focus his entire life on the study of Torah."

Yeruchem's face, which tended to the saturnine, looked even gloomier than usual. He was clearly pained by the exclusionary judgment of the Rebbe Rashab. "What about all other forms of knowledge and learning? What about Greek philosophy? What about Aristotle?" Yeruchem's voice uncharacteristically rose above a whisper on the mention of the ancient thinker. "The Rambam [Maimonides] references Aristotle a bunch. Isn't Aristotle's work of value?"

Two classmates walked past Yeruchem and giggled. "Yeruchem's at it again," they snickered.

Berel tried to be sympathetic. "I hear what you are saying, Yeruchem. It is true that the other *umoys* [nations] have their own wisdom, and *chazal* [the ancient rabbis] acknowledge this. But the fact is that Torah is on a much higher *ruchniasdiker* [spiritual] plane than all other knowledge."

Yeruchem just stared at him. Berel tried another tack. "The Rebbe actually spoke at length on Shabbos Chanukah in the year *tuf shin lamed alef* [1971] about the difference between non-Jewish wisdom, exemplified by the Greeks, and Jewish learning." Lubavitchers often quote the statements of the Rebbe the way others quote the Bible, chapter and verse. All arguments are made infinitely more compelling by including a quote from the Rebbe.

"The Rebbe explained that non-Jewish wisdom, for all its beauty, does not necessarily dictate moral action, whereas Jewish learning is superior because it is not merely abstract thought. It is rooted in this world and always requires moral action. This distinction was emphasized by the Rebbe with a story of Aristotle, who was once caught doing an immoral act. When they asked him how he could do such a thing, he responded, 'Now I'm not Aristotle!'"

Although I was friends with Yeruchem and didn't join those who openly laughed at his ideological questions, I didn't share them. *I don't give a fig about Greek philosophy or the wisdom of other nations. It's obvious that everything the Lubavitcher Rebbes wrote was completely correct, and I wish Yeruchem would just get with the program.*

After two years in Chicago, I transferred with a group of classmates to a Lubavitch yeshiva in Miami's South Beach.

In terms of climate, the shift was drastic. The temperature in Chicago during the winter typically is in the mid-twenties, and everyone always tries to cover every last bit of exposed skin. I remember once during a major snowstorm, the temperature reached sixteen degrees below zero, and while walking to yeshiva my eyelashes froze shut. In South Beach, the typical temperature is in the eighties, and the biggest meteorological concern is hurricanes. During my stay in Miami, we were forced to evacuate the yeshiva on two occasions in anticipation of coming storms.

Culturally, the contrast was also dramatic. I saw very little of the city of Chicago and was exposed to even less of its ethos. South Beach was different. Just walking outside the yellow pastel walls of the yeshiva I saw gay and lesbian couples walking and holding hands and making out, and not infrequently I saw people walking with their hands inserted down the back of their partner's pants. I had never seen anything like this in person. The closest I ever came was when I snuck into a theater and watched the 1996 film *The Birdcage*, which takes place in South Beach and stars Nathan Lane and Robin Williams. I never imagined then that I would live there.

The yeshiva in South Beach was founded in 1972 when a group of eleven students handpicked by the Rebbe were sent there. The Rebbe met with these students in a private audience and announced: "May the Almighty bless you to be successful. It should be from there [Miami] that the wellsprings of Hasidism will be dispersed to the rest of the world." Decadent South Beach may seem like an inhospitable locale from which to launch a spiritual revival, but the Rebbe was nothing if not audacious.

Although I never partied in a nightclub in Miami, it was impossible to live there and not be exposed to its gay ambiance. As fate ordained, the yeshiva was located at 1200 Alton Road, and right next door was a hotel proudly displaying six giant rainbow flags. Out back in the hotel pool area, guests, apparently exclusively gay men, would have sex, which we could see from the second-floor balcony of the yeshiva. The rabbis in the Miami yeshiva were so oblivious to their own surroundings they apparently were unaware of what was happening in their next-door neighbors' pool, so they never tried to prevent us from seeing it.

In the Miami yeshiva, as in other Lubavitch yeshivas, students would immerse each morning in the mikvah, the ritual bath, before prayers. The mikvah had a small window to allow the steam from the showers to exit. The window was right across from the side entrance of the hotel. One morning, when the mikvah was jammed to capacity with naked yeshiva students, someone opened the window to let out the steam. Just then, we saw a guest at the hotel walk by and raise his eyebrows in surprise at his view. The crowd of naked boys and men in the mikvah screamed in unison, and several hands shot up to slam the window shut.

My studies told me that the Bible forbade a man to "lie with another man," and I knew that this prohibition was related to homosexuality, but just as heterosexual sex was never directly discussed, neither was homosexual sex. Students in the yeshiva would occasionally laugh about the "*feigelach*" walking past our building, but that was the extent of the open conversation about it that I was ever exposed to in Miami.

I was at the Miami yeshiva for two years, including during New Year's Eve of 2000. That year, December 31 fell on a Friday, and Rabbi Katz forbade us from going to the party on the beach that evening, the Sabbath, on pain of expulsion. "The dorm counselor will be on the lookout for anyone missing at midnight," Rabbi Katz warned. He must have forgotten King Solomon's words in the book of Proverbs (9:17): "Stolen waters are sweet and bread eaten in secret is pleasant."

After eating our Friday night dinner and hanging out, four of us decided to make a run for it. It was 11:55 P.M. We ran from Alton Road east on 11th Street down a dozen blocks to the party on Ocean Drive. We swerved past groups of SWAT teams in black uniforms holding machine guns. I knew the increased security was due to the hype over Y2K terrorism, but I imagined Rabbi Katz sent them to prevent us from reaching the party.

We passed groups of people shouting and jumping up and down. We kept running. When I was about to collapse, we finally hit the beach, which was already mobbed with thousands of people. Just as my shoes dug into the sand, I heard the crowd scream in unison, "seven . . . six . . . five . . . four . . . three . . . two . . . one." Cascades of red, green, purple, and blue lit up the night sky, and the partiers around me kissed. I just stared. In the crowd of revelers wearing odd hats, glasses, and wigs, we—in our white shirts, dark pants, full beards, and yarmulkes—hardly stood out. After waiting a few minutes to catch our breath, we ran all the way back to yeshiva and snuck into our dorm rooms undetected.

Some rule breakers were less lucky. A group of students arranged with the Latina manager of the laundromat down the block—a kind, chatty Texan transplant—to watch movies on the large screen in the front of her store. For several weeks they rented movies from Blockbuster and watched them there. Although I watched on a small TV screen as I folded my laundry—I remember seeing a music video of Cher singing the lyric, "Do you believe in life after love?"—I never joined the movie club on the large screen.

One night, a rabbi from our school happened to walk by and spotted five of his students watching *Titanic*. For several days, the talk of the yeshiva was his threat to kick out all the conspirators. The students pleaded; the teachers deliberated; and in the end, no one was kicked out. But the club went from watching movies to having to memorize whole chapters of Hasidic texts. The teachers made them promise to refrain from all forbidden activities. Their probation meant giving up everything they had gotten away with until then. One had to give up a cell phone and a scooter.

Although no one in yeshiva would openly violate the laws of Shabbos, there were various levels of religious commitment within the school. Most were devout, but some lifted weights (a thoroughly "goyish" and misguided pursuit); others snuck into hotels and logged into internet chat rooms to talk to girls; and still others ran a poker game on Friday nights, albeit without money. In general, even the devout students were level-headed.

Commonly, Lubavitchers are very good at having one foot in heaven, believing in the Rebbe's power to perform miracles, even after his death, while having the other foot firmly planted on Earth: able to fundraise, organize community programs, and plan for the future.

"Excuse me, are you Jewish?" I asked that question to thousands of (mostly) white men and women during outreach activities standing on street corners, in malls, or in office buildings looking for Jews. And I heard every imaginable response, from the defensive "What, do I look Jewish?" to the comical "What gave me away, my big nose?" to the evasive "I'm not Jewish today" and the technical "I'm only half-Jewish." But by far the most common answer from Jews as they ran past us was, "Yes, I'm Jewish, but I'm in a rush."

I asked people whether they were Jewish rather than whether they were interested in Judaism because the exclusive focus of Lubavitch outreach is nonobservant or less observant Jews. Unlike typical Christian missionaries or those from other religions who seek to bring people from outside of their religion into their fold, Lubavitch has no interest in bringing non-Jews into Judaism. Instead, they seek to interest non–Orthodox Jews to become more religious.

Participating in outreach activities was a key element, both ideologically and practically, in my upbringing as a loyal Lubavitcher. The Rebbe taught us that every mitzvah, every commandment, we encouraged others to undertake brought the messiah one step closer. The Rebbe also taught that, regardless of his or her current level of religious observance, every Jew contains a spark of the divine. Likewise, the true nature of every Jew is to seek a connection to God. As one popular Lubavitch formulation of this idea puts it: "A Jew neither wants nor is capable of being separated from Godliness."

In Jewish legal terms, Lubavitch views secular Jews as falling under the category of a "captive child" raised among the gentiles (*tinok shenishbah bein ha'akum*). They are not responsible for their sins because those sins are performed in ignorance of Jewish law. Maimonides in the twelfth century first applied this concept of the captive child to the children of Karaites, a medieval fringe Jewish group, who were not technically "captured" but simply lacked "proper" Jewish education. Following his lead, the Lubavitcher Rebbe applied this concept to secular Jews today who lack Orthodox Jewish education and instructed his followers to be welcoming and "tolerant" to such Jews.

A popular Lubavitch camp song, which I sang around many bonfires and at Friday night sing-alongs, emphasized this outlook. The song tells the story of a college student who feels lost, turns to the campus Lubavitch rabbi, the *shliach*, for guidance, but complains that he is "too far gone." The punch line of the song is the last stanza: "The *shliach* says, 'Not true / *Hegam shechoto yisrael hu* [Even though one has sinned, one is still a Jew] / No matter where you roam / You can always come back home.'"

The Rebbe sent us out into the world to do the work of returning lost Jews home to their religion, aware that we were at risk of spiritual contamination. The Rebbe compared the spiritual risks we faced with those that confronted the ancient priests of the Temple in Jerusalem who prepared the ashes of a red heifer in a ceremony to purify Jews who had become ritually impure through contact with a dead body. The irony was that the priests themselves became ritually impure as a result of preparing and handling the red heifer's ashes. This is a classic example of how Lubavitch learned to frame necessary worldly duties as self-sacrifice. That is, the priests temporarily gave up their state of purity to help a fellow Jew. The Rebbe viewed the self-sacrifice of his emissaries and their families as analogous to the conduct of the ancient Jewish priests.

While doing outreach, I saw billboards of scantily clad men and women in underwear ads. I also passed by women wearing miniskirts and clean-shaven men in shorts and T-shirts walking in the streets. I understood that there was an entire world beyond the Lubavitch community who lived by a different set of rules. I was told that these people's lives were devoid of meaning and purpose, like a pit devoid of water but full of snakes and scorpions. I was taught that our way of life was superior. We were not just Jews. We were not just Hasidim. We were Lubavitch Hasidim whose Rebbe was the *Nosi Hador*, the Prince of the Generation. I was 100 percent convinced of this.

My classmates and I were taught that to fulfill our mission we had to be a *tefach hecher* (handbreadth higher), than those in the world. We needed to play by our own rules and not be affected by the thinking and standards of the outside world, in both spiritual and practical matters.

As a young child I joined older boys in their outreach activities. In 1980, the Rebbe founded the Lubavitch youth movement Tzivos Hashem (the Army of God), in effect recruiting all Lubavitchers to be his loyal soldiers.

In yeshiva in Chicago, when I was fourteen, my partner and I started doing outreach every Friday afternoon. We went on a designated route to find and talk to Jews. My first route was in the downtown Chicago Mercantile Exchange. After a few months, the rabbi in charge of outreach sent us instead to Evanston, Illinois, a suburb of Chicago and the home of Northwestern University.

In both locations, the mission was to get men to put on *tefillin* and recite a few prayers and for women to agree to light Sabbath candles. We also spoke to them about the weekly Torah portion and its life lessons, derived from the teachings of the Rebbe. When I moved to South Beach, I continued doing outreach every Friday, with a new partner. Our route in South Beach got serious. Not only did we make visits on Fridays, but we also arranged a Chanukah and Purim party, and we distributed round, handmade matzah before Passover. We even distributed individually packaged slices of cheesecake before the Shavuos holiday.

Although all of the students involved in outreach work were deeply committed to it in principle, it developed into a kind of competition. No one in yeshiva bragged about cool sneakers or jump shots. Bragging rights went to the team who managed to get the most men to put on *tefillin*. Extra points went to the students who managed to put *tefillin* on a "*karkafta*," a man who had never donned *tefillin* before in his life.

The term *karkafta* originates in a discussion in the Talmud (Rosh Hashana 17a) about various categories of sinners. It culminates with a Jew who had never put on *tefillin* even once in his lifetime. This most unfortunate individual is destined to suffer in Gehenna for the full twelve months after dying. Then his body and soul will be burned and scattered under the feet of the righteous. We were eager to help our fellow Jews avoid this awful fate.

Like secret agents, we relied on our wits and charm when doing outreach. You would think that in preparation we would receive special training for this work. We did not. To prepare myself, I collected and memorized ideas and explanations I had heard from the Rebbe or from my teachers to be used to answer questions posed by potential "customers."

For instance, if someone asked me, "How could God allow the Holocaust to happen?" I would answer, "We can't understand God's plan. To look for an answer is to assume that if the 'right' answer is found, then the horrors of the Holocaust would 'make sense,' which is a perverse idea."

If asked, "How can the God of the whole universe care whether a simple guy like me eats nonkosher?" I would answer, "Just as with a romantic partner, it's not about what *you* think the other one wants; it's about what they tell you *they* want. God tells us in the Torah exactly how He wants to be worshipped."

If asked, "Doesn't the existence of fossils that are millions of years old contradict the idea that God created the universe in six days and that it is only some five thousand years old?" I would answer, as the Rebbe once suggested, that "God created the universe with the fossils already buried in the ground." (The Rebbe was not the first to put forward this explanation. Philip Henry Gosse, a British popular science writer and pastor of the Plymouth Brethren, made the same argument in 1857.)

If asked, "What do you think about Darwin's theory of evolution?" I would answer, "If you saw an intricate painting, would you accept that the painting had no maker and that all the colors simply happened to fall into a perfect configuration by chance?" I had only a vague sense of Darwin's ideas, but I had my answer ready to go.

If asked, "Why are women not obligated to perform all the commandments, as are men?" I would answer, "Because women's souls come from such a high spiritual source that they don't need the refinement that male souls require, which necessitates all the extra obligations."

If asked, "Is it really true that the Lubavitcher Rebbe can perform miracles?" I would answer the same way the Rebbe himself once did: "Every Jew can perform miracles if he connects his soul to God through fervent prayer, Torah study, and the performance of mitzvos."

And if asked a question for which I had no answer on file, I learned that I could always say, "The reason we do this ritual or recite this prayer is explained 'according to kabbalah.' It's a mystical secret."

In addition to having ready answers to questions, outreach work took chutzpah. We went to malls during Chanukah to give out free menorahs. We knew the malls prohibited soliciting. We would hand out menorahs, and the mall security guards would come over and tell us we weren't allowed to solicit. We would say, "We're not soliciting. We are giving them away for free." The guards would say, "That's still soliciting, and you have to leave." We would leave through one end of the mall and come right back in from the other end.

Sometimes we didn't have to leave the yeshiva to find "customers." The yeshiva itself acted as a magnet to draw them in. A man with long, flowing white hair came by the Chicago yeshiva several times and tried to give us compact discs (CDs) of the Mormon Tabernacle Choir. "They're very spiritual. You guys will like them." He was asked not to return. Another visitor, a member of a different Hasidic sect who wore a tall fur hat on Shabbos, made occasional visits. Anytime someone asked him where he was from, he would respond with an off-color joke by paraphrasing the ancient rabbinic dictum, "Ich kum fun a tipa srucha. Ni, azoy shtayt?" (I'm from a putrid drop. That's what it says, right?). A gay Latino man in his thirties visited the Miami yeshiva. He wanted to convert to Judaism, and the rabbis told him he couldn't convert as long as he was gay. The visitor bemoaned his failure to change his sexual orientation through "conversion therapy."

One day in South Beach a Jews for Jesus devotee named Ben who was in his fifties and heavily suntanned showed up and tried to convince a group of seven of us that the "rabbi" from Galilee was the real messiah, not only for the goyim, the non-Jews, but for us and all other Jews.

Ben lectured the bemused cluster of students surrounding him. "If you read the Brit Chadasha [New Testament] it's so clear how it redeems the Tanach [Old Testament]. The downfall of humanity was caused by a virgin, Chava [Eve]; a tree, the tree of knowledge; and a death, that of Adam. The redemption of humanity came about through a virgin, Yeshua's [Jesus's] mother, Miriam [Mary]; a tree, the tree of the cross; and a death, the death of Yeshua at Calvary." Ben said all this as if he were repeating a scientific formula that was so self-evident that to hear it was to accept it. "Don't be blinded by lies; just open your eyes."

We set our sights and fired at the fortress of his faith in Jesus, but nothing penetrated. Our assaults failed because every time we mounted a charge using Christian sources, Ben would respond, "Well, that's what the goyim think, but I'm talking about what we Jews think." And every time we attacked using Jewish sources, such as Maimonides's writings on the messiah, he would smile broadly and retort, "Well, what do you expect? He didn't accept Yeshua as the Moshiach [the messiah]."

I felt unsettled every time Ben substituted a Hebrew translation for a known Christian name or term. It felt to my training like an unsubtle attempt to transform the foreignness of Christianity into something as homey as chicken soup with matzah balls. For several hours the argument went nowhere. The South Beach disputation ended with seven yeshiva students and Ben standing with our arms around each other's shoulders in a circle, singing, "No matter where you may roam, you may always come back home." Ben was smiling from ear to ear. Who had gone astray and who was at home? Every man in the room was sure he knew the answer.

During my time in yeshivas in Chicago and Miami, I was taught what separated my people from the rest of the world: that we immersed ourselves in the Hasidic way of life, and this made us a higher order of person, one not led astray by baser instincts. Nothing that I observed inside or outside of these yeshivas had shaken my pious commitments. But the handbreadth between me and the outside secular world would not prove steadfast.

6

Forbidden Knowledge

"Gotta sign the passport form in front of me," demanded the Black, female postal worker with a smoker's voice seated behind the bullet-proof glass window. I stared at her the same way I would have if she had demanded I sprout wings and soar across the Brooklyn Bridge.

The trouble was that I couldn't sign my name in English. It was the language I spoke at home but I could barely print it. I was fifteen. The Rebbe strongly opposed "secular education" because it took away time from religious studies and because he felt it was morally corrupting. Many Lubavitch schools, including one of the two boys' yeshivas in Crown Heights, nonetheless taught at least the rudiments of these subjects. My luck, all the yeshivas I attended from second grade on adhered strictly to the Rebbe's wishes and taught absolutely no English reading and writing or any other secular subjects, for that matter.

Although both my parents enjoyed extensive secular education, they seemed to act as if it was something we would never miss, like one's tonsils that could be excised without causing any damage to the body. Maybe they assumed the messiah would arrive any day now and English grammar and multiplication tables would no longer be of use.

My father, who filled out the entire form in advance but left blank the line demanding my signature, suggested to the postal clerk that I go with him to a side table, which happened to be out of her line of vision, to practice. She would have none of it. "Practice right here!" she demanded and pushed a slip of yellow paper through the opening in the glass window.

Was it just my paranoid imagination or was the woman taking delicious pleasure at the sight of a white middle-class young man unable to sign his own name? Although I was only fifteen, with my unshaved beard people often mistook me for eighteen.

My father signed my name on the practice paper in large flowing letters and handed me the pen. Despite being a physician, he had beautiful penmanship. With clammy hands and a wet forehead, I traced over what he wrote and then practiced writing it twice more on my own. He then handed me the passport form and pointed to the line I needed to sign. I squeezed the pen hard and tried to reproduce on the form the mass of unfamiliar scribbles I managed to scratch out on the practice page, with the postal worker eyeing me all the while like a cop on the beat. The hieroglyphics I produced looked nothing like my father's masterpiece, but mercifully the clerk said nothing and accepted it.

Truth be told, the yeshiva I attended for first grade taught some "secular" subjects, and I almost accidentally learned how to read English that year, at age seven. In the mornings, all the students received religious instruction, but in the afternoon the school had two tracks, one to learn English and one to learn more Yiddish. The parents made the choice. On the first day of school, there was a mix-up, and I was placed in the English class, where they were watching the movie *Pinocchio.* Within twenty minutes the principal discovered the mistake and yanked me out. I never saw Pinocchio turn into a boy. I also never learned to read and write English as a boy. I sometimes wonder whether my life would have turned out differently if I had stayed in the first school and learned rudimentary English and the other secular subjects they offered there.

The post office embarrassment was not the first time my inability to write English was an issue. Whether from learning it in school or picking it up on their own, many Lubavitch boys knew how to read and write English (almost all Lubavitch girls' schools taught secular subjects). I, however, still had not picked it up by age nine when I went to a Lubavitch sleepaway camp in Michigan for five weeks. The fact that my schools never taught me English certainly helped keep me ignorant of it, but it is also possible that a learning disability contributed to my troubles.

When I was nine and still having difficulty reading Hebrew, my mother took me to a child psychologist for testing. He concluded I had stronger auditory than visual abilities, but with proper tutoring I could learn to read. I then went to a special tutor for Hebrew reading for a year and came away able to read the daily prayers, not as fast as my friends, but at a reasonable pace.

In my summer camp, the boys wrote letters home every Friday. Most wrote in English, but some wrote in Yiddish or in English transliterated into Yiddish. My parents knew no Yiddish and, anyway, my Yiddish was too poor at the time to be useful.

My father devised a solution for me. I made audio recordings on a small black tape recorder and mailed the tapes home in preaddressed, stamped brownish-green padded envelopes. My parents would listen to them and send back their own recordings. Every Friday while other campers huddled around tables, shoulders bent, writing letters, I would circuit around the trailer bunkhouse with the recorder in my hands, kicking up sand as I walked, reporting on how many lines of rabbinic text I memorized, how my counselors treated me, and how many laps I swam in the lake.

I don't remember being embarrassed by my lack of English reading or writing. I was ashamed, however, that I still sucked my thumb under the blanket when I slept and was terrified that my bunkmates would discover my secret.

My father would send me his recordings, which began with a few "hellos" and giggles from Rivky and Chana Sara, five and seven years old, and updates on the welfare of the tomatoes and strawberries he was growing in the backyard. It seems my father had unnamed saboteurs in his garden. As soon as anything started to ripen, birds and squirrels ferociously attacked them with military precision, as if these creatures were docked for each fruit or vegetable they allowed to reach full maturity. The bulk of the tape consisted of long passages from the Holocaust book he'd begun reading to me before camp started.

Some of the members of my extended family realized that my brothers and I were not being taught how to read and write English in elementary school. The most vociferous of these critics was my father's mother, Bubby Ruth, a veteran public school math teacher and lifelong learner who read multiple books per week well into her eighties. Like clockwork, at the end of each of our periodic visits to her home she would pester my father. "Why don't the boys learn English? How are they going to get jobs if they can't read?" He would always mumble some excuse and hustle us kids out, allowing the slamming of the screen door to settle the matter.

After the incident at the post office, I was desperate to find a way to learn English. Then, a few days later, my mother's brother, Uncle Jeff, a one-time actor who worked at a law firm and did the *New York Times* crossword puzzle religiously every day, visited us in Crown Heights. As my mother stood over the stove outfitted in the "World's Best Mom" apron we'd bought her for her birthday, frying meat kreplach and hamburgers for lunch, I pulled Jeff aside.

"Jeff, it's *meshugah.* Tatty and Mommy got me an English tutor for a year, but all I learned were the names and sounds of the ABCs. I can barely read words that a five-year-old can read." I laughed, but inside I was crying. "I gotta learn this English thing once and for all."

"Don't worry, Zalman, I'm happy to help you," he said as he stroked his neatly trimmed reddish beard. His good looks from the days he shared a stage with Sam Waterston in the Lincoln Center production of *Abe Lincoln in Illinois* were still intact.

A few months later when I saw Jeff next, he gave me a second-grade English workbook. He tore out the first five pages and handed them to me along with a self-addressed stamped envelope. "Take these and fill them out. Then mail them back to me. When I get them, I'll send you the next batch."

I took the pages with me to yeshiva in Chicago. I needed to keep them secret or I would get in trouble with the school, and possibly even kicked out. At first, I tried to work on them at night sitting on the toilet in the bathroom with the door locked, but this overextended my visits, and my roommates got annoyed. After a couple of guys pounded on the bathroom door, I decided I needed to find a new workplace.

Lying in bed one night, I hit on the idea of waiting until everyone else in the dorm fell asleep and tiptoeing into the laundry room at the end of the hall. It had a cement floor, was strewn with broken-down washing machines and dryers, smelled of detergent, and was full of dust, but I figured I would be safe from detection. As I entered the unlit room, I heard a swooshing sound as something sliced the air. I reached for the light switch and discovered my roommate, Peretz Shemtov, swinging a six-foot samurai sword about fifteen feet away from my head.

"What the heck, Peretz?"

"Keep it down, Zalman. You'll wake somebody."

"What is that?"

"I keep it hidden under the luggage in the closet and come out at night to play. What are you doing out of bed, Zalman?"

"I'm trying to finish some pages from an English workbook."

We agreed to keep each other's secret, but with the continuous swooshing sound and the distinct possibility of decapitation, the laundry room was not an ideal workspace.

Over the next several months, as the weather got ever colder—beyond what I thought humans could endure—I managed to finish all the pages of the workbook by stealing a few minutes each time I happened to be alone in my dorm. I mailed the completed pages to Jeff, and we discussed my progress in person when I got back to New York on yeshiva breaks for Jewish holidays.

I was fascinated by martial arts. I had briefly befriended a local master of White Crane Kung Fu until Berel Teibenfeld caught me at his studio one Shabbos and warned me never to return. So I bought several books of Bruce Lee's fighting techniques. Notwithstanding my progress with the worksheets, all I could do was gape at the black-and-white pictures in these books. I could no more read the text than I could execute Bruce Lee's mysterious one-inch punch, which sent his opponents flying across the room as if zapped by invisible lightning.

By the time I started going to yeshiva in South Miami Beach, at sixteen, I still hadn't read a single English book in my entire life. That was all about to change, thanks to my roommate and old friend Peretz, the samurai enthusiast. Like me, he had transferred from the yeshiva in Chicago to the one in Miami, and during the first few months there, he added a BB gun, three throwing knives, and a pair of nunchucks to his arsenal.

In addition to constantly shooting his BB gun at green Dial soap bars in our dorm room and trying to land the throwing knives in the dense brown trunks of the palm trees in front of the yeshiva, he took up lock picking. He bought a lock pick set and practiced all the time jiggling open locks. One night as we sat around, bored, in our stuffy dorm room, Peretz announced, "Zalman, I'm gonna pick the library door lock. Want anything?"

The library in question was located on the second floor in the back of a large building across the street from our yeshiva and belonged to the Lubavitch high school, which had a Hebrew-English dual curriculum. The library consisted of one small room packed with books. I had my own eye on the place, but students in our yeshiva were strictly forbidden from using the library. "Yes," I told Peretz, "get me anything, but it's gotta be easy to read." Peretz nodded his head and started leaving the room.

"Wait, the library is on the second floor, and the back staircase is locked at night. How are you gonna get up there?" He just grinned, revealing his ivory-white teeth, and with his blue eyes sparkling, he walked out.

Twenty minutes later, Peretz ran into the room panting. He had swung a rope with a rock at the end over the banister and climbed up the rope, like a marine on maneuvers. He used his lock pick set to unlock the door and grabbed an armful of books. Then he tied the rope around the banister again and lowered himself to the ground. He handed me four hardcover books: *The Call of the Wild*, *The Merry Adventures of Robin Hood*, *The Three Musketeers*, and *Ivanhoe*. But these weren't ordinary editions. They were part of the Great Illustrated Classics series, which presented the original stories in simple form and had illustrations on every other page. I only needed to read half of the fifty or so pages to finish the book. The type was also large, and there weren't too many words on a page, either.

I felt a surge of excitement. Finally, books I could finish! For himself, Peretz got five fantasy paperbacks. Each one was more than eight hundred pages long and had tiny print. Peretz finished them all off in a month. I was amazed at his endurance. He seemed to me like a weightlifter pressing a thousand pounds.

The first book I tackled was *The Call of the Wild*. I read slowly, temporarily frustrated by tricky words such as *though*, *closeness*, and *ramshackle*, but the adventures of Buck, the innocent wolflike dog who was brutalized and had to become vicious to survive, captured my imagination. I felt as if I was there with him in snow-swept Alaska as he was betrayed and mistreated by his owners and the vicious dog, Spitz. I couldn't put it down. I started the book after morning prayers and finished it before supper.

The detailed portrayal of the dog's physical characteristics, as well as the feelings of an animal, was completely different from anything I had previously encountered. Raised in a community that disdained pet ownership, especially dogs, my most extensive connection to animals—save the few goldfish my father took care of and the short-lived hamster I had once begged for—was the generic and bloody animal sacrifices described in the Bible. Here was a gripping tale all about the inner life of a four-legged creature.

Immediately afterward, I sank my teeth into *The Merry Adventures of Robin Hood*, and once more I was engrossed in its magic. I felt as if I was galloping along with Robin Hood and his colorful crew of outlaws and misfits in the verdant English countryside of Sherwood Forest. I joined Robin Hood raising hell battling against the corrupt Sheriff of Nottingham and his petty minions.

The martial heroism of Robin Hood was completely different from the heroes on whom I had been raised. My heroes were nineteenth-century hidden mystics with supernatural powers and long white beards. (All the mystics had long white beards in my imagination.) They wandered the Polish forests seeking lost souls to bring back to God. My other heroes were these masters' spiritual descendants, contemporary scrappy Lubavitch emissaries who travel the world inspiring wayward Jews to return to Judaism. The idea that one could employ muscle and force to achieve a goal was completely foreign to me.

Each book I read temporarily lifted me up and away, far, far away, from the Talmud, Jewish law, and the Hasidic philosophy I'd been struggling to understand for years. The tales transported me to new and exciting adventures that made me think about and feel things such as gallantry and chivalry, which I'd never felt before. But most important, it was just pure enjoyment over which I didn't have to make a blessing and for which no moral reckoning was required. I just cracked open the book, plunged into its pages, and felt sheer bliss.

As I read these first books—I finished all of them within a week—my ability to make sense of the jumble of English letters on a page increased, as did my speed. I started to read more and more advanced books. Within two years, I would read F. Scott Fitzgerald's *The Great Gatsby* and Elie Wiesel's *Night*, as well as the first volume of Aleksandr Solzhenitsyn's *The Gulag Archipelago*, among others.

I began visiting public libraries in Brooklyn when I was home on vacation. My favorite was the Central Library at Grand Army Plaza, two miles from my house. The library is more than seventy years old; it has three stories, occupies 350,000 square feet, and has more than a million books. Adding to its luster are gilded relief sculptures in the enormous portico depicting modern and ancient themes of science and the arts, including Athena, Zeus, and Walt Whitman, plus a miner and an electrician. It is a palace of knowledge.

I would camp out for hours, wandering among the endless rows of shelves, picking up books at random and leafing through their pages, riveted by each new discovery. These library visits were not, strictly speaking, a secret from my parents, but I knew better than to bring them to their attention. They chose to ignore them. They acted as if these forays were a passing phase I would outgrow as I matured, the way other kids abandon their early fascination with bugs, or dinosaurs, or model airplanes.

Around this time, I began to accumulate books as if by a magnetic force. I hung out at Barnes and Noble as well as used bookstores, picking up a few volumes each visit. But my main source of books was Uncle Jeff. The handoffs took place at each of our meetings, which occurred every few months. It began with a trickle of ones or twos but soon advanced into a torrent of large paper shopping bags overflowing with books of Jewish and world history, memoirs, social science, and literature.

When Jeff handed me the treasures, he went through them one at a time, detailing their history and relative merits and pointing out any personal connection, however tangential, he had to them.

"This book was on my college syllabus, although truth be told, I never did read it."

"I met the author of this book at a lecture sponsored by the Workmen's Circle. I'm not sure about his writing, but he's a real mensch."

"This one was turned into a major film, and I was in a play in New Hampshire with the star of the film."

I felt like I was being guided into a new universe of knowledge by a most loving and informed preceptor.

I came to adopt as my own Jeff's passion for Shakespeare, Dickens, and Molière as a convert adopts a new faith. I even embraced his prejudice against all translations of Molière except the rhyming couplets of Richard Wilbur; I tried Albert Bermel's and Mildred Marmur's translations, and they just didn't measure up. I also adopted Jeff's passion for more contemporary dramatists such as George Bernard Shaw, Clifford Odets, Arthur Miller, and Tom Stoppard.

Like the revolution of the heavenly spheres, the cycle of yeshiva life persisted on its established course. The rabbis continued to deliver their twice-weekly lectures on the intricacies of the Talmud and its generations of commentators, with their myriad arguments and counterarguments, the intellectual equivalent of a series of seemingly endless smaller and smaller reflections produced by two parallel mirrors. But now I attended the mandatory lectures like a prisoner serving time. My body warmed a chair in the lecture hall while my mind was anywhere but there.

The rabbi's lectures weren't inherently uninteresting, but although I was not fully cognizant of it, I'd already promised my heart to another. The object of my affection was not the one my parents wished me to wed and the one my community expected me to settle down with. But I was enchanted by a new love: secular books. I wholeheartedly agreed with the observation of the fourteenth-century Italian humanist Petrarch: "Books give delight to the very marrow of one's bones. They speak to us, consult with us, and join with us in a living and intense intimacy." My heart burned with ardor for my new paramour. I hadn't yet spoken a romantic word to a flesh-and-blood lover in my life, but my books made me feel alive and capable. Books were my dearest companions, always generous and loyal.

I took a large stash of contraband books, about fifty, to each yeshiva I attended. I had to hide them all in different places in my dorms. In case one location was hit by the rabbis' periodic raids, the others would remain safe, just as our patriarch Jacob divided his family to ensure some would survive when they were threatened by his brother Esau's forces. I hid some underneath the mound of suitcases in the back of the closet, others in the dropped ceiling, and still others behind a loose panel in the wall. I agreed to share books with classmates, but, like a cautious drug dealer, I did business only with people I trusted not to rat me out if they got caught.

One Friday night I was in my room, door locked, with two friends showing them my inventory. A classmate, Yonah Chitrik, came over and knocked on my door. He was a short, friendly guy, but I wasn't close with him, so I didn't know whether he could be trusted. He might crack under pressure and give me up. "Zalman, I hear you've got books; I want to borrow one." I put my finger to my lips. The guys inside the dimly lit room fell silent. "Come on, man. I know you're in there. Let me in." Silence. Knock, knock. Silence. A minute went by. The guys inside said nothing. We didn't move. Yonah walked away, dragging his feet and muttering to himself.

The best defense against the rabbis finding them was to ensure that I was never the subject of a search. Simply stated, I needed to make sure that I never fell under suspicion. To do that, I had to make sure that I was never seen by the rabbis with an English book in my hand. Usually this was not too much of a hassle. I would make an effort to show up to each study period exactly on time and hang around for about fifteen minutes, long enough to ensure that the rabbi taking attendance saw me and got the impression that I was learning. Then I would nonchalantly duck out of the study hall and go back to my room to read.

When you add up all the chunks of time I snuck away, I can honestly say I was in my room reading most of the day. The schedule in the Miami yeshiva was divided into five study periods, and usually the rabbis didn't come looking for missing students in the middle of a period. Once I had a close call. I was sitting in bed idly resting my head on the bare white wall, reading a book about the Rothschild banking dynasty in Europe and the splendor of their opulent mansions. Suddenly, the *rosh yeshiva* (head rabbi) stormed into my laundry-strewn dorm suite, which was upstairs from the study hall.

I could hear him tramping through the front room. I was in the back room with the window leading to the back balcony right behind me. I quietly opened the window, snatched my book, held on to the windowsill, and climbed out, almost landing on a tiny green lizard scurrying away. I stood frozen on the balcony a few feet away from the window. The rabbi burst into my room and shouted, "Zalman, *ayeka* [where are you]?" The great Talmud scholar lifted my peach-colored blanket and jostled it, as if coaxing it to give up the location of its owner. Then he threw it down in frustration and retreated.

In those days, the Talmud and I were like friends who were once extremely close and now just nod as we pass each other in the street. We both knew the relationship had fundamentally changed but were too polite to say anything.

I fancied that my extracurricular readings were a total secret from the yeshiva rabbis. But maybe they weren't. One night at a *farbrengen*, Rabbi Pinchus Lipsker, the mystically inclined teacher charged with our spiritual mentorship, hugged me tightly, pressing my head into the effluence of his black beard, and whispered, "You're a *varme neshama* [warm soul] but be careful because you're *yelech beshruras libi* [you stubbornly follow your heart's desires]."

Did he know about my secret stash of books or was he simply able to sense that I was slipping away from the circle of the devout? I didn't worry about him too much. I felt that Rabbi Lipsker had only a tenuous connection to the physical world.

Although after about a year of receiving books from Jeff my father started to give me a few books he found on "the avenue," his term for miscellany he found on the sidewalk—"It's a little bruised on the cover, but the pages are fine"—his main contribution to my secular education was as a walking dictionary. Whenever I was home reading and tripped over an unfamiliar word, I always turned to him.

Me: Tatty, what does *ab-se-cond* mean?
Him: There's no such word. Spell it.
Me: *a-b-s-c-o-n-d.*
Him: Oh, that. It means run away.

My father was not thrilled that I was learning this stuff. I think it was just that he was bursting with information, and he couldn't help but let a little spill over onto me. My mother didn't like when he explained to me the meanings of words out loud. She said, "You should learn to look up words yourself in an actual dictionary, the old-fashioned way, just like I did when I was a child." Maybe. But I think she didn't like the constant intrusive reminder that I was learning English.

My book collecting reached a point that it required two huge clear plastic containers to hold them all under my bed in my parents' house. My mother wasn't shy with her feelings about my new interests. From time to time she would issue broad warnings: "Just remember that Jeff doesn't know everything." Other times she hurled insults at my growing repository of secular wisdom: "Zalman, you shouldn't read such *shtus* [nonsense]."

She occasionally expressed her solution to rectify what she saw as the pollution of her home. "Maybe," she would say with a smile that was a mix of honey and vinegar, "when you're away at yeshiva, I'll just take all your books and donate them to the public library. Finished." I never knew whether she meant it. I dreaded that I would come home and all my treasures would be gone.

Ultimately, she confiscated only two volumes: Dante's *Inferno* ("It's about hell, and it's very goyish") and Harper Lee's *To Kill a Mockingbird* ("It's about rape, and it's completely inappropriate"). Never mind the literary elegance of Dante's imagery of the netherworld or Lee's social message decrying racism and discrimination.

Although lacking the fire of my mother's opposition, my sisters were perplexed by my obsession with secular books. Because Lubavitchers believe that girls lack the same religious obligation to study Torah as boys, Bais Rivkah, the flagship Lubavitch girls' school in Crown Heights, which my sisters attended, provides a modicum of secular education, including classes on literature. All my sisters were A students but didn't take particular pleasure in the secular studies offered at their school. My sisters' lack of enthusiasm for literature may not have been entirely their fault. The lackluster English curriculum taught by bored and clueless teachers seems designed to keep the students uninterested.

Once when I was home from yeshiva and reclining on my parents' couch reading George Orwell's *Animal Farm*, my younger sister Chana Sara walked by and was surprised by my reading choice. "I read that book in school and hated it. Why are *you* reading that book? You don't have a test on it."

She laughed to herself and continued: "I would never read those kinds of books if I didn't have to for school."

"I'm reading it because I enjoy it. It's fascinating stuff."

Chana Sara was unconvinced. "No one in my class enjoys the books we read for school. There's only one girl at school, Pessy Kozlowski, that is interested in the literature class, but she's weird. She also likes baseball and talks about boys." It was clear that, to Chana Sara, evincing an interest in secular books made you odd and potentially irreligious.

While at the Miami yeshiva, every Thursday night as my friends started the *farbrengen* downing cups of vodka, I would take the gray cordless phone from my dorm and walk up and down Alton Road talking to my mother for an hour. Ours was a quiet street six blocks away from the beach and far removed from the wild party scene. Once in a while, a car would drive by blasting Latin music.

My friends couldn't believe I wanted to talk so much to my mother. "What do you have to talk about?" But we had a lot to discuss. I would report on the food the yeshiva cook was serving, and my mother would fill me in on what my siblings were up to:

"*Boruch Hashem* [thank God] Yossi is doing well in the Montreal yeshiva. We just arranged for a classmate traveling from Brooklyn to bring him leftover *cholent* to eat."

"Chana Sara is working hard on her family project. She even interviewed Aunt Marta."

"Rivky is going to be in the school production this year. It's a very big deal. Not every girl in her grade gets to do it."

Standing in the cool February breeze, I spotted Chaim returning from Pita Loca, a kosher Middle Eastern restaurant a fifteen-minute walk from the yeshiva. "Newfield, are ya coming to the *farbrengen*?" he asked as he passed me.

"Yeah, I'll be in soon."

Hearing this exchange, my mother said, "I don't want to keep you if you have to go."

"It's OK, Mommy, I have some more time."

"Ok, I'll just say that Esty's teacher told me when I met her at the grocery store on Monday that Esty is her most *eidel* [refined] student. I hope your teachers also have good things to say about you, Schneur Zalman."

"I'm sure my teachers would also say that I'm the most *eidel* student they have."

"I'm not joking."

"Who says I'm not serious?"

"I hope you are serious. We'd like to *shep naches* [derive pride] from you."

After a second pause she continued her report. "Listen to this. Chaya's class is doing a project in honor of Shimmy. Each child will draw a picture of a mitzvah they will take upon themselves to help bring Moshiach. The idea for this totally came from Mrs. Goldberg, Chaya's teacher. Isn't that sweet?"

"It's a lovely idea. The more mitzvahs the better."

"Exactly. What else is going on? Let me see. Mendy is starting to read from the *siddur* [prayer book] with his class. He's such a big *yingale* [boy]."

"OK, I probably should get going now," I said hesitatingly, not wanting to disconnect from the pleasant conversation but knowing that friends at the *farbrengen* would come looking for me if I didn't show up soon.

"Before I forget, Miriam went on a date last night. I'm not crazy about the guy, but . . ."

"Now you mention this juicy piece of information?"

"There's not much to say. I just wanted you to be in the loop. Now I'll give the phone to Tatty," and I heard her call out, "Shlomo, pick up the phone."

When my father picked up the receiver, we swapped a few brief lines and said goodbye. We still didn't seem to have much to talk about.

This all changed when my father visited me in Miami. He came to the city to spend a few days with his mother, who was ensconced in a

Miami hotel for the winter. When he came to see me, I brought him up to my messy dorm room to talk. I sat on my disheveled bed, and he made himself comfortable on a folding chair nearby. I was worried we would run out of things to talk about, but two hours went by in a flash.

He reported to me on how the small, gift-wrapped photo albums in his luggage intended as presents for his mother were ripped open by airport security but then returned to his suitcase by the would-be thieves. "I guess they figured there was something expensive in the boxes and were disappointed," he said, deadpan. I laughed. From there we just continued schmoozing as if it was the most natural thing to do.

It was the first time I ever had a real conversation with my father in my life. I don't know whether it helped that he was outside his comfort zone of Crown Heights or whether it was just that I was nearing eighteen and no longer a little kid, but somehow the distance that had existed between us for years was suddenly gone. It was like a circuit had finally clicked into place, and now we were both on the same frequency, able to communicate freely.

One thing I didn't mention to my father was just how little I was learning from the yeshiva curriculum. Oddly enough, aside from the one cryptic comment from Rabbi Lipsker, none of my teachers even mentioned it. We seldom had formal exams and the concept of "failing" a course or a grade point average didn't exist. This was because, unlike the yeshivas in some other ultra-Orthodox communities, which were focused on scholastic achievement, Lubavitch yeshivas were focused on inculcating religious piety. So even though I wasn't learning much Talmud, the teachers weren't especially vexed as long as I wasn't rebelling against the religious rules. Since I appeared devout, I didn't get in trouble.

In theory, I could have tried to apportion my time equally between my secular reading and my yeshiva studies. But since the yeshiva system itself dealt in absolutes—either all sacred or all profane—this never occurred to me. The unintended consequence of the Manichean spirit of the yeshiva was that all my attention was focused on profane books.

Years later, when I learned about students in Eastern European yeshivas in the early twentieth century who hid copies of Spinoza or Marx in their Talmuds and read them in the study hall, I felt a kinship to my rebellious brethren across time and space. But when I was in yeshiva sneaking off to read, I just felt a compulsion to do so. I didn't have a plan or a developed agenda. It certainly never occurred to me to try to leave the Lubavitch school system and attend a school that taught secular subjects. I wanted to be part of the Lubavitch system; I just also wanted to read my books.

At that point, I couldn't stop reading even if I had wanted to. I gained so much pleasure from it, but more important, I was too intoxicated by the realization that a whole world existed out there of which I was ignorant. I was like a villager who discovers one day that there are scores of modern metropolises beyond the muddy alleys of his ancestral home. My thirst was unquenchable.

One rainy afternoon, while daydreaming in the Miami yeshiva's study hall, which was incongruously decorated with pastel pink tiles, I was baffled to see a clean-shaven and damp Moti Abramowitz walking toward me. The last time I had seen him was two-and-a-half years earlier, the day he was unceremoniously kicked out of my Chicago yeshiva. I jumped up and hugged him.

"What the heck are you doing here? I thought you were back home in South Africa?"

"I got sick of my parents always spying on me and nagging me to be more *frum* [religious]. I came here to get away. I'm working part time for a Lubavitch family in North Miami driving their kids to school in South Beach every morning."

"That sounds exciting."

"Well, at least I'm free now and no one can tell me what the hell to do with my life."

Over the course of the next few months, I would chat with Moti occasionally after he dropped off his employer's children at their school across the street from my yeshiva. One day, Moti burst into the study hall and ran over to me. His face was flushed, and his gray eyes were dancing. He was so excited he didn't notice or care that we were not alone.

"I met this Lubavitch girl who dropped out of high school. Oh my God! She is so damn hot."

"Keep your voice down," I hissed through gritted teeth.

Moti was indifferent to my admonition. He had this ridiculous grin on his face. "You don't get it."

"I don't get what?"

"We did it, *it*, in my car last night!"

I quickly glanced at Moti and then at the handful of my classmates in earshot.

"*Are you serious?*" I whispered.

"Yes, I'm serious. It was the most amazing thing in the world! There's nothing like it! You don't know what you're missing."

After Moti left the study hall, I sat speechless. *What kind of person would do such a dirty thing and then brag about it publicly?*

One classmate muttered in a voice audible to all in the room. "Ugh. What a mixed-up guy, doing such *prost*, disgusting things!"

Another classmate opined, "That's what happens when you're a bum who drops out of yeshiva. You have nothing of value in your life, so you follow your *tayvahs* [base desires]."

I knew I never wanted to end up like Moti, reviled and denounced by my former friends and classmates. *I'm nothing like Moti. He's a low-life, a bum! I'm a good Lubavitcher. I just read goyish books.*

7

To Russia with Matzahs

"Attention passengers, please find your seats so we can depart on schedule," announced the Aeroflot captain over the loudspeaker. This was the third such request in the past ten minutes. Most of the passengers on the flight from New York's John F. Kennedy (JFK) International Airport to Moscow had already complied. But the targets of his entreaties, who were among the 150 Lubavitch rabbinical students headed to Russia to lead seders for Passover in various cities across that vast country, were oblivious to his polite requests.

The Boeing 767 was taxiing to the runway. I was already seated, with my seatbelt fastened, for fifteen minutes, but a group of guys in white shirts and dark pants, wearing dark sports jackets and fedoras, some of whom I knew from yeshiva and summer camps, were standing in the aisles chatting, as if they were still in the study hall back at yeshiva.

The plane made a slow right turn and lined up on the runway. It started to creep down the runway. The guys didn't budge. Suddenly, the curtain separating first class from economy swung open, and in charged the flight attendant, a tall blond woman—the Hollywood stereotype of a female KGB agent. She wore a smart navy-blue uniform with a military-looking cap emblazoned with Aeroflot's winged hammer-and-sickle logo, a legacy from its Soviet days when the airline was a state-owned enterprise. She pointed her index finger at the offenders and commanded, "Sit down right now."

With that, all the noncompliant passengers scattered for their seats. A minute later, the plane roared down the runway and lifted off.

This was April 2000, and I was eighteen. As the youngest member of the group, I was able to squeeze myself onto the flight through the intercession of a friend related to a prominent Lubavitch rabbi in Moscow. Twenty minutes into the flight, Alter Bernstein, my partner in this seder-hosting effort, was downing shots of vodka with a non–Jewish Russian passenger in the back of the plane. Vodka is produced from grains, making it not kosher for Passover. So Alter was having his fill of the intoxicant with his new Russian friend before the onslaught of the "dry days" of Passover. I was accustomed to seeing Alter polish off one cup of vodka after another. He had assured me many times over the previous two years in the Miami yeshiva, "I'm not an alcoholic. I can stop any time I want. I just don't want to."

It was no mere coincidence that Alter was my partner. He was my best friend, almost a blood brother. He was also my Talmud study partner. We would talk for hours and make each other laugh uncontrollably when we were supposed to be learning Talmud. Compared with me, or just about anyone else, he had a much higher social status in yeshiva. Like the flashy leader of a motorcycle gang, Alter was fearless. He saw every stop sign as a provocation to violate it. As his reliable sidekick, I caught some of his boldness. The price—and perhaps key—of our partnership was that I hesitated to contradict him and had to go along with his decisions, including religious observance.

As I sat in my seat, I reflected on the orientation meeting held the previous night in Crown Heights. The coordinator of the trip, an energetic Lubavitcher in his mid-twenties with glasses and a short black beard, stood up on a table in a large and noisy room and said, "The program is like this. You're flying to Moscow tomorrow. You'll spend three days together near Moscow in a *lager*, a camp."

As he spoke, he swayed back and forth in the same rocking motion used in prayer. He continued, "You'll have a chance to meet representatives from your communities there. Then you'll travel with your *chavrusa* [partner] and the local leaders to your city. You'll spend six days in your city. Then you'll meet back in Moscow for a final day and fly back to New York."

Once he finished his speech, he handed a white envelope to each pair of travelers. I opened our envelope and stared at the contents. In addition to Alter's and my passports with attached Russian visas, there was a thick wad of $100 bills. I counted $3,000. The organizer stood on the table again to get everyone's attention. "Hey, hey," the organizer said, "this money isn't your Chanukah present. We're giving it to you for the program and some extra just in case. Have *rachmonus* [mercy]. Please return whatever you don't spend." Most of the guys chuckled.

To me, this whole trip started to feel like a spy operation—and not one especially likely to succeed. Where exactly were we being sent? Was it safe there? Alter and I didn't speak a word of Russian. How would we communicate with the people at our seders? Where would we get kosher food for the seders?

Cruising forty thousand feet above sea level at 550 miles an hour, I realized that I had two main associations with Russia, and neither was reassuring. Pops, my mother's father, told me stories about his father, Eliezer Yanushewitz, who fought in the czar's army in World War I and was shot in the hand, leaving him with a permanent disability. When he returned to his village, he used his army rifle to scare off anti-Semitic hoodlums. I never learned which battles Eliezer participated in or what tasks he performed as a soldier. I just knew that my great-grandfather, along with approximately 450,000 other Jews, served in the Russian army during World War I defending Mother Russia.

I had also heard stories from my yeshiva teachers of Lubavitch rabbis thrown into Stalin's gulags for the crime of teaching Torah in the Soviet Union. The truth is: I thought of Russia as the place that Jews like my great-grandparents *used* to live in and did everything in their power to escape from. But more than 260,000 Jews still lived in that country, with a much higher number of people of Jewish descent.

The history of the Jews in Russia is as convoluted as the course of the Volga River. During the Soviet era, the regime was strongly opposed to the Jewish religion, just as it opposed the formal observance of all other religions. The result was that those Jews who remained in Russia after the fall of the Soviet Union were highly assimilated and often lacked even basic knowledge of Judaism and its customs. It was with these Jews of Russia that I was planning to spend Passover, my first time outside North America.

Our flight landed at Sheremetyevo International Airport in Moscow, and everyone cheered. Alter, whose face ordinarily sported a smart-ass grin and whose movements were usually quick and decisive, now seemed dazed and lethargic from all his drinking. I stood near him and helped get him through customs. As we moved through the airport, I noticed the drab brown decor hadn't been updated since the Khrushchev era.

We boarded buses that drove us to the *lager*. In Soviet times, the *lager* was a state-run summer camp; it still had a mural in the pool room of a boy and girl in their Komsomol (Young Communist League) uniforms, with matching red neckerchiefs, standing together in warm comradeship. Now the Lubavitch organization in Russia uses the grounds for its outreach programs.

The next day we met the representatives from the community we were to visit. The representatives were non–Orthodox Jews, and most were not especially knowledgeable about Judaism, but they were active in local Jewish clubs and organizations. Alter and I were going to Syzran, a distant city in the southeastern part of Russia, sixteen hours away from Moscow by train. Syzran sent two men: Igor, in his fifties and clean-shaven, and Dmitri, in his thirties with a brown mustache, neither of whom spoke a word of English.

To get acquainted with our hosts, Alter, who was slender but had chiseled arms and a six-pack abdomen, joined an arm-wrestling competition with a group of Russians. I mingled with the crowd, desperate to get some answers to my questions. I looked for representatives from other communities who might know a few words in English. I joined a circle of Russian guys trying to set some Lubavitchers straight. "The Russian language is very," one of our new friends struggled to find the correct word, "difficult to talk."

"Why is it so difficult?" I asked.

"Because it has eight tenses in Russian," he responded. Then he and his friends conferred in Russian for a minute and burst out laughing.

"What's so funny?" I asked.

One of the other representatives in the circle jumped in to explain. "The other day in Rostov, where we live, an American rabbi was trying to sing a Jewish song. The song speaks of the two tablets that God gave Moses, but he not say *tabluchki*, the word for tablets. He say *tapochki*, the word for slippers." All the Russians in the group cracked up all over again.

"Are there any easy Jewish songs to sing in Russian?" I asked, at the risk of sounding foolish.

"*Da, da*, there is one easy song," one of the guys said. "Ochen schastliviy ya, potomu chto ya everei."

"OK, what does it mean?" I asked, wanting to verify they weren't pulling my leg with a string of obscenities.

"It mean, 'I'm so happy because I am Jew.'"

"Oh, that sounds great. Can you sing it again?"

The three Russians in the group sang it. I took out a pen and paper and wrote down the words in English letters as best I could. I planned on singing it at the seders I would soon be hosting.

Later that day, five of us Americans set out to do some sightseeing. We packed into a taxi for the thirty-minute drive from the *lager* to the center of Moscow. Our destination was the Kremlin. Before we left, one of the Russians advised us, "You must to carry passport at all times during travels in Russia." But we were scared the passports might get stolen in Moscow, so we left them in the *lager*.

As soon as we entered downtown Moscow, we stopped at a traffic light. I heard a knock, knock, knock, on the car window. I turned around and saw a Kalashnikov pointed right at me. The police officer holding the rifle, wearing a gray uniform with a white belt, was a bear of a man with pudgy cheeks and a wide neck. He looked like a walking and talking oversize potato. He motioned with his hand to roll down the window. I did. He ordered, "Pasporta, pasporta."

We all pretended we had no idea what he was talking about. "We're Americans. We don't speak Russian. What do you want?"

"Pasporta, pasporta," he repeated, more insistently this time.

"What? We don't understand."

He motioned with his hand for us to get out of the car. We followed him fifty paces into a small police station to see the captain. The policeman and the captain could have been brothers. They were molded out of the same Play-Doh. The captain demanded, "Pasporta," and we played dumb again.

"We're Americans. We don't understand."

The captain scrutinized the five of us with bushy beards and wearing yarmulkes. He tilted his massive head and asked, "Amerikansky?"

"Yes," we all answered, nodding our heads. "We're Americans."

"Bill Clinton. Monica Lewinsky," he said to no one in particular and laughed out loud, sending shockwaves through his large frame.

The captain's laugh terminated our interrogation. We were free to go. We got into another taxi and drove to Red Square. We were eager to take pictures standing in front of the Kremlin. We stood in front of what we thought was the Kremlin and took a few pictures of each other. Then a Russian passerby asked, "Do you want me should take picture of you all in front of the cathedral?"

"The cathedral?" Alter asked in horror. "We want to take pictures in front of the Kremlin."

The passerby shook his head side to side. "That," pointing to the building with the colorful domes that looked like the swirly tops of ice cream cones, "is St. Basil's Cathedral." Then he turned to the right and pointed at a squat yellow brick building partially obscured by a long red brick wall. "That is Kremlin!"

"Wow, we had no idea," I said. "Thanks."

We had the passerby take several snapshots of us in front of the actual Kremlin.

Before the passerby walked away, I asked him, "How do you say Red Square in Russian?"

"Krásnaya Plóshcha," he answered.

As I stood on Krásnaya Plóshcha, now populated by commuters and tourists, I remembered the Cold War newsreels I'd seen of military parades with trucks carrying enormous missiles on this same spot. I imagined that Joseph Stalin and Lavrentiy Beria, his chief of secret police, must have stood on the very cobblestones on which I was now walking. I shuddered.

Still, I was eager to tour the Kremlin, the site of so much Russian history. Alter agreed to join me. We walked toward the line to pay the entrance fee of thirty rubles when a corpulent Russian in his fifties carrying a bulging black binder approached. "Je parle français. Ich spreche Deutsch."

"We're Americans," I said.

"Amerikansky. I speak good English. I give you Kremlin tour." He flipped through his binder looking for some brochure.

"How much?" I ask.

"Hundred rubles."

"That's too much," Alter said. We started to walk away.

"It's good," the tour guide protested. "I show you the bell tower, the crowns of the Romanovs, and the churches."

Alter, his eyebrows raised, broke in. "There are churches in the Kremlin?"

The tour guide answered. "Yes, it has numerous churches."

"Forget it," Alter said, as he sliced the air with his hands. "We're not interested in churches. Let's go, Zalman."

The tour guide suddenly realized the nature of the situation and suggested, "It is not necessary to visit churches."

But it was too late. The repulsive word had already been uttered and could not be reclaimed. For my part, I really wanted to visit the Kremlin and would have hired the tour guide and circumvented the churches, but Alter was adamant that it was inappropriate for us to enter a building that contained churches. I could have ignored Alter's objections and gone by myself. But between the two of us, Alter was the religious authority, and I felt uncomfortable disregarding his decisions on spiritual matters.

After giving up on touring the Kremlin, we figured it would be safe for us to visit the embalmed body of Lenin, which is on display in a gray-and-maroon granite mausoleum in the center of Red Square. We ambled over to the mausoleum to join the line, where we heard that visitors had to take off their hats inside as a sign of respect. That would mean we would need to take off our yarmulkes. I was contemplating the feasibility of complying with the head-covering rule when Alter proclaimed, "Lenin, *yemach shemoi* [may his name be erased], spent his whole life trying to get Jews to abandon *Yiddishkeit* [Judaism]. We could never allow him in his death to get us to take off our yarmulkes, even for a second." All the pain of the Russian Lubavitchers who were banished to the gulags on Stalin's orders for spreading Judaism in the Soviet Union seemed to pour out of Alter at that moment. That was the end of our attempt to gaze at the father of the Bolshevik Revolution.

We decided to visit the State Historical Museum, which faces St. Basil's Cathedral on the opposite side of Red Square. The museum, built in 1881, occupies an enormous red brick building with intricate towers and windows. It looks like an elaborate gingerbread house designed by a child with a very active imagination.

We toured the museum, which contains artifacts from Russia's prehistory and its monarchs but seemed to gloss over the sixty-nine-year span of Soviet history. I saw only one image of Stalin in the entire museum but noticed numerous royal thrones of the Romanovs, along with their jewels and elegant paintings. Things seemed to be going well. I was standing in a small room inspecting a painting of Catherine the Great dressed in a green riding outfit astride a white horse when I detected several Russians staring at me and giggling. I was shocked. Were they so blatantly anti-Semitic that they would laugh in my face?

I narrowed the lids of my eyes and stared right back at them with all the meanness I could muster. I felt my body temperature suddenly rise. Then one of the bystanders looked right at me and said something in Russian while putting his hand on his head. He then dropped his hand down to his side as if dropping a yarmulke. Was he telling me to throw my yarmulke on the floor? My face reddened. How could these anti-Semites be so open with their hatred—and in a museum of all places?

I thought of my great-grandmother, Miriam Feiga, a woman known for her strong personality, who spoke no English and frequently repeated the Yiddish aphorism "Men ken lebn ober me lozt nisht" (We could live, but *they* don't let us). It was clear that the "they" referred to non-Jews. She was always on the lookout for manifestations of anti-Semitism. Once, after watching a performance in English of *Romeo and Juliet*, she observed, "Of course. It's always the same story: the anti-Semites bothering the Jews!" Standing in the museum, I wondered whether her obsession with non-Jewish hatred of Jews wasn't a natural outgrowth of living the first forty years of her life on Russian soil.

As I stared down my adversaries, wishing I could shoot fire out of my eyes, as in the Talmudic legend of Rabbi Shimon Bar Yochai and his son Elazar, who scorched farmland just by looking at it, a young Russian woman entered the room. Sensing the tension, she inquired, "I speak English. Can I help?"

"Yes, what does that guy want?" I asked, pointing to my nemesis. She walked over to him and conferred.

She came back to me and said, "He wants to know, what keeps the hat on your head from falling off?"

Back at the *lager*, the organizers were explaining how to rearrange the usual order of the seder. This can be a problem because some of the seder rituals must be performed at night, but in many regions of Russia in this season, sundown is quite late, after 9 P.M.

I was more concerned with how we would make enough food to feed all those who would attend our seders. The organizers provided each group with an old industrial blowtorch and a can of fuel to use to render a nonkosher kitchen kosher. I doubted whether the steel contraption with the enormous nozzle would even turn on. Besides, I could hardly explain to an English-speaker, much less in pantomime, the logic of the rules for making a kitchen kosher. Essentially, to turn a nonkosher stovetop into a kosher one, intense heat needs to be applied to burn out the residual ingrained flavor previously absorbed from the nonkosher food. Hence, the blowtorch.

The next morning, Alter and I, along with Igor and Dimitri, boarded a train for the sixteen-hour ride to Syzran. We had a sleeper cabin to ourselves, but it was cramped and smelled awful, like an overstuffed crate of rotten onions.

When we finally arrived in Syzran late at night, our contacts took us to Otel Chayka (Hotel Seagull) and left. The austere atmosphere of our room was partially offset by a homey touch, the dark green diamond pattern of the wallpaper. We plopped down on the narrow beds and fell fast asleep.

The next morning, our hosts Igor and Dimitri returned along with a teenage girl named Galina, who would be our translator. Now we could get down to business. Alter and I proceeded into town trailing behind Galina, with her bob haircut, blue-and-white checkered pants, and brown sweater. Her English wasn't fluent, but it was more than adequate. At one point, I complained that Russian was so difficult to understand. Galina smiled and said, "Russian is not hard to learn. I mastered by age three."

Galina informed us that the Lubavitch organization in Moscow had shipped a dozen boxes of matzah, two cases of kosher wine, and containers of prepared foods to Syzran for our seders. With the sun outside shimmering in the sky, forcing me to squint, our group packed into Igor's dark-blue Zhiguli, dating from the 1970s and the product of the Volga Automobile Plant nearby. He drove us to the small house that served as the Jewish community center. Miniature Israeli flags adorned its walls, along with portraits of Theodore Herzl, David Ben-Gurion, Moshe Dayan, and children's paintings of menorahs.

Igor opened the fridge and showed us the inventory: six large, white, round plastic containers full of carrot and cucumber salads and two large square containers of fist-size tan patties. They didn't smell like fish, but they looked like gefilte fish. It turned out they were actually ground chicken masquerading as gefilte fish.

Igor spoke to Galina, who translated. "Igor arranged two seders. The first night the old persons will come; the second night the young persons will come."

"That sounds great," I said.

"How many people are going to come each night?" Alter asked.

Galina conferred with Igor. "Igor thinks approximately seventy-five persons each night." She pronounced *thinks* as *sinks.*

"That's a lot of people," I said.

Galina relayed my reaction. Igor nodded his head a few times. "Igor says many persons eager to come to the program."

I told Galina, "We want to arrange for extra food to be cooked for the seders to make them special. And please tell Igor we have money to pay for the extra food."

Galina spoke to Igor. "Igor wants know what you want cook?"

"What does Igor think would be good to have at the seders?" I asked.

"Igor thinks it would be good to have borscht, potatoes with onions, and tomato salad."

"That sounds great," I said. "Is there someone in the community who could cook this food for us? We would pay her."

"Igor thinks Svetlana could do the cooking, but money not required."

"Perfect," I said. "Where will Svetlana do the cooking?"

"Svetlana will cook in her home."

"OK, the only thing is we need to make her kitchen kosher," I said.

Igor scratched his head and then looked at us wide-eyed. Galina asked, "What does that mean?"

"Well, it depends on exactly how her kitchen is set up," I said. "But we will probably need to use a blowtorch."

"What is this?" asked Galina.

"A blowtorch, a small machine that shoots out fire." As soon as I said those words, I realized I said the wrong thing. Igor shook his head from side to side and said something in Russian.

Galina said, "Igor thinks this is not good idea. Svetlana will not agree to this."

"It's OK. It's OK," I said. "It will be fine."

Galina said, "Igor says he will speak Svetlana and see what she feel."

We were about to set off to buy the needed vegetables when Igor's car came to a sputtering halt in the street. We were out of "petrol." Galina said, "Igor says he has plan."

Igor got out of the car and removed a four-foot length of garden hose from his trunk. He flagged down a car and spoke to the driver.

The other driver nodded his head and parked his car right next to ours. The other driver unscrewed the cap of his gas tank. Igor unscrewed the cap of his gas tank and placed one end of the hose inside the other car's gas tank. He held on to the other end and sucked on it.

Once he got the petrol to reach his mouth, he placed the end of the hose into the gas tank of his car. He waited a few minutes for enough petrol to transfer from the other car to his and then removed the hose and put it back in his trunk. Igor thanked the other driver, handed him a few rubles, and the other car drove off. The other driver, Igor, and Galina all acted as if this was as ordinary an interaction as wishing a neighbor good morning. Alter and I were quite impressed with the Russian ingenuity.

I didn't know what to expect at the marketplace. As a schoolkid, I'd heard stories of Lubavitch American yeshiva students going to Russia and returning with suitcases laden with mink hats and full military uniforms they snatched up for pennies after the fall of the Soviet Union, when the country was in complete economic chaos. I also heard that the shelves in stores were often empty.

We drove to a fruit and vegetable market and were surprised to find heaping tables of ripe tomatoes, onions, zucchini, apples, oranges, and grapes, and stout vendors wearing neat blue aprons who weighed the produce on large white mechanical scales from an earlier era. By the time of my arrival, the economy had stabilized. The official exchange rate was twenty-eight rubles to a dollar. The produce was affordable, but it was not being sold at fire sale prices. After purchasing five large paper bags overflowing with produce, we drove to Svetlana's apartment to discuss the issue of the blowtorch. As we bumped along the streets, we passed a tram and several kiosks selling cigarettes and beer.

Svetlana's building was probably built in the 1950s and in a hurry. The gray brick, nine-story building with no elevator was a monument to no-frills construction. We walked up several flights to her apartment. I brought the blowtorch along. Svetlana greeted us at the door. She was a trim woman in her sixties with white hair and a graceful posture. Galina was not with us, and Svetlana spoke only a few words of English. So holding the blowtorch, I tried to demonstrate in pantomime using it to make her kitchen kosher. I handed it to her. Svetlana took it and turned it all around as if inspecting a small meteorite with fascination mixed with fear. Then she said, "*Da, da*," nodded her head, and led us into her kitchen.

Alter stood in front of the stove and turned the nob on the back of the blowtorch. A raging flame shot out of the wide nozzle, blackening the stovetop and the formerly white wall behind the stove. I thought how ironic it would be if this building survived the Cold War only to be burned down by two rabbinical students sent from New York.

Alter and I decided to ditch the plan to make Svetlana's stovetop kosher. Instead, we agreed it would be wiser to spend some of our money to buy a new electric hot plate and several pots and have Svetlana cook in them.

Before leaving her apartment, Svetlana proudly showed us the medals her father, an officer in the Great Patriotic War, as Russians termed World War II, earned for his valor in combat. She lovingly displayed them on the kitchen table. One was made of silver and had a red star surrounded by a pattern of rays. In the center was a Mosin rifle crossed with a saber. Another one consisted of a brass disk depicting a stern-looking Comrade Stalin in the uniform of the Marshal of the Soviet Union and was attached to a black-and-orange silk ribbon. The third was also a brass disk that depicted a helmeted Red Army soldier, a sailor, and a worker, all three with rifles at the ready. It was attached to an olive-green silk ribbon with a darker green stripe. Svetlana handled the medals the way someone would handle precious jewels. These medallions represent a kind of birthright. They proved that her family—and, by extension, all Russian Jews—were loyal citizens who thus deserved equal status in their country.

Back at our hotel room, I was surprised to discover that all our purchases of food and supplies had barely made a dent in the wad of bills given to us in New York.

The following night was our first seder. I had no idea how the Jews in the city ran their public seders in the past. Was this the first public seder held there for at least fifty years? Did they conduct it exclusively in Yiddish? Did they conduct it exclusively in Russian? Did they read through the entire Haggadah, the special prayer book of the seder? Did they cover only the main rituals, such as drinking the four cups of wine and asking the Four Questions?

Alter and I decided that he would read aloud several passages of the Haggadah in Hebrew and that I would explain in English the meaning of each ritual, with Galina translating. We revised the order of the seder because sundown was close to 9:30 that night. The first night's crowd arrived and took their seats, the men in suits and ties and the women in formal dresses. The men also wore black yarmulkes provided by Lubavitch in Moscow. We began by reading the Four Questions in Hebrew. Then I explained their significance and told the story of the Israelite exodus from Egypt.

At first, I spoke in a New York torrent. Galina whispered to me, "You must to speak slow for me to translate." I started to speak slower and paused after each sentence. It forced me to choose my words more carefully and to cut out extraneous comments. After my speech, we served dinner. Once they had eaten their fill, our guests were more than happy to continue on with the recital of the Haggadah. We made kiddush, distributed the matzah, and drank the four cups of wine. Each blessing in the seder we said out loud as a group, one word at a time.

By 10 P.M. the seder and its rituals were completed. For the grand finale, Alter and I danced with arms interlocked and sang the Russian Jewish song I had been practicing since leaving the *lager*: "Ochen schastliviy ya, potomu chto ya every" (I'm so happy because I am a Jew). The audience, which had largely maintained a respectful silence throughout the seder, came alive.

Luckily, they recognized our version of the Russian song and loved it. They clapped and sang along for more than five minutes, repeating the same one line over and over again. On the second night, at the young adults' seder, we followed the same schedule. All the young people, dressed casually in jeans and sweatshirts, were also moved by the song at the end. Several of the young men even joined in the dancing while the women sat in their chairs and clapped to the beat.

The day after the second seder was a Saturday, so we stayed in Syzran and made a gathering Saturday afternoon for the young adults at the community center. I told the group about the weekly Torah reading, then we relaxed and had an informal conversation. Galina was on hand to translate.

A man in the group cautioned Alter and me to be careful what we said in Russia. "You never know if other persons is listening."

"I don't understand," I said. "I thought the KGB is finished."

The man laughed. "FSB [the Russian Federal Security Service, the successor to the KGB] is same thing as KGB, just change name." I felt a chill go through my body. There was still a shadow network of secret police surveillance in place of which I was ignorant but my seder guests were well aware.

A teenage boy in the group told a joke about a *kulak*. "What is a *kulak*?" I asked.

"*Kulak* is lazy peasant," he answered. I didn't know at the time that the term *kulak*, which literally means "tight-fisted," was a political term for independent farmers who resisted Stalin's plans for farm collectivization.

I was surprised by how much I learned about Russian history, politics, and culture in the course of a few days, notwithstanding the obvious language barrier.

As the gathering was breaking up, an attractive brunette teenager offered her hand in a handshake. She had a mischievous twinkle in her eye.

I wanted to touch her hand. Moti Abramowitz's boasts flashed in my mind, and here, it seemed obvious to my teenage perception, was my opportunity to see what he meant. But I'd been taught that these were disgusting things to do, shameful things to do before marriage. Only *oysvorfs* (lowlifes) do such things. The *Tanya* is very clear that even to think such thoughts contaminates the soul and causes it grievous pain. These are things that Moti would do, but not me! I was a soldier in the Rebbe's army and on a mission. I needed to push these *machshva zaras*, these impure thoughts, out of my mind so I could focus on my mission.

I told her through Galina, "I'm not allowed to touch women." The persistent brunette tried again to shake my hand. I backed away. She moved in closer. I took two steps back. She came forward again, closing the distance. Instinctively I jumped back a few feet to avoid making physical contact with a woman. She and her friends hooted.

A few minutes later, I spied the same teen frolicking with one of the Russian boys in the grass nearby. I was jealous. I wished I was the one she was hugging and whispering to. I wished she was laughing and playing absentmindedly with my hair. Would I ever get to experience that?

Back in Moscow, Alter and I rejoined the group of rabbinical students at the central Lubavitch headquarters at the Marina Roscha Synagogue, whose dignified marble and wood prayer hall seats two thousand worshippers. I was disconcerted to learn that several years ago, the synagogue was bombed and later attacked by an arsonist. "Don't worry about it," reassured Gershon, one of the rabbinical students on the trip. "Berel Lazar is tight with Putin, and Putin won't let these *mamzarim* [bastards] do anything to *Yiddin* [Jews] in Russia."

Vladimir Putin had assumed the position of prime minister of Russia nine months earlier and seemed to have embraced Rabbi Berel Lazar, the head Lubavitcher in Russia, as his official representative to the country's Jewish community. Between this assurance and the team of security guards patrolling the facility, I figured the chances were decent that I would make it back safely to Brooklyn. Twenty-four hours later I was home.

The Russian Jews I had met lived very different lives from mine, religiously and culturally, and we spent less than a week together. Still, I felt a kinship with them. My Lubavitch upbringing taught me the uniqueness of the Jewish people and the necessity to love all Jews because every Jew was "a spark of the essence of God." In theory and in fact, all Jews were my brothers and sisters.

I also had a personal bond linking me to the Jews of Russia. It was only ninety-two years since my grandmother's mother, Mildred Byer (née Sachnovsky), boarded the S.S. *Lithuania* and sailed for America. And it was only seventy-one years since my grandfather's mother, Miriam Feiga Yanushewitz (née Rothenberg), left Russia and sailed to America. But for a quirk of history—had my great-great-aunt Yochved not earned enough money from her tiny candy store on the Lower East Side of Manhattan to purchase steamship tickets for Miriam Feiga and her children—I might have been born somewhere in Russia, several generations later, to assimilated parents, waiting for Lubavitch rabbinical students from America to visit and teach me how to make a Passover seder.

I hadn't realized until that trip how much I enjoyed public speaking and exploring foreign countries. But as I reflected on it in the following weeks and months, I began to feel uncomfortable representing Lubavitch and telling other Jews to be more religious. I felt burdened by the constant admonishments to refrain from making a "*chillul* Lubavitch," a desecration of the name of Lubavitch. The handbreadth I'd been told to imagine between myself and them seemed smaller than ever.

It was hardly a fully formed thought at that early stage, but I began to feel as if doing outreach work was not my life's mission. Still, I was firmly enough entrenched in Lubavitch at that time to be outraged by the teenage girl's attempt to touch me—or was I outraged at my instinct to reciprocate—and to continue my studies in yeshiva as a matter of course. But Russia was only my first trip abroad. My travels and my hesitant steps away from the Lubavitch path had only just begun.

8

On the Doorstep of Freedom

"Listen to this," my friend Dovid Tiechtel said as he handed me his CD player and black headphones. Dovid was always laughing, as if he was privy to a constant comedy routine the rest of us couldn't hear. I placed the large earpieces on my ears and adjusted the wide bar on top of my yarmulke. "It's Slim Shady. Ya like?"

"What's Slim Shady?" We were standing in Dovid's small dorm room in the Lubavitch yeshiva in Buenos Aires, Argentina.

"Just listen."

I did, but I didn't understand much. I understood that I was listening to non-Jewish music, which was forbidden in Lubavitch because the rabbis believed it contaminated the soul. I also understood that it was rap music and that the song was studded with profanities.

I was nineteen, and I was not one of those Lubavitchers who listened only to Nichoach, an austere, all-male Lubavitch chorus. I listened to the kitschy Shlock Rock, the soulful Shlomo Carlebach, the hip Diaspora Yeshiva Band, the folksy Moshe Yess, and the touching songs of Journeys. But all these singers and music groups were Jewish, and they were all Orthodox. Now I was listening to non-Jewish music and, even worse, a song brimming with curse words. "Got anything else?" I asked, handing him back the CD player.

"Of course. Try this." He put in another CD. "It's 'Gangsta's Paradise.'"

I listened. The music was slower, and I could understand all the words, but it didn't grab me. "Nah. Something else."

"How about this? It's called 'It's My Life.'"

I heard the pounding of drums and the cry of an electric guitar, and above it all, I heard Bon Jovi howling: "It's my life. . . . I ain't gonna live forever. I just want to live while I'm alive."

My body swayed to the beat, and my heart sped up. I felt unstoppable. I imagined myself alternately surfing a massive tidal wave and racing a wild horse up a steep rocky cliff with the wind blowing in my face. I also thought about my brother Shimmy. It had been two-and-a-half years since he had passed away. Bon Jovi's lyrics hit home. I felt like you never know how long you're going to live and you have to make the most of the time you've got. How was I making the most of my time?

In September 2000 I completed my two years in the Miami yeshiva. Then I transferred with a group of ten American friends to the Lubavitch yeshiva in Buenos Aires. It was common for Lubavitch students to attend Lubavitch yeshivas abroad. Some of my friends went to Lubavitch yeshivas in France, England, and South Africa. We ended up in Argentina because one of the students in Miami was from Buenos Aires, and he arranged with the yeshiva in his hometown to accept us.

Argentina was not terra incognita to my extended family. My great-great-uncle Avrum, the brother of my great-grandmother Miriam Feiga, emigrated from the town of Ostrow-Mazowiecki, in Poland, to Argentina in the mid-1920s and lived there until 1947, when he left for the United States. He was a suave dresser and taught himself to speak Spanish fluently.

Had Uncle Avrum arrived in Argentina twenty years earlier, he might have been drawn to one of the Jewish agricultural settlements such as Moisés Ville in the province of Santa Fe, which was supported by Baron Maurice de Hirsch. But by the time he arrived, more immigrants were making their homes in the cities. Instead of becoming a farmer, Avrum became a door-to-door peddler in Buenos Aires, selling bedsheets, suspenders, and other household items. But he longed to be reunited with his siblings who immigrated to the United States, and with their help he was able to join them after World War II.

The yeshiva in Argentina is located in Palermo, the largest and one of the richest neighborhoods of Buenos Aires. Buenos Aires isn't all goyish. The area close by the yeshiva has many psychoanalysts and is known as Villa Freud.

The Argentine yeshiva is run like Lubavitch yeshivas everywhere else. They share a single curriculum, dress code, and ideology. It's like a McDonald's franchise. Although the language spoken by the employees may vary, and although the environment *outside* of the establishment may be quite different, what happens *inside* the walls of the establishment is remarkably similar across the globe.

Culturally, all yeshivas I attended were like bunkers, but the large brown brick building of the yeshiva in Argentina is actually physically a sort of fortress. This was in response to two deadly attacks in Buenos Aires: one against the Israeli Embassy in 1992 and the other against the main Jewish community center in 1994. The yeshiva building has seven stories with two subterranean floors, housing a community synagogue, a children's day school, and the adult male yeshiva. The building is surrounded by large cement barriers to prevent car-bomb attacks. Teams of security guards patrol the building and search all incoming mail for explosives.

Most of the thirty Argentine students in the yeshiva spoke Spanish at home and at yeshiva. They were the grandchildren or great-grandchildren of European Jews who had immigrated to Argentina in the 1920s and 1930s. My Argentine classmates' parents or grandparents were attracted to the Lubavitch community once they settled in South America.

Before going to Argentina, I didn't speak a word of Spanish. My father purchased from the William H. Hamilton book catalogue a six-part Spanish crash course on audiotape. I packed the tapes in my luggage but felt no urgency to learn the language. During the first few weeks in Buenos Aires, I listened to the first tape and learned the phrase "Permiso, me llamo . . ." (Excuse me, my name is . . .). But I lost interest and sold the tapes to an American friend for $10. Out of the ten Americans, only one learned to speak Spanish, and he arrived already speaking French.

I mostly spoke to other Americans or to Argentine students and rabbis who spoke Hebrew or Yiddish. I seldom traveled more than a few blocks from the yeshiva. In truth, partly due to the language barrier, partly to our intentionally crammed yeshiva schedule, and partly to religious restrictions, I never watched a tango show at a café, or listened to an opera performance at the majestic Teatro Colón, or visited the brightly painted buildings in the La Boca neighborhood.

My main use for Spanish was to speak to the non-Jewish female food servers at the yeshiva's cafeteria. I learned to ask for *carne* (meat) and *pollo* (chicken) and to avoid the two foods I was allergic to: *pescado* (fish) and *huevos* (eggs). I also learned the word for eyeglasses, *anteojos*, which stuck because it sounded like Antiochus, the villainous Greek king in the Chanukah story. I had to learn a few words to communicate with the laundry lady across the street who washed my clothes. I learned to say *hoy* for "today," *mañana* for "tomorrow," *cuánto cuesta* for "how much?" and *gracias* for thanks.

The only other Spanish phrase I picked up was from the head Lubavitch rabbi, whom my Argentine classmates nicknamed *papa grande* (the pope). He would speak at communal *farbrengens* in Spanish. After several of these events I learned the phrase that he used to begin all of his remarks: "Esto es muy importante para todos los judíos" (This is very important for all Jews). After that, ironically, I had no idea what he was saying.

After several months in Argentina, I realized that some Spanish words were identical to English with an *o* added to the end of the word. Once I needed a postcard. I went to a supermarket and asked for "el post cardo." As the cashier looked at me, perplexed, I tried to make conversation about the cold weather outside. "Mucho coolo," I said, and rubbed my hands together. The woman turned red in the face and screamed something in Spanish. I ran out. Afterward I learned from an Argentine friend that *coolo* (which in Spanish is spelled *culo*) means rear end, and my phrase meant something like "fat rear end."

We Americans had difficulty adjusting to Argentine food, especially the breakfasts. The yeshiva served boiled eggs, bread with *dulce de leche* spread, and sliced tomatoes. No cereal, no oatmeal, no fruit. Lunch and dinner were not much better. In the land famous for delicious beef, hardly any meat was served. The elderly Jewish couple who served dinner gave each student one squirt of ketchup, no more. One night I made the mistake of requesting an additional squirt. The laconic Yiddish-speaking husband with a pencil mustache warned me, "Es iz sam" (It's poison).

With limited food options from the yeshiva, the American students looked for alternatives. There was a kosher McDonald's a few blocks away, which, to the chagrin of some customers, didn't serve cheeseburgers. To my surprise, the food there was not very tasty and wreaked havoc on my digestive system. A cheap and convenient option was to buy large sticks of halva from a grocery store around the corner. The halva only cost a dollar and was delicious. Once we tired of halva, the American entrepreneurial spirit came alive in the hearts of two of my classmates. One cooked onion rings in his dorm room on a George Foreman sandwich maker full of sizzling oil and the other cooked French fries on a single burner in the sub-basement of the yeshiva. They each charged $2 a serving. Between the halva and the fried foods, I gained fifteen or twenty pounds.

The culinary highlight of our time in Argentina occurred when one of the guys in our group befriended a Jewish American expatriate and bank owner. He invited us all to his penthouse for an *asado* (barbeque). We were served beef slowly grilled over an open fire. We also delighted in heart sweetbread from a calf.

My fellow Americans at the yeshiva were repeatedly called by Argentine students *el estúpido yanqui*. The Argentine students pronounced the *y* of *yanqui* as if it were a *j*, which was confusing. More confusing still was why they were calling us stupid.

After a month of this treatment, I confronted the only Argentine student who spoke decent English, a soft-spoken soul named Mayer. "Why do you all call us stupid yankees?"

"Because all yankees are millionaires," Mayer said, without a moment's reflection.

"What? That's ridiculous. My father is a doctor, but we're far from millionaires, and most of the other guys from America come from families with even less money than mine."

"You don't get it. Compared with families in Argentina, all you guys are rich. My cousin is a doctor and he makes $35,000—and that's considered a lot of money here."

"Wow, I see." I decided that was not a good time to tell him that the white Big Oxford Gap shirt I was wearing, ten of which hung in my dorm closet, each cost $35.

"And another thing. People in Argentina are angry at America for supporting our right-wing governments."

"What are you talking about?"

"America supported the right-wing military junta that ruled Argentina from 1976 to 1983. They were terrible. They 'disappeared,' like, thirty thousand people, including many Jews."

I was bewildered. "What do you mean, 'disappeared'?"

"The government accused them of being left-wing guerrillas. So they kidnapped them, tortured them, and flew them in airplanes over the Atlantic Ocean and dropped them in the water. Then they claimed not to know anything about what happened to them."

I was shocked. "And the American government still supported them?"

"Absolutely. The United States gave the junta millions of dollars and helped them build their military."

I stared at Mayer wide-eyed. I was raised to believe that America was a bastion of democracy; the Rebbe would often refer to it as *medina shel chesed* (a country of kindness). How could the government of this country support a regime that perpetrated such brutal murders? What's more, growing up in the United States, I had never once heard mention of these atrocities, let alone the fact that America was supporting them. The more I encountered the world outside my own, the larger it grew.

Mayer saw my response and tried to comfort me. "Don't worry, Zalman," he said with a chuckle. "Most people in Latin America hate Argentines."

"Why?"

"They say we are *soberbio*," Mayer said, and pushed his nose up with a finger.

"What does that mean?"

"That we think we are better than them."

"Is it true?"

"Maybe a little. We are one of the richest countries in South America."

Even though I was more than five thousand miles from my family, I didn't feel homesick because since age twelve I had lived away from home. Still, I was eager to communicate with my family. Many of the American students used email at an internet café a few blocks from the yeshiva to stay in touch with their families back home. I didn't have an email account because I still could hardly write in English. One day, a friend made me a Yahoo account and showed me how to send an email. I started emailing my family letters full of spelling errors that sometimes taxed the decryption talents of the receiver. Even though at that point I had read many books in English, reading and writing are two different skill sets that can develop separately.

A good example of my writing abilities at that time is the following email I sent to my Uncle Jeff and his wife, Kathryn, on December 2,

2000, just as the contentious George Bush-versus-Al Gore presidential election was being decided:

> dear jeff and Katherin,
>
> It's bean a while since I heard from you. I whant to late you know that I resev the pakag that you seant me and have wread some of it, but still don't understand how ther could be a scenario wher somwon can lose the total popular vote but still win electoral college, I think it has to do with the big stats smwol stats.
>
> I joust wread over shabbos I. B. Singer's Enemies and Love Story, it was great, he writes so brilliantly, it was trouly spellbinding, one of the greatist books I aver wread! (although it was wroend a bit becuos I knew the ending befor I started wreading it).
>
> With love,
> Zalman
> p.s. please writh backe soon.

Along with expanding my English writing skills, I spent a lot of my free time watching movies that year, when I wasn't busy reading or emailing. Growing up, my family had a videocassette recorder (VCR), but my mother was strict about the movies we could watch. We were forbidden to watch movies that contained immodesty (including even just kissing) or violence. If a movie unexpectedly had a kissing scene, my father would fast forward it or, if the remote control was out of reach, jump up and stand in front of the screen, blocking our view. My family ended up watching old Disney films and episodes of *I Love Lucy* and *The Little Rascals.*

The Rebbe was vehemently opposed to his followers' owning television sets, warning that it was likely to bring Christian messages into a Lubavitch home. In 1982, the year I was born, as if a personal rebuke to me, the Rebbe proclaimed that owning a television was like "bringing inside the home the church, the priest, and the cross, Heaven forbid." Nonetheless, many Lubavitch yeshivas had VCR monitors to play video recordings of the public gatherings of the Rebbe, which had become a common educational pastime after his passing in 1994. The videos were a means of keeping the charisma of the Rebbe alive in his absence. But some of us American students in Argentina used the monitor for other purposes. Mostly out of boredom we rented "goyishe"

Hollywood films from a Blockbuster store near the yeshiva and viewed them on the monitor.

Watching these videos was a serious offense against the rules of the yeshiva, and watching them on the "Rebbe monitor" was an act of sacrilege. We turned down the volume almost to the point where it was inaudible and placed rolled-up towels under the door to block out the monitor's glare. We watched action movies and comedies but also the erotically charged 1996 masterpiece *The English Patient*, starring Ralph Fiennes, Kristin Scott Thomas, and Juliette Binoche. I felt uncomfortable watching the sex scenes sitting next to three Lubavitch friends. Oddly, watching those scenes with my coconspirators felt similar to going to the mikvah surrounded by other naked men. In both cases, my solution was to go about my business as if the others weren't present.

Where the Rebbe videos always had the same leading man, the Rebbe, and only one plotline—exhortations to be more pious—the Hollywood films depicted scores of main characters and pursued endless plots and subplots. Despite several close calls, our illicit film club was never busted.

My love affair with books and bookstores continued in Argentina. That year we were supposed to be studying the tractate Kesubos of the Talmud, which focuses on marital contracts, but I hardly cracked the volume open. I was too busy sneaking off to my dorm room two flights up from the study hall and reading my own books. I spent so much time hiding out, reading, in my dorm bathroom that I eventually developed the practice of bringing the desk chair in with me for added comfort.

When Pedro de Mendoza, the Spanish conquistador, founded Buenos Aires in the 1500s, he brought with him seven black leather-bound volumes (we don't know their titles), along with a collection of Petrarch's poems, a book by Erasmus, a book by Virgil, and a volume by C. de Bridia (*Tartar Relation*). I surpassed him tenfold with my literary baggage. That year, I read several novels by Isaac Bashevis Singer and E. L. Doctorow, four books on Zionism and the creation of the modern state of Israel, eleven books on the Holocaust and the Nuremberg trials, and Stephen Birmingham's trilogy on the history of Jewish immigration to America.

I also read several books by Arthur Conan Doyle and was both delighted and bothered by the character of Sherlock Holmes. The private detective living at 221B Baker Street was super-rational and able to deduce all sorts of facts from minor clues that others would never even have noticed, such as the worn-out knees on the pants of a suspect or the clay gathered on the boots of another suspect. But he was a cold fish who treated his one friend, the long-suffering Dr. Watson, poorly. He reminded me of certain rabbis in yeshiva who were adept at analyzing Talmudic texts but were unable to deal with people.

I read *Death Be Not Proud* by the journalist John Gunther, which tells the story of his son's brain tumor and death at seventeen. Gunther's son Johnny and my brother Shimmy both possessed great promise that was snuffed out by childhood illness. Reading about Johnny's two operations, daily X-ray treatments, and medication upset me greatly. I couldn't stop thinking about Shimmy and all he suffered trying to treat his leukemia.

The title of Gunther's book is based on a poem of the same name written by the seventeenth-century Anglican minister John Donne, which tries to humble death by highlighting its limitations. The poem concludes with the lines: "One short sleep past, we wake eternally / And death shall be no more; Death, thou shalt die." The last stanza echoes a verse in Isaiah (25:8) which prophesies that the Lord "will destroy death forever." At that time, I still believed in the messianic era with the end of death and the promise of resurrection of the dead. I took comfort in looking forward to being with Shimmy again. But I didn't focus on this as I used to.

One book I read that intrigued me was *Hitler's Willing Executioners*, by the political scientist Daniel Jonah Goldhagen. He argued that most ordinary Germans willingly went along with the Holocaust due to the unique "eliminationist antisemitism" that was embedded in the German culture in which they grew up. I wondered, *Was Goldhagen right? Were all Germans conditioned to hate Jews and want to kill them?* This view certainly fit with the Lubavitch worldview that saw all non-Jews as suspect, at best. However, this broad criticism of close to seventy million people seemed hard to accept. But it was ten years before I would read the historian Christopher Browning's meticulously researched book *Ordinary Men*, which explores the five hundred members of Reserve Police Battalion 101, who personally massacred Jews in Poland. Browning shows that these men were not necessarily uniquely anti-Semitic but, rather, acted out of peer pressure and obedience to authority.

To further complicate my attitude toward Germans who lived during the Holocaust, eleven years later I read Anne Nelson's *Red Or-*

chestra, which details the efforts of a substantial (if informal and poorly coordinated) network of German artists, railroad workers, administrators, military personnel, and aristocrats who resisted Hitler and Nazism before and during the war. Many members of this network were caught and ultimately killed by the Gestapo. Some members of this loose network were communists, while others were not.

Nelson explains that the full story of German anti-Hitler resistance was intentionally suppressed for years. The West largely ignored the story because of its distrust of the communists central to the story; the Soviets and East Germans promoted their own version of the story that glorified the communist members at the expense of the historical record.

Although I came to Buenos Aires with a large box of books, I couldn't resist visiting used bookstores near the yeshiva to hunt for treasures. Most of these bookstores' inventory was in Spanish, but they carried some strays in other languages. Among these orphaned books I noticed several in Yiddish. I regret that I snubbed them and didn't pay them any attention. In my ignorance, I associated Yiddish books with my yeshiva education without realizing that many Yiddish authors were rebels against their own yeshiva upbringing and its mindset. I regret unintentionally spurning the companionship of these like-minded authors.

Maybe it was fitting that it was in Jorge Luis Borges's old neighborhood that my labyrinthine schemes of hiding a secret library and my dream of acquiring forbidden knowledge finally came under threat. It was mid-December, and I was nursing a cold, having just finished reading *Hitler's Pope*, by John Cornwell. This was especially eerie fare, given that I was living in Argentina, where the Catholic Church helped countless Nazis escape justice and hide incognito. I had taken all my books out of their hiding places to select my next read when in burst Rabbi Grossbaum, tugging on his short pointy beard. His sharp black eyes darted around the small room as if summoning the bare walls to help explain the mysterious sight of one of his students surrounded by a heaping pile of forbidden books.

My heart pounded, and sweat dripped down my forehead like a marathon runner. I shot up from my chair and moved away slightly from the table, as if creating a bit of distance, even a few feet, between myself and the books would make me appear less guilty. The thought that he would start screaming terrified me. I have a fear of being screamed at and always imagined that if I got caught, the first thing the rabbi would do is hurl insults in Yiddish. I also feared that I would be kicked out of the yeshiva immediately. I remembered how, in the Miami yeshiva, a fellow student, Zeev Lebovic, almost got kicked out for the sin of possessing a single biology textbook. I had enough books to start a small bookstore. Was I going to be ignominiously shipped back to Brooklyn for my offense?

We had several rabbis in the Argentina yeshiva, but Rabbi Grossbaum boasted the largest personality. He had a brilliant mind and a quick sense of humor. At a *farbrengen* a few weeks earlier, he had repeated the Yiddish aphorism: "Too smart is a heretic, too pious is a priest, too generous is an adulterer."

Pacing in my narrow dorm room, Rabbi Grossbaum took a deep breath and asked, "Nu, vus iz dus? (What is this?) Are these non-Jewish books?"

Here, I had a slight advantage, since Rabbi Grossbaum was fluent in Hebrew, Yiddish, Aramaic, and Spanish, but hardly knew a word of English. "It depends what you mean by non-Jewish," I said, trying not to stutter. "Most of the books are written by Jews or about Jews, but they are certainly not religious books." Rabbi Grossbaum listened, nodded his head gravely, and left the room.

The next morning after prayers, Rabbi Grossbaum, in his customary socks and slippers, called me over and in a singsong rhythm honed by years of Talmud study began a parable:

> *Du vaist, Zalman, amal is geven a katshkele. . . .* You know, Zalman, there was once a baby duck whose owner loved him and gave him special food to eat to keep him strong. One day the duck became tired of eating the food prepared by the farmer and went to a neighbor's farm to forage. The duck swallowed a rusty nail and died. The farmer cried, "I gave you all the best things to eat. Why did you have to go to other people's fields to find food?"

He paused, but then continued: "Katshkele, katshkele, vohin gayst du?" (Little duck, little duck, where are you going?).

I looked at Rabbi Grossbaum and smiled faintly. Then I raised my right hand, palm out, in protest. I did not think I was striking a Faustian bargain, sacrificing my soul in pursuit of earthly knowledge. "But I'm not trying to change the way I think or to become less religious. I'm only trying to learn about what's out there."

Rabbi Grossbaum was unmoved. "You think you're safe reading these books, but you're playing with fire."

I was grateful that he didn't throw me out of the yeshiva or take any punitive steps against me. He treated me like an adult. It was my choice whether or not to read such books; he only wanted to warn me of the risks involved. I figured he was exaggerating the risks to my soul and continued blithely consuming books at a feverish pace.

When the academic year came to a close that June, I packed my suitcases in the cold, dark days of the Argentine winter and flew back home looking forward to the bright and sunny American summer. The seeds of my future rebellion were already planted in the soil of my consciousness.

I had spent a year in a Lubavitch "bunker." Although we watched Rebbe videos every Thursday night and spoke at *farbrengens* about remaining connected to the Rebbe, the Rebbe had passed away six long years earlier, against all prior teachings, and the bonds that tied me to him were slowly loosening. And then there was Shimmy. The more I thought about his early death, the more I felt the urgency of making the most of however much time I had on this Earth. I had managed to enjoy illicit movies and books. My attitudes and values were imperceptibly changing. It was like the metamorphosis of a caterpillar into a butterfly. At one stage it is clearly a caterpillar; at another it is a butterfly. But when exactly did it shift from one organism to the other? There were tiny steps in the process that might go unnoticed and are identifiable only once the transformation is complete.

9

Posting to China

"*Ich ret in yiddish* [I'm speaking in Yiddish] because you never know who's listening," Eli Rubin, the Lubavitch rabbi in Beijing, said to Alter and me as his eyes darted around the green-and-orange taxi we had just squeezed into that was taking us from the airport to his home. Rabbi Rubin, a portly forty-year-old with an enormous brown beard, continued: "And never say anything on the phone against the Chinese government." Alter and I gave each other a look. Was he for real? Rabbi Rubin sensed our incredulity. "I'm serious."

"*Beseder* [fine]. We'll be careful," I said.

"Good. So here's the situation," he continued in English with a hint of a British accent. "My family already left for our trip to England, and I'll be leaving on Sunday to join them. Which of you cooks?" Alter and I were dumbfounded. We were two twenty-year-old yeshiva students. Not only would we be left alone in China, but we were expected to cook? We were both silent, hoping this was just some kind of twisted joke.

Alter and I were in Beijing in June 2002 because three months before we had used a plastic fork to jimmy the lock on the office door of the yeshiva in Morristown, New Jersey, where we were studying for the year. We had slipped into the office and commandeered the phone to call all the Lubavitch rabbis in Asia and Africa. We were searching for a rabbi who wanted two yeshiva students to assist him for the summer.

We weren't picky about where we ended up, as long as it was exotic. My allegiance to Lubavitch held strong, but so did my curiosity to discover more of the world. Five times no one picked up, so we left messages. Another half-dozen times, the rabbis said they had all the help they needed.

When we reached Rabbi Rubin in Beijing and gave him our pitch, we high-fived as he replied, "I could use help over the summer, and I'll pay all the expenses for when you're here. Can you raise money to pay for your flights?"

"How much are they?" Alter asked.

"Two tickets are about $1,500."

Alter, without a moment's hesitation responded, "No problem. We'll buy the tickets."

I was worried about Alter's assurance that we could come up with such a large sum, but I wasn't surprised by his chutzpah. Alter and I were like brothers. We had been close friends for four years and had traveled to Russia together. Our personalities complemented each other. Alter was daring, a real *chevraman*. I was cautious. He would push me to take risks, and I would help ground him.

We immediately began raising money from people we visited on our Friday outreach route in New Jersey, as well as from a few Lubavitch families living in the Morristown community. We collected about $1,300, and I topped it off from my savings.

We had never discussed the details of the "help" Rabbi Rubin needed over the summer and assumed we would be his sidekicks assisting in the programs *he* was running. As we zoomed along the smog-filled highway toward Beijing, Rabbi Rubin sensed our confusion. "You thought I brought you here for vacation? I'm leaving the country for seven weeks to fundraise. I need *you* to keep things going."

As our taxi zigzagged around thousands of bicyclists, many wearing white medical masks over their faces for protection against the enveloping smog, Rabbi Rubin returned to the issue of cooking. "We have twenty to thirty guests for Friday night dinner and the same for Shabbos lunch. They're going to be pretty disappointed if there's nothing to eat."

"Rabbi, we never cooked a meal in our lives," I confessed.

"What, you think *I* did? Don't worry. My wife wrote out foolproof instructions. Even a klutz could do it. I also need someone to lead services Friday night and Shabbos morning."

I got nervous any time I had to lead services, worried I might trip over the Hebrew words. I jumped in and said, "Alter will lead the services."

Alter, sensing an opening, said, "And Zalman will do the cooking."

After driving for about forty-five minutes, the taxi pulled up to the Grand Hills gated community in the Jing Shun Lu neighborhood of the Chaoyang district of Beijing, where many foreign businesses and most foreign embassies are located.

Grand Hills was graced with neat rows of houses and manicured lawns; it looked like we could have been in suburban New Jersey. The taxi stopped at a large, two-story pastel orange house. "This is my house, and for now it's also the Lubavitch center," Rabbi Rubin said. Looking at the row of houses, he continued, "Most of my neighbors are foreign ambassadors, like from the United Arab Emirates and from Bulgaria." He laughed, shaking his massive frame. "You guys are in good company."

We arrived in Beijing on a Thursday. That night, while Alter sat on one of the comfy brown couches in the living room looking over the portion of the Torah he would chant for our congregation on Saturday morning, I joined Rabbi Rubin in the modest kitchen in the back of the house to prepare the food for Shabbos. I felt like a character in a Jules Verne novel forced to develop new skills in response to dire circumstances. If I didn't cook, there would be no Shabbos. If only my mother had shared with me some of her cooking secrets!

Sure enough, Rabbi Rubin had three white pieces of paper with typed-out instructions for cooking Shabbos meals. He followed them the way an engineer follows a blueprint. We baked eight challahs and four noodle kugels; cooked three chickens, a huge pot of chicken soup, and cholent, a traditional Ashkenazi Jewish meat stew; and chopped several salads. "You see Zalman, if you follow what the boss wrote, you'll be fine." I had my doubts, but I kept quiet.

Rabbi Rubin and his wife, together with their two daughters, had been living in Beijing for several years. Rabbi Rubin's flock consisted mostly of secular Jewish expats and visiting businessmen, academics, and tourists from America and Israel. It did not include any native Chinese Jews.

Rabbi Rubin invited four Israeli backpackers, two men and two women, to sleep on the basement floor for Shabbos, while we slept in the bedrooms on the second floor. Our first Shabbos in Beijing was delightful. Rabbi Rubin, blessed with a booming baritone voice, regaled us with Hasidic *nigunim* (wordless melodies) for hours on Friday night. He possessed a forceful personality, delivered captivating sermons, and masterfully entertained his guests. Like a talented artist at work, he excelled at running every aspect of his operation.

Before Rabbi Rubin left for his flight Sunday morning, we sat down to discuss plans for the following weeks. "I have some frozen chop meat. Go to town. Finish it. I have thirty-two chickens in the basement freezer. Try to save the chickens for Shabbos, if you can. I get the chickens shipped from the Lubavitch rabbi in Shanghai. He slaughters them himself. I can get more sent if you need. You brought twelve containers of cream cheese from New York, and I have a ton of bagels in the freezer."

"Where did you get the bagels from?" I asked.

"A Chinese woman makes them in her bakery a few blocks away. I oversee their production and give them a kosher certification. Anyway, there's also a ton of stuff in the cabinets. You should have enough to eat till I get back."

Rabbi Rubin got up and put a book in his carry-on case and said, "The main thing I need you to do is prepare the Shabbos meals and run the Shabbos services. During the week, people will call up and make reservations for Shabbos. If they want to come over during the week to talk or learn, that's good, too."

Rabbi Rubin handed me a wad of American bills. "Use this to buy whatever fruits and vegetables and other stuff you need. You'll get more money from donations from guests. If people ask if there's a fee for the meals, tell them, 'The meals are free, but all donations are accepted.' Guests often end up giving some donation." Then he looked at me and said, "Zalman, don't burn down my house."

And with that pep talk, Rabbi Rubin walked out the front door. Our training was over. This was not a drill. That night I paced around the large quiet house. I felt like a "stranger in a strange land," as Moses called himself in Midian. What on Earth were we doing in China?

China has a long history of opposing the imposition of outside religions and ideas, especially the proselytizing efforts of Christian missionaries. This was one of the motivations behind the violent struggle of the Boxer Rebellion, which erupted at the turn of the twentieth century and sought to cleanse China of foreign domination by America, Austro-Hungary, Britain, France, Germany, Italy, Japan, and Russia. Alter and I were hardly an invading horde of conspirators spreading foreign ideas and sedition, but it felt strange to know that I was in a country doing something that the authorities in the country opposed.

Alter and I walked around our gated community. For a city notorious for over-congestion, it felt odd not to meet a single person on our stroll. We found an empty park with a swing set. We sat on the swings, rocking slowly in the cool dark night. We both knew that we were in Beijing on a mission from the Rebbe to bring Jews to Judaism, but also to satisfy our budding wanderlust. Alter said, "We're like elite soldiers who train for years to go on a mission." My lips parted in a half-smile. Alter fixed me with a stare and continued: "This is our mission now, to do the Rebbe's work in Beijing. We're ready. Zalman, we're gonna kick ass." Alter's strident tone didn't upset me. I was used to it. He was always the more ideologically driven one.

Over the coming weeks, Alter and I explored Beijing. China was still nominally communist—the image of the communist leader Mao Zedong graced the country's paper currency, the yuan, and there were many public displays of his picture, including a massive one at Tiananmen Square. Yet under the leadership of Deng Xiaoping, China had introduced aspects of a market economy in 1979. In the decades since then, it has become deeply integrated into the global capitalist economy. We noted scores of shiny new buildings being built and tons of Starbucks cafés dotting the capital.

We befriended a talkative Chinese cashier at a nearby supermarket who insisted in broken English that we call him Tony. "Is that what your mother calls you?" I asked, knowing the answer but wondering how he would respond. He burst out laughing. "No, no. My name Zhang Qiang but too difficult for Westerners. Now my name Tony."

One muggy afternoon, I took a bus to go shopping at an open-air market. Nothing about the New York City subway prepared me for the congested and overcrowded conditions of Beijing public transportation. The bus even had a metal cage surrounding the driver to protect him from the press of passengers. It felt odd to have so many strangers squeezed up against my body. Glancing out the window, I saw scores of workmen squatting on the side of the road eating lunch with their shirts rolled up above their bellies to cool off.

At the market, amid the cries of hawkers selling everything from live chickens to English translations of Mao Zedong's *Little Red Book* and pirated DVDs of new American films still not out in the United States, a small crowd of wide-eyed bystanders gathered around me and were pointing at my substantial beard and laughing. It took me a few minutes to decipher their pantomime. I was informed that interest in my beard owed to the generalization that most Chinese men cannot or do not grow much facial hair, and the onlookers were astonished by my bushy growth.

Alter and I made a point to visit the Great Wall of China. We hiked up the wall for hours. Like a three-dimensional version of M. C. Escher's optical illusion drawings, every time we thought we had reached the summit we would discover that the wall continued on into the distance.

We climbed until we reached a large metal sign painted white. The top line had Chinese characters in red. Below this Chinese was an English translation in blue that read: "Dangerous Ahead No Walking." The path seemed safe enough to us so we kept trekking along. After another ten minutes the neat path ended and was replaced by loose rocks. We climbed up the rocks and suddenly realized we were hundreds of feet above the ground without any protective railing or barrier. If we made a wrong move, we would fall to certain death. Beads of sweat dripped down my face, even though it was already getting dark and the night was chilly.

I don't know if it was Alter's belief in the reliability of his own muscles and sinews or his belief in God, but he seemed perfectly calm and wanted to keep on going. My faith in both those forces was less secure. I was petrified. I convinced Alter that we needed to turn back. Slowly, ever so slowly, we lowered ourselves down the craggy rocks and walked on until we got back to the well-preserved path.

Despite these adventures, most of our time in Beijing was spent in the house waiting for the phone to ring and answering questions about Saturday services and meals. Rabbi Rubin had a large black Jacuzzi in the upstairs bathroom. I soaked in it for hours reading Solzhenitsyn's *Lenin in Zürich.*

A key concern of mine was my ability to cook for all the people who showed up and whether the food would have any taste. Rabbi Rubin employed a young Chinese woman named Fang to keep house, buy groceries, and assist in the kitchen. Fang, a mother of two with long black hair, stayed on in Rabbi Rubin's absence, but she didn't speak a word of English, and she didn't actually do any of the cooking. That was my domain.

When the first Thursday arrived, I was eager to start the cooking early. I followed all the recipes to the letter. The egg-glazed challahs came out soft and golden, and the roast chickens looked and smelled delicious. I was starting to rebuke myself for ever having doubted the magical power of the "boss's" recipes. Then I inspected the chicken soup. Disaster. The pot of soup was tasteless and looked like a swamp with floating debris consisting of chopped carrots, onions, and celery, with a scrawny boiled chicken bopping around.

I had spent enough time in my mother's kitchen watching her in action to know she used Domino's dark brown sugar, Wesson vegetable oil, Gold's sweet-and-sour duck sauce, and Droste's Dutch processed cocoa powder—the kind that comes in a bright red box. But I had no clue what exactly she did with them to produce edible food. I had never asked to be let in on the mystery, and she had never offered. Turns out, cooking is like swimming: You can't learn to do it just by watching a pro. You have to jump in and get involved.

It was 6 P.M. in Beijing, and I was in a panic. I dialed my home number. It rang a few times, and then I heard the handset get knocked off the base and someone's hand poking around trying to find it. "Hello?"

"Mommy."

"Zalman, is that you?" I heard a sleepy voice say.

"Yes."

"You OK?"

"Yes. I've got a cooking question."

"Now? It's six in the morning by me."

"Sorry, I forgot."

"Why are you cooking? Why isn't the rabbi's wife cooking?"

"It's a long story. The rabbi and his wife left the country to fundraise. Alter and I are taking care of the show, and I'm cooking."

"How are you supposed to eat? This is so irresponsible of the rabbi."

"Mommy, we'll be fine. I just need help making a pot . . ."

"It's just . . . it's not right."

"Don't worry. I made a big pot of chicken soup but it's colorless and tasteless."

I could hear her yawn. Then she said, "How many chickens did you put in?"

"One."

"You need at least three."

"We don't have a lot of chickens here and it's hard to get more."

"Then you should put in bouillon cubes. They give soup more taste and color. You know the kind I'm talking about?"

"Yes. The little yellowish cubes—but we don't have any."

"Well, you should put in at least two chickens and parsley. Did you put in parsley?"

"No."

"So, put in a lot of parsley, like two big handfuls. That'll help. And a lot of salt and pepper."

I did everything she suggested, and eventually the soup became edible but not particularly tasty. The closest any guests came to complimenting my soup was when an American tourist called it a step up from the tasteless broth he was subjected to in his youth at a Jewish summer camp in the Berkshires.

Despite the soup, twenty to thirty guests joined us in our living room each week for Friday night and Saturday morning services, just as Rabbi Rubin predicted, and they stayed on for a meal. The men shook our hands; the women smiled and nodded and thanked us over and over again. We routinely heard, "It's amazing that you run these services in Beijing." Those who attended our makeshift synagogue inside Rabbi Rubin's house—white Jewish Westerners—found it remarkable to encounter such a community within the very different culture of the Chinese capital in which our synagogue was nestled.

In addition to the Sabbath meals and services, we held services that summer for the fast day of Tisha B'Av, commemorating the destruction of the Holy Temple in Jerusalem two thousand years ago. On Tisha B'Av, religious Jews sit on the floor, chant the biblical *Book of Lamentations* and other poetic elegies, and reflect on the history of Jewish suffering.

I delivered my sermon to the half-dozen visitors who gathered in Rabbi Rubin's dimmed living room that night. I spoke softly and slowly, trying to keep my face and hands as still as I could, working hard to avoid my usual gesticulations. I spoke about the Temple and the tragedy of its destruction and other afflictions we Jews have suffered.

Unfortunately, most of the congregation was made up of young businessmen from Georgia—the country, not the state—who spoke only Georgian. One of the men in their group spoke Hebrew, but since my spoken Hebrew wasn't great, and since I was the designated preacher, we used a three-way translation relay. I spoke in English; Alter translated into Hebrew; and the visitor translated into Georgian. It was like a water bucket brigade, where some of the contents are lost each time it passes down the line. Tisha B'Av services don't usually include quite so much muffled laughter.

Through our services and informal gatherings I met people who taught me things I had never been exposed to before. I learned about AIDS research from a Los Angeles infectious disease pioneer who started studying the disease when newspapers still called it GRID. I met an American political scientist who had studied at Princeton and told me that the mathematical genius John Nash, the subject of the biopic *A Beautiful Mind*, starring Russell Crowe, would wander around campus muttering anti-Semitic nonsense. I met a slim fiftyish brunette tourist from Ohio who informed me as we chatted after dinner Friday night that I had "very gentle eyes." She also told me about her search for the remains of the ancient Jewish community in Kaifeng, in the Henan province of China. She had not found many physical remnants of the community, which had been destroyed hundreds of years earlier, possibly by a flood, but she was optimistic and planned to continue her exploration.

The most memorable friendship I made that summer was with an American Jewish college student named Andy Birnbaum, who was part of a study abroad program in China. When I first met him, I had known very little about modern China. The only book I had read on China before arriving was the historian Barbara Tuchman's *Stilwell and the American Experience in China*, which focuses on the feeble American efforts during World War II to support Chinese resistance against the Japanese occupation. That book was about as helpful for understanding modern China as reading the same author's *A Proud Tower*—about Europe on the eve of World War I—would be for understanding contemporary French or German society.

Andy, a bespectacled Maryland native with thinning hair who salsa-danced across our dining room floor, was majoring in Chinese studies at Brown University. He informed me that Mao Zedong, the Chinese communist leader, had spearheaded the economic and social campaigns of the Great Leap Forward and the Cultural Revolution, both of which were news to me. Andy offered to take me sightseeing. I was eager to visit as many temples and cultural sites as possible. I readily accepted Andy's offer. I was determined not to make the same mistake I had made in Russia of missing the opportunity to visit cultural landmarks just because of the strictures of Jewish law.

On a sunny afternoon we visited the Forbidden City, weaving our way past swarms of tourists following guides who held up bright green and blue flags to identify themselves. Andy told me, "The Forbidden

City served as the center of the imperial court for five hundred years. It contains more than nine hundred buildings and covers 170 acres." As we walked around the grounds, I marveled at the maze of palaces, halls, and ornately decorated temples, with their yellow-glazed tile roofs and countless images of coiled dragons.

We also visited the colorfully decorated Temple of Heaven. Visitors lit incense sticks outside the temple and stuck them in large metal receptacles. I entered the temple and saw a massive wooden statue of Buddha. Despite the biblical verses from Leviticus that swirled in my mind, railing against graven images and idolatry, the Buddha didn't seem sinful or evil to me. It seemed peaceful.

Andy informed me, "Each year, the Chinese emperor would visit this temple and perform a secret ceremony to ensure a good harvest." I wondered whether the Chinese emperor's annual temple visits were very different from the high priest's Yom Kippur ritual in the ancient temple in Jerusalem, performed to ensure a healthy and prosperous year for the Jews. The handbreadth separating me and those around me grew smaller still.

A few days later, Andy returned to our place to chat. Andy spoke Chinese fluently, at least in my estimation, based on the ease with which he communicated with Fang. He tried to teach me a few words. "You have to make sure to pronounce the words exactly how I do," Andy instructed.

"Or what?" I asked.

"Or else no one will know what the heck you're talking about. Mandarin Chinese has four basic tones, and the same word could mean four different things depending on the tone you use."

"Wow. That sounds extremely hard."

"It is, but you're just going to learn a few words. An easy word to learn is *Shuǐ*, which means 'water.'"

I practiced saying the word a few times, trying to mimic exactly how Andy did it.

"Not bad. You should also learn the phrase *Nǐ hǎo ma*, which means 'How are you?'"

I tried to repeat it but seemed not to get it exactly right.

"Don't worry, Zalman. Keep practicing. You might want to know the word *Yóutài*, which means 'Jewish.'"

A week later, I took a taxi with Andy. We were sitting in the back seat, and Andy struck up a conversation with the driver in Chinese. At one point, the driver turned around and looked at me and said something. "What's he saying?" I asked.

"He wants to know what religion you are."

I responded immediately, "Yóutài," trying to remember which tone I was supposed to use. I apparently got it wrong, because Andy and the driver both laughed. Then the driver said, "Karl Marx," and tapped his index finger to his temple.

"The stereotype of Jews as smart is prevalent in China," Andy said. I was impressed that a random Chinese taxi driver knew of Marx's Jewish origins.

Although I learned a lot from Andy, what he taught was not nearly as shocking as what I learned from Smadar Ne'eman, an Israeli of Yemenite descent who visited our Chabad house with her Ashkenazi husband, Yonatan, for a Shabbos that summer. After the other Friday night guests had left, Yonatan, Smadar, Alter, and I sat down to talk. Smadar, a petite woman in her late twenties with dark skin and a thick Israeli accent, recounted her travels through Asia, including the time a man in a crowded Mumbai bus catcalled to her and she slapped him in the face. After about an hour, Alter excused himself and went to bed.

Eventually Smadar mentioned that she was a doctoral student studying the Hebrew Bible. I didn't quite understand. "What exactly do you study? You read all the *meforshim* [the medieval rabbinic commentaries] on the Bible?"

"Not exactly," she said and smiled. "I study Ugaritic and Akkadian texts to compare them with the Bible and understand the historical context the Bible was written in."

Yonatan got up and said, "This is my signal to go to sleep." As he left the room, he added, "Watch out. She could talk about this all night."

As Smadar started to explain to me what biblical criticism was, she suddenly blurted out, "Are you sure you want to know this? It could affect your *emunah* [your belief in God]."

"Don't worry about it," I said. "I want to know."

"Look, the Bible is full of internal contradictions and contradictions with science and what we know about the world."

"Really? I never knew that."

"Yes, of course, but you should also know that many of these contradictions were addressed by rabbis hundreds of years ago, especially by Ibn Ezra in twelfth-century Spain."

"I see."

"It just depends on whether you find the question or the answer more compelling. I find the questions more compelling, but you might find the answers more compelling," she said as she twirled several strands of her long black hair.

"I understand. I want to know the questions." I felt as if I was standing on the doorstep of a secret palace of knowledge and was anxious to gain admittance. I didn't think these questions would shake my faith, and if they did, how strong could my faith have been?

"OK, let's get down to business," she said. Then she walked over to a bookshelf and picked up a copy of the Bible. She flipped through the pages and stopped. "Look, Zalman, in Berashit [Genesis 14:14] it says how Abraham was told that Lot, his nephew, was kidnapped. So Abraham pursued the captors 'till Dan' to get him back. The only problem is that according to Shoftim [Judges 18:7–30], which supposedly took place, like, five hundred years later, the place was still called La'ish at the time of Abraham and only changed its name to Dan once the descendants of Dan conquered it with Joshua, centuries later."

"So what does this mean?" I asked.

"It means that although the traditional view is that Berashit comes before Shoftim, the truth is that Shoftim was written first."

"I see. What's another example?"

Smadar thought for a moment and said, "Here's a simple one. In Yehoshua [Joshua 8:29] it talks about Joshua burning down the city of Ai and turning it into ruins. Then it says that it remains a ruin 'unto this day.' Now, if the book of Yehoshua was written by Joshua, which is what the traditional view is, this verse doesn't make much sense. To say that a city was burned down and was still desolate a few years later, big deal. If the book was written hundreds of years later, then it would make sense for the author to point out that the city that Joshua burned down is still desolate. This is pretty clear proof that Joshua didn't write the book that has his name."

The conversation continued for hours this way, until the rays of the morning sun crept through the dining room windows. It was like the scene in the Haggadah where Rabbi Eliezer and his colleagues in B'nei Berak stayed up all night speaking about the exodus from Egypt. We also spoke about Exodus and other books of the Bible besides, but our conclusions were different from those of the ancient rabbis.

I wished Smadar "good night and good morning" and tiptoed to bed for a few hours of sleep before morning services began. Once I woke up, I couldn't stop thinking about everything Smadar told me. Could it be that there were basic logical problems with the Torah that proved that it was not written by God, as I had been taught since I was a child? For the first time in my life, I began to think seriously about the possibility that God didn't write the Bible.

Smadar's questions, perhaps more than her answers, contributed to my independent thinking, which set off a crisis of faith in years to come. But a week after Smadar left, two other Israeli backpackers set off a more immediate crisis. Alter and I met Efrat Bitton and Noa Segel on a Friday morning while we unsuccessfully searched for kosher products at a large "international" store in a shopping mall. (I found a kosher cheesecake from Australia in the freezer section, but Alter claimed it wasn't kosher enough. No dice.) The two women were at the end of their Asian travels and their money and were desperate to find cheap lodgings. We invited them to crash in our basement for free. They were thrilled.

We brought them back to our place and got them settled in the basement. Then we sat down to talk, and Noa, who had striking red hair, which is unusual in Asia, amused us with stories from her travels in Mongolia and the many marriage proposals she received, sweetened with the offer of dozens of sheep and goats. Efrat and Noa insisted on helping me with the cooking, and when Shabbos came around and the house filled with guests, they helped entertain the crowd. Everything went swimmingly.

Then, as I sat on the couch Sunday morning, the phone rang. Efrat, who just happened to be standing next to the phone, picked it up. "Hello," she said in her slight Israeli accent. There was a pause. Then she said, "My name is Efrat Bitton. I'm staying here with my friend Noa. Who are you?" I couldn't hear what the caller was saying, but she turned to me with a stricken look on her face. "He wants to talk to you," she said and handed me the phone.

I may have gotten the words, "Hello Rabbi," out of my mouth, but that's it.

"Are you completely *meshugah*?" Rabbi Rubin screamed into my ear. "You invited two girls to stay with you—in my house?" He reacted as if we had turned his domicile into an underground sex club.

"Nothing happened. They're staying in the basement, just like you had other Israeli backpackers stay in your basement the first Shabbos we were here."

"Have you completely lost your minds? You think it's the same if I'm there or you two *shnooks* are there by yourself?"

I tried to calm him down. "OK, I see what you're—"

"Never mind," Rabbi Rubin growled. "They need to leave right now."

"OK," I said. "I'll speak to them."

"Forget about it. I'll speak to them. Put Efrat back on the phone now."

My face was pale. I handed the phone back to Efrat.

Rabbi Rubin spoke to her for a minute. Efrat nodded her head several times and said, "I completely understand, Rabbi. No problem." She hung up the phone. The house was silent. Noa and Efrat packed their bags and were out the door in minutes.

I felt humiliated by Rabbi Rubin's overreaction. Any sense of independence that I nurtured from living in a beautiful house in Beijing by ourselves and running the show for two months vanished. We had no carnal plans with the Israeli backpackers. At most, we could be faulted for having an oversize sense of chivalry to help two young Jewish women find a safe place to sleep for a few nights—two women who had managed to fend for themselves in rural Mongolia.

A week later, as I worked to rebuild my confidence, I found myself at a loud bar near Rabbi Rubin's house talking to a German businessman in his fifties. Hans's English wasn't great, but we felt a kinship since we were both foreigners who didn't speak Chinese. When we were finished drinking, Hans and I left the bar and walked down the busy street when a Chinese man walked past us and whispered, "Lady bar, lady bar?" He was weaving in and out of the crowd whispering to all the men he passed. I assumed he meant he was asking us if we were interested in going to a strip club.

I had never been to such an establishment before, but in the movies it seemed like fun. Hans nodded, so I did the same. The man gestured for us to follow him. We walked together to the corner and then he gestured that we should get into his taxi. Hans and I exchanged glances and then climbed in. We drove for about ten minutes and stopped in front of a small house on a darkened street. It seemed odd to me that a strip club would be located in a residential area, but this was China, so all bets were off.

We entered the house and saw five nubile Chinese women in lingerie, all with shoulder-length black hair. They stood in a semicircle behind a plush jade-colored sofa. The women giggled. One of the women rested her hand alluringly on the back of the sofa and smiled invitingly at me. Her private parts were only flimsily covered by a pair of black silk undergarments. Her slim body was only inches away from mine. A light brush from my hand would uncover her nakedness. A jolt of excitement rushed through me.

My heart raced so fast I thought I was going to drop dead right there. I had seen pictures of topless women in *National Geographic* and fully naked women in my father's dermatology textbooks. Years earlier, Uriel Ben David had shown me pornography in Morristown. I found some photos on my own on the internet. But now I was standing in front of a group of women with whom, for $100, I could actually have sex.

All at once, the fear of contracting a sexually transmitted disease (about which I only vaguely understood), the fear of Chinese police in the mold of Jackie Chan crashing down the door and arresting me, and the fear of God above seeing and punishing me raced through my soul. I was in the inner sanctum, facing living and breathing available women in lingerie. I could hardly take in the details of how they looked. I was blinded by terror and the sensation that I needed to escape. I dashed out of the house. The taxi driver followed me. I told the driver to take me back to the bar. When we arrived, I paid him for the trip and walked out of the car in a daze, still shaking. I have no idea what happened to Hans.

Three days after my abortive visit to the brothel, the phone in our house rang. It was Rabbi Gershovitz, the head rabbi from our yeshiva in Morristown. He called to tell us the official news that Alter and I were being sent along with our two friends Zev and Naftuli to Singapore for a year of community service. This was in accordance with contemporary Lubavitch practice of studying for four years in a yeshiva and then spending the fifth year doing outreach.

Alter put the call on speakerphone. I could hear Rabbi Gershovitz's heavy breathing. Then he said, "You know that this is a tremendous *zchus* [merit] and a tremendous *achrayus* [responsibility]. I trust that you will make me and the Rebbe proud." With Rabbi Gershovitz still on the line, Alter scrounged up a bottle of vodka and two plastic cups. It was 10 A.M. in Beijing. Alter said, "*L'chaim, l'chaim*, we should be *zoyche* [merit] to do the Rebbe's work as he wants us to do it." Then we both downed the vodka and hung up the phone.

I was about to spend twelve more months in Asia as the Rebbe's foot soldier. Another opportunity to spread the Lubavitch message and explore the outside world.

10

Conflicted Soldier

After our flight to Singapore, the small English-speaking city-state nestled between Indonesia and Malaysia, landed, my three pals and I were greeted by Rabbi Chaim Srugo, the Lubavitch rabbi who served the country's established Jewish community. He smiled broadly and said, "*Shalom aleichem.* I'm so excited that you're here. Welcome. Welcome." The reinforcements for his outpost had arrived.

We all piled into Rabbi Srugo's blue Toyota Sienna minivan, and he drove us the half-hour to what would become our apartment. It was dark outside, so we couldn't see the pool in the back of our building, but once inside I was thrilled to find that we had two bedrooms with two bathrooms, a large dining room, an office, and a kitchen. It was no Buckingham Palace, but our digs were far more than four twenty-one-year-olds who had been accustomed to living in dilapidated yeshiva dorms had imagined or even hoped for.

The next morning, Rabbi Srugo picked us up and drove us the ten-minute trip through the winding streets of the city center to one of the two functioning synagogues on the island, the lavish Ma'gen Ahvot Synagogue at 24 Waterloo Street, built in 1878. The equally magnificent Chesed-El Synagogue was built in the Renaissance Revival style in 1905. Chesed-El boasts a white marble floor and fluted columns, is located slightly more than half a mile away from its sister synagogue at 2 Oxley Rise, and is used only occasionally by the community.

As we drove, Rabbi Srugo pointed out: "You see those fellows watering the trees and bushes along the streets? They are paid by the government to do it every day." The streets were extremely clean and orderly.

With time, I would discover that the entire city-state was well maintained by a government that oversaw every detail of daily life, like a fastidious retiree attending to his rose garden. Spitting on the street was forbidden, and violators could be shamed by having their photo printed in the newspaper.

The Ma'gen Ahvot Synagogue was built in the neoclassical style and influenced by the Late Renaissance architecture in Britain. The high-ceilinged, massive main sanctuary boasts a white marble floor and is flanked by tall Roman columns embellished with gold trim. The congregants sit in rows of black wooden and wicker benches. There is a second-floor balcony reserved for women. The sanctuary lacks air-conditioning, which is noteworthy given Singapore's location eighty-eight miles from the equator.

As I stood taking in the new sights, a tall dark man in his sixties walked up to me. His skin had the texture of sandpaper, and his personality was equally abrasive. He extended a firm hand. "I'm Ezra Harari."

"So nice to meet you. My name is Zalman Newfield."

"Your name is Suleiman. That's a good name."

"No, my name is *Zahl-man*." I added, "I'm Ashkenazi, not Sephardic." Both Zalman and Suleiman derive from the biblical name Solomon, but Zalman is Russian and common among Ashkenazi Jews, and especially so among Lubavitchers, while Suleiman is Arabic, the language of many Sephardic Jews.

"Here we are Sephardim, proud of our heritage." And then, as if not to leave any wiggle room or doubt, he added for good measure, "We are not Lubavitch!" and wagged his finger at me. Then, with a nod toward diplomacy, he continued, "But Ashkenazim are also Jewish, so your name is Zalman." He repeated my name but pronounced it in a way that still sounded suspiciously like Suleiman.

The cantor, a burly Sephardic man in his forties with a pockmarked face and a three-day beard, sauntered up to the podium. In a gruff voice, he began the morning prayers. I picked an empty bench in the front of the sanctuary and joined the prayers. Throughout the service, the cantor chanted the entire liturgy similarly to how a *qari* in a mosque recites whole passages of the Quran out loud. This was not the custom in the Ashkenazi synagogues I had attended up till now. My sense of bewilderment increased when the Torah scroll was taken out of the ark during the service and I noticed that it was housed upright in a cylindrical wooden case rather than being covered in a simple velvet mantle, as is the Ashkenazi custom.

To my surprise, after the service was over all the congregants sat down in the synagogue for breakfast prepared by the Indian cook on staff. The menu consisted of paratha (small, round Indian flatbreads), white rice with spicy red sauce, and sliced tropical fruit.

As I nibbled on the sweet white almond-shaped fruit of the mangosteen, Mr. Harari, the president of the Singapore Jewish community, took it upon himself to school my pals and me on the role Jews played in Singaporean history.

With a very stern expression, which I would come to learn was his default resting face, he began: "Jews were very important to Singapore's history. The first chief minister of Singapore in 1955, David Marshall, was Jewish. Before him, Manasseh Meyer, a wealthy businessman, gave a lot of money to the Jewish community. He also gave money for the university and for the British war effort in World War I. That's why King George V knighted him in 1929. Meyer Road nearby is named after him. And later there was Jacob Ballas." Several of the men around the table nodded their heads, but no one dared interrupt. "Jacob Ballas was an important businessman. He started the Stock Exchange here."

When Mr. Harari left the table, another old timer, the soft-spoken Mr. Isaac Kadoorie, continued the lesson. "The Jewish community came here from Iraq when the British opened a trading post in Singapore in the early 1800s. Singapore was very British for a long time and the Jews who lived here were also very British."

Mr. Kadoorie chuckled to himself and then almost in a whisper said, "You see that man on the other side of the synagogue?" He pointed to a thin man with white wispy hair who was stooped over and was placing his prayer shawl in its velvet bag. "He used to wear a top hat, walk with a cane, the whole thing." He laughed. "He used to be more British than the British." All the old men seated at the table chortled.

Clearly the Baghdadi Jews who settled in Singapore, unlike their brethren who settled in present-day Indonesia or Myanmar, were granted full civic inclusion and became completely integrated into their adoptive homeland. One thing the men around the table did not tell me was that the early Iraqi Jewish businessmen in Singapore, including the revered Manasseh Meyer, were heavily involved in the opium trade between India and China.

In time, the old man, with the help of a female aid, shuffled towards our table. Hearing talk of the British, his jaw stiffened, and he blurted out, "Churchill was a bloody liar."

"What do you mean?" I asked. "I thought Churchill was a good guy?"

"Rubbish," the old man sneered, and sliced the air with his hand. "He was a rascal. Churchill promised in 1942 he would never surrender Singapore to the Japanese and three weeks later he ordered the British to pull out." The man banged the table with his hand. "For the next three years the Japanese occupied Singapore. Very bad. Very bad." Everyone around the table was quiet. Later I learned that the speaker, along with many other Jewish men, women, and children who were considered British subjects, were placed in prisoner-of-war camps and suffered miserably until the end of the war.

After all of the congregants left the synagogue, leaving only Rabbi Srugo and his four new lieutenants, we sat down to talk. Rabbi Srugo wanted to add his own thoughts about the place of Jews in Singapore. In time, I was to discover that Rabbi Srugo had the personality of an absent-minded professor who managed to cram all the contents of his bulging Judaica library into his head. He loved nothing more than to speak for hours about the most obscure topics in Jewish thought. Rabbi Srugo, whose beard was neatly tucked under his chin and kept in place with several bobby pins, was of Sephardic descent with family roots in Morocco. His speech was an uncommon combination of Lubavitch lexicon with a Sephardic pronunciation of Hebrew words.

With his eyes only half-open, Rabbi Srugo gazed down at the wooden table we were seated at and launched into his spiel, carefully enunciating each word he spoke. "You need to understand that this country has three major ethnic groups, Chinese, Malay, and Indian, and four official languages, English, Mandarin, Malay, and Tamil, although most Singaporeans speak English. There are four main religions, Buddhism, Islam, Hinduism, and Christianity, and then there is our small Jewish community. All told, there are approximately five hundred Jews living in Singapore today, down from its peak of 1,500 before World

War II. In the past there have been instances of tension among some of these groups, so the government is extremely supportive of interfaith cooperation. I'm on a council, the Inter-Religious Organization, that represents all the religions."

"What kind of tensions?" I asked.

"Well, I'm not supposed to say this, but once someone spray-painted a swastika on the wall of the synagogue. I called the police. They came with a bucket of paint and painted over it and told us not to publicize the incident. They don't want to draw attention to any holes in the interfaith alliance."

"That's not exactly a brilliant scheme for dealing with the issues," I said.

"No, but in general everyone gets along here now. Having said that, we do have a Filipino security guard named Andrew, a real mensch, at the synagogue, and a special Gurkha police force to protect the Hebrew school."

"So you feel safe here?"

"Absolutely! Nothing to worry about."

The local Jewish community began to refer to the four of us endearingly as the "Chabad boys." Within a few days, we proceeded to divide up our responsibilities. Zev would cover programming for the adults; Alter would take care of the teens; and Naftuli and I would oversee the children and senior citizens. And all four of us would work together on community programs for Jewish holidays.

I was shocked to see that the large sanctuary was filling up Saturday morning. During the week, the synagogue struggled to attract the ten men necessary for a prayer quorum, but on Saturdays, about 150 men, women, and children attended. After the morning services, the synagogue provided a communal lunch, featuring a hot curry stew, called *chammim*, that included whole chickens and hard-boiled eggs.

A few weeks after we arrived we learned that Lubavitch was not the only Jewish institution with an eye on Singapore. The Jewish Agency for Israel was sending two Israeli women to volunteer for a year. Shortly after they arrived, someone made the mistake of calling them the "Chabad girls." They were mortified. "We are not Chabad, and we are not girls!" This was all true. They were decidedly non-Chabad, Modern Orthodox women in their twenties. These volunteers mainly taught at the Jewish day school (which we did not do) and arranged Israeli cultural activities, such as a celebration for Israel Independence Day. But their presence made us feel pressure to stay on top of our own game.

Each day, the four Chabad boys would attend all three services at the synagogue, ensuring a prayer quorum. Each week I tutored six children—four boys and two girls, ranging in age from five to eleven—in Hebrew reading at their homes. Along with Naftuli, I visited the local Jewish home for the aged every Friday and met with two men, the Solomon brothers, and a woman, Rachel Elias. We helped the Solomon brothers put on *tefillin* and say prayers, and we discussed the Torah portion with Rachel. Rachel was quite elderly, and her memory wasn't great, but she made an effort to tell us stories about the network of Jews who lived in Indonesia, where she grew up. Rachel's stories hinted at the complex history of Jews in Asia.

Zev, Naftuli, Alter, and I organized a Chanukah-on-ice event at an indoor snow slope, where we celebrated by sliding down the slope on round plastic tubes. For the Purim bash, a carnivalesque celebration that sometimes includes cross-dressing, we hit on the idea of getting decked out in traditional Chinese dresses. With our nonexistent Chinese and the saleslady's limited English, how could we possibly explain to her that we were straight guys trying to find women's dresses to celebrate a 1,500-year-old holiday about a Jewish woman who saved her people by marrying a foolish Persian king?

The saleslady and her friends all giggled at the sight of four bearded men trying to fit into extremely tight fitted dresses. We ended up going with a different costume idea, (men's) colonial American outfits with tricorn felt hats, which seemed fitting given their similarity to the three-cornered Purim cookies, the *hamentashen*.

At the large public Passover seder in the synagogue, there was a near-mutiny among our ranks when the waiters brought out heaping trays of rice and chicken. We were warned in advance that the community recites the Four Questions in Arabic rather than the Yiddish to which we were accustomed. But serving rice, which Ashkenazi custom considered a forbidden grain on Passover, was too much for Zev. He jumped to his feet, as if he had just spotted a ghost floating across the room. He started to order the waiters to remove the offending platters when he was informed that Sephardic tradition permits the eating of rice during Passover. Clearly struggling to control his emotions, he proclaimed, "All those who follow Sephardic customs may eat the rice. All those who follow Ashkenazi customs may not!"

The tension between the historically Sephardic community and the Ashkenazi Chabad boys had been festering since we arrived. When we introduced the Hasidic practice of dancing around the synagogue platform (*bima*) during Friday night services, as we had done for years in yeshiva, the president of the Jewish community was not amused. His posture and demeanor were a close approximation of a seated statue of the Egyptian pharaoh Ramesses. Likewise, several other community members joined the president in disapproval.

It never occurred to us to try to find out about the Sephardic traditions of the indigenous community. Our instincts told us, as our teachers had always maintained, that *our* traditions were the best. We knew this with the same certainty with which the British colonial officials assumed that British forms of dress, speech, and religion were superior to those of the natives.

We even carried out our own version of gunboat diplomacy. At one particularly prickly point in the tensions, it was arranged that our delegation's big gun, a very large cannon in the person of the renowned and rotund Rabbi Binyomin Marazov of Brooklyn, would visit the community. A formal dinner was organized in his honor at the elegant home of a community leader, during which the guest of honor, with his signature bulbous red nose, tried to convince those in attendance of how lucky they were to have us. "These boys are the elite," he proclaimed in deep measured tones. "They could have gone to Harvard, to Yale, to Columbia. Instead, they chose to spend a year of their lives helping to strengthen Judaism in your community."

I stood holding my heaping plate of chicken nuggets and spicy peanut sauce and tried not to burst out laughing. Not only was it highly doubtful that we could have been admitted to such schools without having any formal secular education, but it was absolutely forbidden for Lubavitchers to attend college. I was appalled by Rabbi Marazov's ridiculous lies and felt angry that he was taking advantage of the audience's ignorance of Lubavitch culture. His confidence in our superiority, rather than strengthening my own, shone a new harsh light on my own, similar assumptions.

Our year in Singapore, 2003, coincided with the lead-up to President George W. Bush's invasion of Iraq. We strained to watch the news on the small TV in our apartment, which received only one channel and suffered from a thin white line that ran across the screen. But when the BBC World Service came on, it was clear enough that the American government was preparing for war. One of the older men at synagogue joked that, if America invaded Baghdad, he would go to reclaim his family home in the city. "My family had a nice house. We had to leave it. Now Bush will get it back for us." All the synagogue regulars tittered.

Global affairs were not my only distraction. My time in Singapore corresponded to the year of the goat, the eighth in the twelve-year cycle of animals that appear in the Chinese zodiac. The goat year is thought to herald promise and prosperity. It certainly did for me.

Even with all our communal responsibilities, there was plenty of downtime for personal pursuits. I continued my feverish consumption of books. I ploughed through Jared Diamond's *Guns, Germs, and Steel*, Viktor Frankl's *Man's Search for Meaning*, B. F. Skinner's *Beyond Freedom and Dignity*, and Somerset Maugham's *Of Human Bondage*.

It was then that I first stumbled upon a collection of short stories by the Argentine writer Jorge Luis Borges. I loved them. Borges was the closest non-Jewish counterpart I found to Hasidic stories. He described supernatural phenomena in a way that made them feel natural and ordinary rather than weird and spooky, just as in the Hasidic tales I had heard growing up.

However, the supernatural elements in Borges's stories functioned in different ways, new ways that left my mind spinning and wanting more. Borges's fantasies allow his readers to engage hidden dimensions of the known universe and to imagine alternative versions of our reality. The purpose of Hasidic stories, at least in the Lubavitch context, is to inspire the listener to further cleave to the oneness of God and the ways of the Torah.

I also discovered Homer's *Odyssey* and was deeply moved by it. Odysseus's ingenious journey back from the Trojan War to his homeland of Ithaca—overcoming the wrath of the sea god Poseidon, outsmarting and escaping the murderous cyclops Polyphemus, protecting himself against the fatal allure of the songs of the Sirens, and many other travails—was breathtaking.

I admired him and identified with him up to a point. I didn't face any supernatural creatures to subdue, but in my own modest way, I, too, was on a journey facing obstacles I needed to overcome. One advantage Odysseus had over me was that he knew exactly what his goal was: to return to Ithaca, reclaim his title of king, and reunite with his devoted wife, Penelope, and his son, Telemachus. For my part, after my year in Singapore was up I would be returning to the United States, but what kind of life would I live?

The other Chabad boys saw the stacks of nonreligious books in my bedroom and knew I was devouring them. But they never said anything to me about my extracurricular reading. They saw it as a harmless hobby that would lead nowhere.

In addition to reading in my apartment, I also read during the hour-long morning prayer services at the synagogue. I made sure there to read only books related to Zionism, the Holocaust, Jewish history, and theology. One of my favorite synagogue readings were the books by Jonathan Sacks, the late Orthodox Chief Rabbi of Britain. I was impressed with the sophistication of his writing and the way he connected Jewish concepts with Western philosophy to argue against materialism and consumerism and in favor of a more community-minded ethos in society.

I thought this restrictive reading list kept me safe from reproach. One day, Ezra Harari, the community president, who sat on the opposite side of the synagogue but right in my line of sight, caught me reading a book during services. He marched over to me and, in his low drawl, proclaimed: "Mr. Newfield, this is not a library. We are here to pray." My face turned red. I couldn't say a word, and I closed the book.

I'd spent years in yeshiva and was almost a rabbi, I raged to myself. This putz could barely read Hebrew. How dare he dictate to me how I should behave in a synagogue? Why was I such a coward? Why didn't I stand up to him and tell him off? I fantasized. My rage at his undermining my supposed authority kept me from reckoning with why I felt more called to read than to pray and what the implications were for my adherence to my faith.

A few days later, I decided that there was no way in the world that I was going to let this bully, who had absolutely no authority over my religious life, stop me from reading during services. This was a key time for me to read. Rather than confront him, however, I decided to change my seat to the back of the synagogue, far away from Mr. Harari's scrutiny. I moved to the back and continued reading. A month later, during the Torah procession that circled the entire sanctuary, he peeled away from the crowd and snuck up behind me as I sat reading my book. Catching me completely off guard, he hissed in my ear: "Mr. Newfield, I can still see you!" I almost had a heart attack.

Rabbi Srugo was entrusted to "watch" us and make sure we didn't get into trouble, either with the city authorities or with God above. But he was overwhelmed with his other responsibilities. He oversaw the three daily prayer services; gave weekly Torah classes for adults; officiated at all circumcisions and funerals; arranged for kosher certifications of locally produced food; slaughtered chickens for the whole Jewish community; and had a wife and five children to look after. And when he wasn't doing those things, he enjoyed reading rabbinic literature in his own well-stocked home library. Rabbi Srugo and his fashionable wife, Gila, were both gracious hosts and often invited us to their tastefully decorated home for Friday night dinners. Still, for the most part we Chabad boys were on our own.

For the first time in my life, I had tons of free time and no one checking up on me. I went to the movie theater in Orchard Tower multiple nights a week and watched every new American release, including the Holocaust movie *The Pianist.* One of the most jarring scenes in that film occurs as a troop of Nazis rounds up Jews in the Warsaw Ghetto. During the mayhem, a pair of Nazi soldiers throw a wheelchair-bound elderly Jewish man out of a second story window to his death.

As I gasped at the horror on the screen, I was shocked to hear many of Singapore's moviegoers sitting around me laughing out loud. How could our emotional responses be so at odds? *Were all these people anti-Semites enjoying the portrayal of Jewish suffering?* It took me some time to realize that for people who are unfamiliar with the history of the Holocaust, it was very difficult to comprehend this horrific scene. It occurred to me that they probably laughed to cover the awkwardness of the moment, to grapple with the shock. This interpretation calmed my nerves enough to allow me to continue my jaunts to Orchard Tower.

In addition to books and movies, I also started to take in the foreign culture—in both senses of the word *foreign*—that surrounded me. I went to one of the main thoroughfares to observe the Hindu parade celebrating the festival of Deepavali. I had never seen anything like it. Thousands of celebrants walked past, many of them carrying elaborate, tall decorations containing metal spokes whose ends dug into the skin of their torsos and backs. Some celebrants had additional hooks an inch or two in length piercing their chests and backs; these had golf ball–size weights attached to them to increase the intensity of the experience. It looked excruciating, but those participating in the celebration didn't give any indication that they were experiencing any pain at all.

As I stood watching the parade, I was shocked to discover many celebrants carrying decorations that contained what seemed to my Brooklyn eyes like Nazi swastikas. The symbol consisted of a cross with arms that were bent at a ninety-degree angle. It's true the symbol also contained four dots tastefully located in the spaces created by the bent arms, but I thought these dots hardly removed the ugliness of the Nazi icon. Was it possible that all these Hindu celebrants were anti-Semites? Was this the kind of religious tension Rabbi Srugo told us about when we first came to Singapore?

After stewing quietly for a few minutes, I could take it no more. I stopped one of the celebrants and pointing at the symbol asked, "Is that a swastika?"

The young man smiled broadly, showing off his full set of teeth, and in heavily accented English replied, "Yes, yes. That is a *svastika*."

My face scrunched up, and I stared right at him. He could tell that something in his reply missed its target.

He tried again. "It's an old Hindu symbol of prosperity, yes," he said as his head bobbed from side to side. "It is found on the bottom of the foot of the elephant god Ganesh, the Lord of Good Fortune." I learned later that the Hindu symbol is spelled in English with a *v*, in contrast to the Nazi symbol, which is spelled with a *w*, but with the man's thick accent and the clamor of the parade, these linguistic subtleties were lost on me.

When the Chinese New Year rolled around, I learned of the custom of giving little red envelopes with money—*hóngbāo* in Mandarin—as gifts to friends. A wealthy Chinese woman connected to the Jewish community came by the synagogue and handed each of the Chabad boys a small red envelope with $200 cash. This holiday beat Chanukah hands down.

My knowledge of the world outside of Judaism and America was expanding rapidly, but my knowledge of Jews and Judaism was also broadening. Naftuli and I made Shabbos parties on Saturday afternoons and "Sunday Funday" programs the next day. One Sunday, we arranged to do an arts-and-crafts project with a group of about twenty children. The boys would decorate yarmulkes, and the girls would decorate challah covers for Shabbos. Deborah, one of the American expat kids I tutored in Hebrew—and who, at nine, understood more about Hebrew grammar than I ever did—wanted to make a yarmulke. "You want to make one for your kid brother?" I asked.

"No, I want to wear it myself," she calmly explained. As far as I knew, only boys were supposed to—and ever did—wear yarmulkes. I was dumbfounded. And forced to imagine new forms of Jewish ritual practice.

I became especially close with a small circle of adults in the Jewish community who taught me secular subjects unknown in the Hasidic world. I became friends with Michael Chan, a Chinese convert to Judaism and a local TV celebrity. I taught him the Code of Jewish Law, and he taught me about Shakespeare and Mozart. I was no yeshiva luminary, but I had managed to absorb some things from the yeshiva curriculum, despite the hours I spent away from the study hall and reading my own books. I was able to decipher the basic text of the Talmud, had a decent grasp of Jewish law, and had a firm understanding of the Jewish mystical teachings in Hasidism. So although I mostly worked with children in Singapore, I was prepared to teach adults as well.

As it turned out, Michael was extremely knowledgeable in Jewish law. He had actually already read through a two-volume Code of Jewish Law, so my role was mainly to review and fill in some details. I, by contrast, knew little about Shakespeare and zilch about Mozart.

I also became friends with Daniel Rosen, a Venezuelan expat and business consultant, whom I would meet with once a week to discuss Hasidic philosophy. He was in love with math and was always trying to explain mathematical concepts to me. Once he tried to teach me Fermat's Last Theorem on the back of a napkin at a baby's ritual circumcision. Although my experience that morning could not compare with the baby's, the math lesson didn't go especially well.

But the most important friendship I made in Singapore was with Rebecca Ackerman. I met Rebecca my first Shabbos in Singapore at the synagogue community luncheon. I was intimidated by the large crowd filling up the long and narrow black wooden tables and benches arrayed in the back of the sanctuary, so I tried to dodge by planting myself on the last bench. A few minutes later, and perhaps for the same reason, an American woman in her thirties with brown hair, large glasses, and a broad smile sat down next to me. She introduced herself and told me that she was a professor of sociology at the National University of Singapore (NUS).

I immediately felt comfortable speaking to Rebecca, and our conversation that afternoon at Shabbos lunch effortlessly zigzagged from topic to topic. She seemed to know everything about everything. They say about the second Lubavitcher Rebbe that if you cut his finger, Hasidic thought would pour out instead of blood. With Rebecca, it seemed a cut on her finger would bleed sociology, philosophy, and world literature. Rebecca's petite frame seemed too small to bear the heft of her vast knowledge. We talked for more than an hour that first time, then we kept seeking each other out at synagogue and other community events to continue our discussions.

On one especially hot Sunday in April, I met with Rebecca at the park behind her apartment building and chatted with her as she walked her golden retriever, Dr. Davka. As the dog chased tennis balls, Rebecca told me about the books she loved, including Albert Camus's *The Plague*, and how she used that novel in her sociology of medicine course to teach about how communities respond to disasters.

We sat on a bench in the shade, thankful for the brief respite from the intense sun. I felt my damp shirt cling to my body. Paying no attention to the stifling heat, Rebecca spoke at length about her commitment to sociology. Rebecca also expressed how important Judaism was to her. "Notwithstanding the fact that I interpret the Torah differently than you, and I disagree with Lubavitch in terms of just how much latitude humans have in interpreting it, *Yiddishkeit* [Judaism] is at the core of my existence."

I had sensed this about her all along, but it was odd to hear Rebecca say it openly. After all, she was a graduate of Harvard and Cornell, did research on the local response to AIDS in rural Thailand, and spoke fluent Thai. Now she was a professor at a prestigious university. I viewed her as the epitome of worldly secular learning and success. And Lubavitch viewed religious commitment in binary terms: You were all in or all out.

What Rebecca said next truly shocked me. "You know, when I was in college, I got involved with the local Chabad rabbi and seriously considered joining Lubavitch."

"Really? I can't believe it. What happened?"

"I was attracted to the sincerity of Lubavitch but ended up realizing that all of the rules and restrictions of the lifestyle just weren't for me."

In addition to my parents, I met many people who had joined Lubavitch from the outside, but I had never met someone who thought about joining but decided against it. Rebecca's disclosure emphasized how joining Lubavitch—or, for that matter, remaining Lubavitch—was an individual life choice that a person could make. I realized that it's possible, even for someone with my background in Lubavitch, to one day make other life choices.

The more I spoke to Rebecca and the more I heard about sociology, the more intrigued I became. So Rebecca invited me to observe one of her lectures at the NUS. On the chosen day, I made my way across the leafy campus, with its multitude of sleek modern buildings. The university, originally called the Straits Settlements and Federated Malay States Government Medical School, was founded in 1905. In 1928, Sir Manasseh Meyer, the Sephardic philanthropist who sponsored the building of both synagogues on the island, donated $150,000 to the institution that later became the NUS. The university has certainly expanded and flourished in the intervening decades and is now a first-rate research university.

Seated in a cushioned lecture hall chair, I reflected that I was twenty-one years old and this was my second time in a college classroom. The first was when I was twelve and sat in on an art history lecture at the University of California, Berkeley. My family had been visiting my Aunt Philippa in northern California. While attending the synagogue in Berkeley, my father befriended an art professor and told him about my budding interest in the subject. The professor extended an invitation to me to visit his class two days later. Although I found the art lecture and slides fascinating, I hardly felt like a college student. I was only a child at the time, and in any event, with the lights off in the lecture hall, I had only a vague sense of my surroundings. But now I was approximately the same age as the other students, and for the first time in my life I could imagine myself as a college student.

Just as in traditional theater where there exists an invisible barrier, the fourth wall, between the performers and the audience that is not supposed to be broken, so, too, there exists an invisible and unspoken wall between Lubavitchers and those they are trying to "convert" or influence to be more religiously observant. I knew I was in Singapore to "win" them over to "our" side. I knew I was a soldier in the Rebbe's army and that he was watching me as I discharged my duties. I had been taught this by my teachers my entire life. I had stayed up late at summer camp singing songs glorifying this mission. But I began to realize that now *they* were winning me over to *their* side.

The rabbis, my teachers, and my camp counselors had taught me that Hasidic thought was oil and the world was water. The oil could never be diluted or influenced by the water. But I found myself taking greater and greater interest in the water around me. It wasn't Rebecca. It was the slow and steady accumulation of exposure. An ancient story, popular in Lubavitch, is told about the great Talmudic sage Rabbi Akiva, who was inspired to begin studying Torah at the age of forty when he saw that gentle but persistent drops of water could carve a hole into solid rock.

The secular world had been seeping into me for years by the time I arrived in Singapore, from Aunt Marta's retelling of her global travel adventures to touring art museums with my father and receiving stacks of books from Uncle Jeff and going with him to Broadway shows. But now I began to feel the impression all these influences were making on me.

After months of thoughtful conversations with Rebecca, she began to encourage me to attend college. One day she said, "It's obvious that you enjoy the give and take of intellectual discussion. Well, that's exactly what college is all about. You'll love it, and it will provide you an incalculable opportunity to learn and grow." Rebecca was the first person ever to suggest that I would be able to manage a college curriculum, let alone that I would enjoy doing so.

The more I thought about Rebecca's words, the more convinced I became that I absolutely wanted to go to college once I finished my year in Singapore and returned to Brooklyn. I still believed in God and the Rebbe. I still identified as a Lubavitcher, and I was still committed to fulfilling the requirements of Orthodox Jewish law. I just wanted to discover the world beyond my Lubavitch cocoon.

In the unlikely event that Balaam's ass showed up to register for college, he would have been better prepared to succeed than I was at that time, given my total lack of formal secular education. But I decided to try. I knew that to enroll in college, one needed a high school diploma or a GED (a high school equivalency certification). Since my high school didn't teach secular subjects, it also didn't provide a high school diploma. I would have to sit for the GED exam.

By now I'd read several hundred books on various topics, so I wasn't particularly worried about the science, social studies, or reading comprehension parts of the exam, but I was positively terrified about the math portion. I knew almost no math and felt panic just thinking about the subject. My hands trembled and grew clammy when I thought about taking a math test. I had nightmares about it. I was twenty-one years old, and I struggled with basic multiplication and division examples. How would I pass the exam, which included questions on algebra and geometry? I feared I was sunk.

When I told Abigail Mizrahi, a friend in the Singapore community who was an elementary school English teacher, about my predicament, she suggested that I hire a colleague of hers who was a math teacher to come to my apartment and teach me math. "It's not as hard as you think. You just never learned it," Abigail reassured me.

Maybe. Time would tell.

I arranged for my tutor to come when the other guys were out of the apartment. A few days later, Jing Yi, a Chinese woman in her mid-thirties, knocked at my apartment door. As I walked the few steps to open the door, I wondered what would be considered more scandalous to Lubavitch sensibilities: that I was learning math when I was supposed to be doing religious outreach or that I was about to be alone in my apartment for an hour and a half with a non-Jewish woman?

I met with Jing twice a week for the next month, and she patiently proceeded to stuff my cranium with the twelve years of mathematics I was missing. After illuminating the mysteries of negative numbers and how to convert fractions into decimals and decimals into fractions, she began to usher me into the secret society of the elect who knew the Pythagorean theorem and could solve algebraic expressions. She gave me stacks of worksheets, and I spent hours each day poring over them. I felt the same way I had when I was sixteen and began to learn how to read English. It was painful and slow, but I could see that I was improving.

As I prepared to leave Singapore, I met with Jing for the last time. She asked me to complete twenty basic algebra problems. I had an hour. I tried to remember everything I had learned from her and completed the exam in fifty minutes. I felt a sense of accomplishment, of having slain one of my personal dragons. Jing reviewed my answers and said I did a good job, but she didn't express amazement at my achievement. "You don't seem very impressed," I needled her.

"No, no," she said in her quiet voice. "Good job."

"I bet you never saw a student do so many problems so quickly," I declared. I figured I might as well go for broke. She smiled but said nothing. "What is it?" I pressed.

"Every student is different, and you did a good job . . ."

"But what?"

"Well, I give my nine-year-old students sixty problems like this and they do it in twenty minutes."

I could only laugh. Still, I was making great progress. The trouble now was that this education operation was still undercover. I hadn't let my parents in on my scheme of attending college. I knew the Rebbe railed for years against his followers attending college because he believed it to be morally corrupting. And I knew that even though I was thinking only of attending Touro College—an Orthodox institution that offered gender-segregated night classes—my mother would have none of it.

Although my decision would not be considered an official desertion from the Rebbe's army, it was certainly a deviation from its rules and regulations, and she would consider it an outrage. I was supposed to return to Brooklyn, go back to yeshiva for one last year of formal instruction, and receive my *smicha*, the rabbinic ordination. All good Lubavitch men did that, even if they were not planning on becoming pulpit rabbis. I knew that she would oppose anything that interfered with this plan. I was scared of her wrath.

When I was in yeshiva, I used to call home every Thursday night and chat with my mother for hours as if we were best friends. My sisters would always say that I had a special relationship with her. Now, as I called from Singapore, our conversations had become contentious. I would make vague references to my desire to attend college when I got back home, but she never engaged the subject. She pretended that she didn't hear me. One day I just blurted it all out: "Mommy, I'm going to college next year."

To explicitly state my college plans to her was a kind of coming out. Although I didn't say anything about religion directly, the fact that I was unwilling to go back to yeshiva and finish preparing for my rabbinic ordination was bucking the Lubavitch system, and she wasn't going to accept that.

She stalled, "We'll talk about it when you get back."

"No," I said. "I'm telling you right now: I'm going to college next year."

She realized that I was serious, so she tried to bargain. "Maybe, once you finished learning *smicha*, in a year from now, we'll talk about you going to college."

But I couldn't wait that long. "No, I'm going this year."

When my mother got angry she used my full name, Schneur Zalman; when I got angry I shortened her name and called her "Ma."

"S-c-h-n-e-u-r Z-a-l-m-a-n," she said my name so deliberately, enunciating every syllable, it was as if the 9,521 miles between us had disappeared and she was now standing an inch away from my face shouting at me. "You are not going to college next year. End of discussion!"

How could my parents join this Lubavitch cult, which demands that the faithful remain ignorant of the ABCs? What kind of religious piety is threatened by knowledge of arithmetic? What exactly were Lubavitchers afraid of? That someone is going to learn how to multiply fractions, and then they're going to go out and eat a cheeseburger? Or if someone learned how to conjugate a verb, they're going to realize that God actually doesn't exist?

My temper was up, and I needed to respond. Even before the words escaped my mouth I knew they wouldn't convince her of anything, but I couldn't resist pointing out the irony of the situation. "You know, Ma, the Rebbe went to college when he was a young man. In fact, he went to two: one in Paris and one in Berlin."

Without a moment's hesitation she shot back, "So now you think you're the same as the Rebbe?" There was enough venom in that line to fell a herd of charging buffalo. She persisted, "Once you learn the whole Talmud and all of Hasidic thought you can also go to college!"

We each took a deep breath, hoping to pull the conversation back from the abyss.

My mother, trying to be constructive, suggested, "At least learn *smicha* in the morning and go to college at night."

This was a reasonable suggestion, but I just couldn't do it. Having spent a year tasting freedom, being able to do what I wanted whenever I wanted, it was unimaginable to me to willingly accept the strict, dawn-till-dusk yeshiva schedule, with the religious scrutiny it entailed. It felt like willingly replacing a straitjacket I was just barely wriggling out of.

"I'm sorry, Mommy, but I can't do that. I can't go back to yeshiva for a year, even only in the mornings."

My mother began crying. I could almost feel her tears on my cheeks. "Schneur Zalman," her voice quivering, "you're ruining your life. No *smicha* and going to college. What decent Lubavitch girl will want to marry you?!"

Until I was in yeshiva and started reading English books, I hadn't had any real fights with my parents. Sure, as a kid I argued about what time to go to bed, whether they would take us ice skating in Prospect Park on Saturday nights, and whether I would be allowed to take martial arts classes (I wouldn't be allowed, because my mother considered it "too goyish").

But these were minor tiffs compared with the soul-shaking reprimands I got for reading my "goyish books." But even *these* flare-ups were nothing compared with that phone call about attending college. In the earlier disagreements, it was obvious that I was a faithful Lubavitcher just trying to broaden my horizons. Now that assumption was not as obvious. No one said anything about it, but we felt it.

Both my parents were on the call, but my father didn't say a word throughout the entire conversation. I got the impression that even though he opposed my college attendance as a matter of Lubavitch principle, his opposition contained much less of the heat, the fear, the disappointment that fueled my mother's opposition.

My nature is to prefer going with the flow rather than opposing it. I loathe confrontation and have tried desperately for years to avoid even minor disagreements. But in this case, I couldn't help myself. It was as if I was being forced along this path by a wind stronger than myself. I was propelled by an inner drive. What exactly that drive consisted of I was only partially aware. Was it a thirst for knowledge, a desire to make my own decisions, a yearning to be free of the burdens placed on me by my community? I couldn't then, and I still can't, pin it down exactly.

Once when we were kids, my family watched a documentary on animal life and saw a mother lioness carry her cub by biting on the scruff of its neck. After the film, my mother commented, "I should pick you kids up by the back of your necks, just like the mother lion." This perfectly captures her parenting style, a combination of caring and force, with a little bite. Now I was feeling the bite.

Within a week of that painful conversation, I had packed all my belongings, including the hundred or so books that I had brought with me to Singapore and those I had collected there, taking special care to individually wrap inside T-shirts Michael Chan's present, J. M. Roberts's massive *History of the World*, and Rebecca's present, the equally massive two-volume autobiography of Lee Kuan Yew, Singapore's first prime minister.

I was departing the Lion City and returning to Brooklyn possessed of some certainties and many doubts. I was certain that I couldn't return to yeshiva life and that I was committed to attending college and expanding my intellectual and social horizons. But I was in doubt as to how the expansion of my horizons would affect my personal and religious life.

11

Deserter

"I know what you're up to, Zalman," Bubby Ruth said as she sat on an Eisenhower-era kitchen chair at her dinette table while paring away the spots on two pears she had purchased at the "reduced for quick sale" section. I stood behind her, eyeing the micro wave and waiting for it to defrost the frozen brick of leftover cholent my father had given for Bubby Ruth and me to share. I feared the jig was up. She had discovered my clandestine adjustment of the thermostat from her frugal fifty-nine to an indulgent sixty-three degrees. Aunt Philippa had warned me that Bubby Ruth, my father's mother, put on only enough heat to "take the edge off," but it was a freezing February night, and I found it difficult to turn the pages of my textbooks while wearing gloves.

"I told you when you take a shower not to turn the water on all the way. You have to let the water just drip onto you. I've been hearing it turned on full force. The pipes can't handle it," she asserted as she shook her head, the way one does with an errant child. I suspected that the pipes were fine, and this was a pretext to prevent the water bill from creeping above the minimum charge. But it was her house, so I had to oblige—or to figure out how to get away with pretending to.

Whatever socialism Bubby Ruth espoused as a youth was long gone, although she retained a deep disgust of Ayn Rand's novels that venerated selfishness and she maintained the left's abhorrence of religious cant. She repeatedly told me how, after the Soviets signed a nonaggression pact with the Nazis, her communist friends would enjoin her to "believe" that Stalin knew best. She would respond, "If I wanted to believe, I would be an Orthodox Jew." Her personal religion was a devotion to work, which is why, as a financially secure pensioner who had reached voting age in 1937, she still rode the subway into Manhattan every day to work in the office of a nonprofit organization.

After returning from Singapore and passing the GED exam, I enrolled in Touro College, as I had planned. Although the composition courses I took helped me begin to learn how to craft a decent English sentence, and although I relished the anatomy course I took—we got to dissect a sheep's heart and a fetal pig—the course offerings were limited. Worse still was the stifling homogeneity of Touro's social environment. It had as much diversity as a cocktail reception of the Daughters of the American Revolution.

My classes at Touro were composed almost entirely of Orthodox men who sounded like Rush Limbaugh's kid brothers. I was shocked to discover how similar my clean-shaven, non-Hasidic but still ultra-Orthodox classmates were to the Lubavitchers with whom I'd grown up. Once, in a writing class discussion of the 9/11 tragedy, the professor asked why the terrorists committed such an atrocious act. The response from several students was, "All Muslims are terrorists and hate America." This was a far cry from the intellectual paradise Rebecca had spoken of in Singapore.

To be clear, many non-Hasidic ultra-Orthodox men who shared the disdain Lubavitch felt toward college had come to the realization that a bachelor's degree was necessary to secure their financial future. For most of my Touro classmates, their attendance at college did not represent a rebellion against their parents or community. On the contrary, their parents were glad that their children had found a program that was sensitive to Orthodox needs (for example, being gender segregated) while still able to provide the necessary education to get a good job.

After two semesters at Touro, I thought of transferring to Brooklyn College. The fervor of my mother's opposition to my attending college hadn't diminished, and she was particularly opposed to my transferring to Brooklyn College because it has both non-Jewish and female students—two suspect groups. So I planned to move in with my nonreligious grandmother, Bubby Ruth, who lived a mile and a half from the campus.

A week before I needed to make a decision about what school to attend, my mother took me out to lunch at her favorite dairy restaurant, Café K, to convince me not to transfer to Brooklyn College. As we waited for our food to arrive, my mother, looking down at the bare wood table, began. "You know I love you and only want what's best for you. I was opposed to you attending Touro, but you went anyway. At least it is a *frum* [Orthodox] environment. Brooklyn College is totally full of goyim. It is the wrong place for you."

She then looked straight at me and delivered her warning. "Going there will ruin your life. Mark my words."

I sat squirming in my seat, trying to think of how to respond. But she wasn't finished. "And going to Bubby Ruth's house is a terrible idea. *Boruch Hashem* [thank God] you have a family who loves you. You should live with us until you get married, like a normal Lubavitch boy."

It was the family image that had brought her to Lubavitch, and it was this image that I was threatening. But why couldn't Mommy understand that I had changed. That I was not the same naïve boy she had sent off to yeshivas across America and around the world? I'd grown up. I needed different things now.

But I couldn't say any of this to my mother. I couldn't fully articulate this even to myself. I just felt claustrophobic, desperate for air. Moving in with Bubby Ruth wasn't just about being closer to Brooklyn College. It was about creating some distance between me and Lubavitch so I could figure out how I wanted to live my life.

Living with Bubby Ruth allowed me to attend college rent-free, but not headache-free. My housemate had lived through the Great Depression, and in her its frugal spirit thrived. She saved everything that crossed her path: plastic containers, pieces of string, paper bags, empty coffee jars, used pencils, rubber bands, and postage stamps. "You never know when you might need it." By far, though, she valued most her overflowing accumulation of books. She owned thousands of them, filling up her bookcases, her tables, and every available surface of her house.

Bubby Ruth was a gray-haired eighty-nine-year-old with failing hearing and stooped shoulders, but she was as sharp as a *shochet*'s knife blade. One morning over breakfast, a few weeks after the water pipes invocation, she announced: "Zalman, you need to be more judicious with your toilet paper use. One or two squares is plenty."

Although dealing with Bubby Ruth could be tricky, we generally got along. She was thrilled that I was attending college, and although she was too independent to admit it—she had lived alone since my grandfather had died more than four decades earlier—I felt that she enjoyed the company.

As the months passed, I got into a routine. I walked to college early in the morning, attended my classes and did research in the college's newly renovated library, walked home, ate supper with Bubby Ruth and gave her a short rundown of my day, and then camped out in my room the rest of the night prepping for my courses.

I was lucky to have several professors at Brooklyn College who took an interest in my education. They encouraged me and provided guidance along the way. But my secret resource was, ironically, closer to home. Although my father initially opposed my attending college, he took pity on me and helped me edit all my college papers. In addition to his Ivy League education, my father had years of experience editing my sisters' book reports and assignments.

As was typical of him, my father took a nondogmatic approach to my college work. He was in a position to help his desperate son, so he did. We would sit together late at night and review my papers on the computer. He would often read a passage I wrote and exclaim, "I have no idea what you're talking about." I would respond by clarifying what I meant in the essay. He would then say, "What you just said is nowhere in your paper. Put that idea in your paper." Taking inspiration from *New York Times* articles by Paul Krugman, my father sought to transform my convoluted and verbose writing into clear and concise sentences, with a zinger or two thrown in, whenever possible. It was the best training I could have received to ensure that I wrote what I meant and I meant what I wrote. When my mother would spot us huddled at the computer editing my papers, she would huff at my father. "Why are you helping Zalman with his college *narishkayt* [nonsense]?" My father ignored these rebukes.

With my father's assistance, I was managing to keep up and turn in my work on time, but I had a nagging feeling that I didn't belong in college. I felt like an imposter, a modern-day Yentl in reverse, a Lubavitch rabbinical student playing the role of a college student. I still had my full Lubavitch beard, large black velvet yarmulke, dark pants, and colored button-down shirts, but this was unremarkable among the college's diverse student body.

I pulled off the role of college student convincingly enough that none of my professors or classmates suspected me, but it felt like a sham.

I was anxious whenever I walked down the halls in college. I waited for a security guard to discover the ruse and send me back to 770.

As I racked up semesters, college expanded my intellectual universe. I studied biology and physics, music and art, philosophy and history, sociology and psychology. In yeshiva, I was taught that the entire world's knowledge could be located in the Torah because, as the Zohar states, "God looked into the Torah and created the world" (*Istakel b'oraysa ubara alma*). The more subjects I explored at college, the more convinced I became that the dictum of the Zohar came up short. I was learning innumerable things that seemed to me completely beyond the scope of the Torah, by any stretch of the imagination.

I learned for the first time about atoms and about cells. I learned about Prokofiev's score for Sergei Eisenstein's film *Alexander Nevsky*; I fell in love with the haunting movement of "The Battle on the Ice," with its dramatic buildup using French horns in the background as the Russian forces led by Nevsky eagerly wait to repel the Teutonic invaders. I learned about the symmetry, balance, and logic of Renaissance paintings.

I learned about Plato's allegory of the cave and René Descartes's "Cogito, ergo sum." I learned about feudalism, capitalism, and socialism. I learned about Max Weber's three types of legitimate authority—traditional, charismatic, rational-legal—and Peter Berger's theory of the social construction of reality. I learned the difference between correlation and causation and the difference between a dependent and an independent variable. I learned about the id, ego, and superego and about cognitive dissonance.

The more I thought about my upbringing, (and I couldn't help but constantly compare it with the outside world I was being exposed to—like someone in a fresh relationship comparing his new partner with his ex), I came to see Lubavitch culture as austere and rigid. Yes, Lubavitch has an inviting veneer of singing and dancing and drinking *l'chaims.* It can seem to outsiders, and often felt to me, even as an insider, like a community that embraces joyfulness and celebration of life.

But at the heart of Lubavitch was a concept of the human drama as a struggle between the two souls inside each individual: the Godly soul and the animal soul. It was the mission of every person to use their Godly soul to subdue their animal one. It was this denigration and denial of the basic pleasures of life that I came to despise and reject. I wanted to explore. I wanted to taste nonkosher ideas, "heretical" ideas, and enjoy them for their own sake. I didn't feel that this pursuit was sinful or degrading. I felt it was exhilarating and enriching.

I thought back to the proverb I had heard several rabbis say at *farbrengens*: "Only a live fish swims against the current." These rabbis thought of the current as the outside world and the live fish as pious Lubavitchers who were defying it by maintaining their faith and customs. I now thought of the current as the Lubavitch system and of myself as the live fish bravely rushing against the flow to seek out my own way.

I came to understand that if I was to live and grow and thrive, I would need to detach from—or, at least, change the nature of my bond with—the two main religious figures in my life: the Rebbe, my spiritual father, and my flesh-and-blood mother.

My flesh-and-blood father, through his academic training and extensive reading, knew about the conflicts between science and Torah but chose to embrace an *emunah peshuta*, a simple faith that accepted the truth of the Torah, God, and the Rebbe without asking any questions. Since my father pretty much kept his opinions to himself, he was not a key player in my drama.

By the time I was in college, the Rebbe had been dead for thirteen years, but he was still alive inside me—what Lubavitchers would call my *neshama*, my soul. My mother was, fortunately, very much alive in every sense.

I had countless heated arguments with her. But she had spent only a year in formal Lubavitch educational institutions before her marriage. Most of her understanding of Lubavitch, and her appreciation, was derived from living the Lubavitch lifestyle after getting married and attending occasional Torah discussions for women. So we didn't argue about Lubavitch theology or Jewish law. Aside from her constant bemoaning, "What did I do wrong to cause this disaster?" we mostly argued about the idea of personal freedom and the obligations of children to their parents.

Once this debate erupted as she was doing the laundry. I avowed, "Every adult has a right to decide how to live his own life."

My mother, who was just finishing filling the washing machine with a load of towels, countered, "You think I'm going to just stand there like a lump if I see my own son doing something I know is harmful? I'm going to try to do everything in my power to get him to change."

Then, as she twisted the knob to colors and pulled it forward to start the wash cycle, she added, "Do you know how many nights I stayed up crying and *davening* [praying] for you in the intensive care unit when you were born with all those complications? You're crazy if you think I'm going to sit around and watch you ruin your life."

"But it's my life, so I get to decide how to live it."

"Even if you're making a huge mistake—one you will regret forever?"

"Yes, it's my *right* also to make mistakes for myself. Everyone has that right. Your father thought you were making a terrible mistake by joining Lubavitch, but it was your right as an adult to decide to do that."

"Oh, please!" she huffed, as she headed down the stairs to go grocery shopping. "How can you even compare? When I joined Lubavitch I was going from a bad thing to a good one. Now you're going from a wonderful thing to a terrible one. No connection."

After enough of these exchanges in which we both kept repeating ourselves and neither of us conceded any ground, I felt confident that it was my life, not my mother's, and that I needed to decide for myself how to live it. I would be the one who would have to live with the consequences of my decisions.

The truth was, although I knew that I found Lubavitch to be claustrophobic, I wasn't sure exactly where to turn. Did I still believe in God? In the Rebbe? About this time, a year or so after I started living with Bubby Ruth, my older brother Yossi joined me in Bubby's *ir miklat* (city of refuge). Yossi was in the midst of a religious evolution of his own and had shaved his beard while in San Francisco visiting relatives. When he returned home, because of hurtful comments from my mother, he no longer felt welcome in her home.

Yossi was two years my senior, still had a slight lisp, was a few inches taller than me, and was much more athletic. He had a great jump shot; a classmate of his once told me that Yossi "was the Michael Jordan of our yeshiva." (Yossi's yeshiva was not quite as strict about sports as mine in Chicago under Rabbi Lefkowitz. Yossi's looked down on sports but grudgingly tolerated them.)

More important, Yossi was a *talmid chuchum*, an erudite scholar of the Talmud and its commentaries, unlike me, who always struggled with these subjects in yeshiva. Unsurprisingly, given his intellectual connection with rabbinic literature, when Yossi began to question his upbringing, he was focused on textual contradictions and logical flaws in the Bible and the Talmud. For me, even if those textual problems didn't exist, those texts would still be limited, and the Lubavitch community and its worldview and strictures would still be overbearing.

I was in touch with Uncle Jeff and Rebecca, who both provided a sympathetic ear and helpful guidance. But Yossi was the only other person I was in touch with who was also going through a personal religious crisis. Yossi and I were like two lost souls alone at sea clinging to each other for survival. We had endless conversations about Lubavitch, the Rebbe, the Bible, the Talmud, literature, rationalism, the scientific method, my parents, and what we should do with our lives.

Yossi was forever doling out book recommendations, like a boy who discovered a hole in the schoolyard fence and couldn't help sharing the secret with his friends. "You gotta read Chaim Grade's *The Agunah* about two rabbis arguing over whether they can give a dispensation for a divorce to a woman whose husband disappeared. It gets to the guts of Jewish law. One rabbi represents the stringent side of the law and the other the merciful side. You'll love it. I promise." Another time he was pushing Saint Augustine's *The City of God*. "It's *mamish* an amazing book. It's like reading one of the *rishonim* [the medieval Jewish commentators]. He takes a verse from the Bible and gives a whole *pilpul* [a hairsplitting exegesis]. It's *gevaldik*, the best."

I followed Yossi's recommendations and was never disappointed. One night at Bubby Ruth's Yossi said, "You absolutely must read Rabbi Louis Jacobs's *We Have Reason to Believe*." He applied a thick coat of hummus to a piece of rye bread as he spoke. "It deals with whether the Torah was actually from God."

"Don't leave me hanging," I said as I unpacked my lamb shish kebab. "What's he say?"

"You really should read it. He writes beautifully. But basically, he argues that just like when we make a *brachah* [a blessing] on bread saying, 'Hamotzi lechem min ha'aretz,' thanking God for 'bringing forth bread from the earth,' we don't mean that the loaf actually comes directly from the earth. The kernel from the earth must go through a long process of development until it's turned into a loaf of challah. So when we say that the Torah is *min hashamayim* [from Heaven], we don't mean that it comes directly from God. We mean that the divine inspiration went through a whole process of human development and only then was the Torah produced."

"So, bottom line, he says the Torah was written by humans?" I asked as I shoveled a spoonful of lamb and rice into my mouth.

"Yes."

"And he's an Orthodox rabbi?"

"He's his own kind of Orthodox, but he's Orthodox, and he's a massive Torah scholar. Jacobs is actually British, and he almost became the Orthodox chief rabbi of England, but his radical ideas about the divine origin of the Bible caused a scandal and killed his chances." Yossi chuckled and added: "They say he's the greatest chief rabbi England *never had.*"

I was intrigued, and I read the book. Jacobs does indeed argue that one can be a good Orthodox Jew and not be limited by the traditional view of the divinity of the Torah. I went on to read other books that dealt with biblical criticism, including Spinoza's *A Theological-Political Treatise*, Thomas Paine's *The Age of Reason*, and Robert Ingersoll's *Some Mistakes of Moses*, all of which detail logical flaws and contradictions in the Bible.

Although I agreed with them, I continued to feel that these were not my biggest problems with my upbringing. My upbringing was just too narrow culturally, morally, and socially.

I can't pinpoint the day when I stopped believing in God. But sometime during college I realized I simply didn't believe anymore—just as children stop fearing the dark gradually and imperceptibly. I realized there was no one above peering down at me and judging me or keeping a tally of my merits and demerits. It was just me and billions of other people trying to live our lives on this pale blue dot of a planet, to use the astronomer Carl Sagan's phrase.

It's as if you're walking with someone along a trail and eventually realize that no one is walking beside you. You are alone, and the sensation of the other presence was all in your head. You were told that it was there, so you believed it; you accepted it without question. You wanted the companionship, so you imagined the other entity into being. But all the wishing in the world and all the hoping couldn't change the simple reality that you had been alone all along.

There was no "Aha!" moment when I realized I no longer believed in God. I only came to realize that my belief was gone when one afternoon in a Mexican restaurant I felt comfortable ordering nonkosher chicken. I no longer feared a lightning bolt tearing through the sky to strike me dead. It was anticlimactic. I just sat there listening to Marc Anthony sing "Y Hubo Alguien" and munching on my *arroz con pollo.*

Growing up with a mother who was a talented chef and surrounded by tons of kosher restaurants and pizza shops, I didn't for the most part envy or fantasize about nonkosher food, except for Wise Onion Rings (which were technically kosher but not kosher enough for Lubavitchers) and the large soft pretzels sold at the ice-skating rink at Prospect Park. Their aroma was heavenly, but they were strictly off-limits.

The kosher restrictions started to really bother me when I was traveling abroad and I realized that these restrictions created a substantial separation between me and the local population. Only then did I begin to resent the elaborate planning that went into every trip, making sure we had enough food so that we would not have to rely on what was available locally to the general public.

Although I had no problem eating nonkosher chicken and beef, I couldn't imagine eating pork. After years of hearing that "*hazeirim* are disgusting; they roll around in the mud—yuck," I just couldn't imagine putting that in my mouth. The taboo was too great, like the taboo against eating bugs for most Americans. The association between pigs and "uncleanness" is very old in the Jewish tradition. The Talmud (Berachot 25a) records a rabbinic opinion that "the mouth of a swine is as dirty as dung itself."

Some Jews have taken their disgust of pigs beyond merely not consuming them. Wilhelm Rothschild, a banker and a head of the Frankfurt House of Rothschild, who was also very pious, refused to shake the hand of any person who had touched pork that day. But then again, as one of the wealthiest men in Europe, he had the luxury of being insulting. Regardless, for better or worse, I never got over my abhorrence of pig.

Around that time, I also stopped believing in the Rebbe. The Rebbe was there to connect me to God. Once I stopped believing in God, my belief in the Rebbe disintegrated. The Rebbe had tremendous personal charisma: He was a firebrand who couldn't help but ignite and set aflame those around him. I still respected his commitment to the Jewish people and his vast learning, but I no longer believed he possessed supernatural powers.

Although so much of my thinking had shifted while I was in college, my clothing and outer appearance had remained the same. This disjuncture sometimes caused consternation on the part of others, in particular one Sunday afternoon at the Metropolitan Museum of Art on Manhattan's Upper East Side. I was there fulfilling a class assignment from my art history teacher, Professor Cronin, to explore an installation and write a two-page visual analysis of it.

I chose as my subject the Renaissance painting *Madonna and Child Enthroned with Saints Mary Magdalene and John the Baptist*, painted by Bugiardini on the side of an altar for the Church of Santa Maria Maddalen all'Isola at Incisa, in the Arno Valley south of Florence, in the early sixteenth century. It stands more than six feet high and five feet wide and was prominently mounted in a gilded wooden frame. I settled onto the hard wooden bench in front of the painting and began to explore.

Bugiardini depicts the Virgin, pious and maternal, seated on a golden throne holding a plump naked infant Jesus in her lap. Jesus, in turn, is holding a crystal globe in his right hand, and his left hand is resting on his mother's breasts. Bugiardini paints two cherubic winged angels in the background kneeling on a ledge bestowing a gold crown on the Virgin. John the Baptist, suntanned and muscular, and Mary Magdalene, rosy-cheeked and devoted, are standing in the foreground. John is holding the cross, and Mary Magdalene is extending a chalice to the Virgin.

I stared at the painting for some time, transfixed by its vitality and luxurious gold, blue, red, green, and orange colors. "Excuse me," asked a middle-aged white woman holding a sketch pad. "Is there a problem?" "No, of course not," I answered, not sure what sort of "problem" one could have in a quiet room full of Renaissance art. I tried to return to my thinking. A few minutes later, a middle-aged man, not wearing a yarmulke but visibly Jewish, walked by and just glared at me. *What is wrong with all these people?*

I tried to cast out these intrusions. The more I looked at the painting, the more I felt how realistic, logical, and even mathematical it seemed. The figures are presented proportionately, and the painting has great symmetry. There are two central figures, two angels, two figures in the foreground, and two pilasters in the background.

Twenty minutes passed. A young Modern Orthodox Jewish couple walked by, the man clean-shaven, sporting a small blue yarmulke with a New York Yankees emblem, and wearing a striped button-down shirt and gray pants, and the woman wearing a purple top that was stylish but modest and a tight black pencil skirt. The guy came over to me and, with a knowing grin, asked, "Oh, so you're doing an art project?" Only then did it dawn on me. All these people were staring at me and were somehow oddly troubled by the sight of a Hasidic Jew with a long beard and big black velvet yarmulke sitting intently looking at a massive painting of Jesus.

After the couple walked away, I could feel my heart tighten. OK, he happened to be right this time, but why did it have to be so? Why couldn't a guy who looked like me be entranced by a Renaissance painting of Jesus simply for the joy of it?

It was as if I was somehow violating an unspoken pact that we each keep to our own turf. It wasn't a Jew–versus–non-Jew thing. It was a worldly-versus-cloistered thing. "They" would not disturb us in "our" synagogues in Brooklyn on Saturday mornings as we swayed in prayer, and we would not show up at the Met on Sunday afternoon.

After four hours, I felt I had gathered enough information for my assignment and scooped up my notes and coat. As I entered the subway station to take me back to Brooklyn, I quickly bundled my coat to keep out the cold. It suddenly occurred to me: The painting captures a magical moment, a snapshot of distinct elements coming together—but it can't last.

We each have a mission. The angelic cherubs need to ascend to heaven. Baby Jesus needs to grow up and be crucified. The mother of Jesus needs to mourn the loss of her son. John the Baptist needs to travel the Earth to proclaim the good news. Mary Magdalene needs to be absorbed into myth and await Dan Brown's retelling of her sexual relationship with Jesus. And I . . . I need to go back to Brooklyn where onlookers will not be disturbed by my presence. I vowed right there and then, on the grimy and dank subway platform of the 4 train at 86th Street, that I would return.

Although my thinking about God and the Rebbe was beginning to solidify, the question of the kind of life I should live was far from settled. I was like a dreidel that had already been spun but hadn't yet come to rest.

One morning as we explored Bubby Ruth's vast book collection, Yossi and I debated whether we could put our Lubavitch upbringing and indoctrination behind us and move on. Yossi stood in the dining room encircled by legions of potted plants and overstuffed bookcases, neither of which had changed much in forty years. He played with his black baseball cap that shielded him from the sun and from criticism for not wearing a yarmulke and said, "Maybe we were born Lubavitch and we're just stuck with it for life. We can't escape."

I stood in front of a bookcase and spotted a well-worn copy of Chaucer's *The Canterbury Tales* and said, "What you're saying is medieval. Modernity, the Enlightenment taught that people can choose their own path, that birth is not destiny. We are not the descendants of cobblers who are forced to continue in our forefathers' trade. So what if we were born Lubavitch? We can decide to be anyone we choose." I picked up the copy of Chaucer and opened its cover to discover my father's name written inside: My father who had made his own active choice to join Lubavitch.

Yossi wasn't convinced and tried to enlist into his argument Solomon Maimon—the eighteenth-century Russian-born philosopher who struggled to gain entry into Berlin's high society. "Solomon Maimon wrote that he couldn't get rid of the sing-song melody and rhythmic swaying of his Talmud study and that he never felt completely at home in secular society. If Maimon couldn't manage to gain acceptance in mainstream society, *man d'char shmei* [it goes without saying] that we have no chance."

"Well," I said as I leafed through a stack of Yiddish socialist pamphlets I'd found on a bottom shelf tucked behind a jar containing my father's collection of fossilized shark teeth, "that was hundreds of years ago, and things aren't the same today."

Yossi just kept going. "According to Yosef Hayim Yerushalmi, the historian from Columbia University, although Freud played down his Jewish roots, in the end psychoanalysis was still accused of being a 'Jewish science.'"

"Come on," I said.

"I'm just saying, many Jews have found a path out, but they're always stamped as a Jew."

"You think there's some kind of conspiracy against Jews that prevents them from being fully accepted?"

"Well, Rashi does say that it's a *halacha* [a law] that Esav [Esau] hates Yaakov [Jacob], meaning that non-Jews will always hate Jews."

"You're seriously quoting Rashi? He was only quoting the Sifre [a midrash from the second century C.E.]. So now you are basing your argument about the prospect of integrating into mainstream society in the twenty-first century on an eleventh-century biblical commentator who is quoting an ancient rabbinic source."

We discussed this as if our lives depended on it—because our lives did depend on it. What's the point of attempting to assimilate if the outside world would always view us as Lubavitch weirdos, even if we shaved and plastered our office walls with fancy diplomas?

12

African Summer

"I forbid you to go," my mother exclaimed when I told her about my plans to travel to Ghana for the summer. It was my sophomore year of college, and I had recently learned that the American Jewish World Service (AJWS) organizes summer volunteer trips for Jewish students to assist impoverished non-Jewish communities around the world. For the summer of 2005, the AJWS was sending groups to Ukraine, Peru, and Ghana. As soon as I heard that a group was going to Ghana, I was determined to be on that trip. I wanted to see Africa—the one continent besides Antarctica that I hadn't been to—and I liked the idea of doing good at the same time.

When I informed my mother, "I'm going with or without your permission," she started to cry. I felt terrible that she was distraught over my decision, but it didn't dissuade me. Then I spoke on the phone to Pops, my mother's father, who was non-Orthodox, and told him my summer plans. He became hysterical and warned me, "Africans will jump out of the bush and kill you and eat you!"

Undoubtedly, Pops had watched too many Hollywood African adventures, but his comments made me worry for the first time that I might not be completely safe in Ghana. So I decided to ask my father what he thought. Unlike my mother, who was forever hounding me with her "advice," I would sum up my father's attitude as, "Those who know do not speak," the Chinese maxim recorded in the Dao De Jing.

It was difficult to get him to give advice on personal matters. I asked whether he thought I would be OK in Ghana. He hesitated and then said, "I'm sure you'll have a great time, but it might not be good for you religiously." His reassurance of my physical well-being buttressed my confidence, and I applied the next day.

After a long selection process and an in-depth personal interview—which included the question, "Do you have experience with manual labor," to which I responded, "I help build my family's sukkah every year"—I was accepted into the program. I also learned that my group would have fifteen members, ten women and five men, and that our project would be to construct a small library in a rural village in Ghana. Our group consisted of secular and liberal Jews, with a smattering of Modern Orthodox. As a bearded Hasid, I stood out, but, I hoped, not apart.

The day before our flight to Ghana, the fifteen members of our group plus our two group leaders had a seven-hour orientation in a spacious lounge in Carman Hall at Columbia University. We discussed the Jewish motivation for social justice work and practical information on Ghana.

Ziv Vered, a Jewish Renewal rabbi who studied mysticism and had a trimmed black beard and an earring, spoke to us and then sang a Hasidic melody. This was my first encounter with a rabbi who blended Hasidic traditions with non-Orthodox Jewish practice. When he began to sing the Hasidic melody, I burst out crying. He appeared so distant from the Lubavitch world I knew, yet he tapped into something so familiar to me.

Aviva, one of our group leaders, who was pursuing her doctorate in education at Columbia Teachers College, had frizzy hair and the warmth and calm of a yoga instructor. She used statistics along with real-life examples to inform us about the poverty in Ghana. "You may not realize, but we are all extremely privileged. Take out your money belts and look through them. What do you see? You see U.S. passports, credit cards, insurance cards, university IDs. These represent tremendous privileges that most of the world's population can only dream of." As Aviva snapped out of her usual temperament, her hands became animated and gestured wildly. Like me, Aviva is a Jew who uses hand motions to punctuate ideas.

Aviva waited for a moment for her information to sink in and then continued. "You need to understand that the average Ghanaian earns about $1,000 a year. You heard me. You will see unimaginable poverty, and it's very upsetting. Our job is to help where we can. Then when we come back home, we need to help people here understand what's actually going on in Ghana so they can work to change it."

The next morning, with a sense of both excitement and trepidation, I joined our boisterous group as we made our way through the crowded JFK International Airport. Once again, I was standing in this airport with a group of Jews on a mission, but my companions now were so different from those on my Passover trip to Russia.

This time, more than half of the group members were women sporting T-shirts over shorts or multicolor wraparound skirts. The men were similarly casually dressed in T-shirts and jeans (except for me in my button-down shirt and dark pants). The goals of the two trips were also so different. The Russia trip had a clearly religious, and specifically Orthodox, agenda. The Ghana trip participants were motivated by a general humanitarianism that was only loosely connected to Judaism. And even that connection centered on the amorphous notion of *tikkun olam*, the Jewish imperative, promoted by liberal Jewish denominations, to heal the world through social justice.

The ten-and-a-half-hour flight to Kotoka International Airport in Accra, the capital of Ghana, was uneventful. Once we landed, we were bundled into a battered orange Iveco Turbo Daily van that drove us the six hours to Gbi Kpeme (pronounced *b' PEH-me*), a village in the Volta region, which we would call home for the next seven weeks.

As we drove farther from the capital, we saw fewer tall buildings. The scenery changed to lush open land dotted with trees and occasional one-story homes. For a time, we drove alongside the magnificent Lake Volta, the largest artificial reservoir in the world. As we approached the village, the paved road ended, and we continued on a bumpy dirt track marked by large craters that the driver only partially succeeded in swerving around.

The nongovernmental organization we were partnered with to build the library arranged for our group to stay in a two-story house that belonged to a Ghanaian who lived in London. We were lucky to have running water, even if only cold. The first thing we tackled was the sleeping arrangements—the guys would sleep on the first floor and women would sleep upstairs. We laid out our sleeping bags on the carpeted floor and hung up our mosquito netting.

Once we were settled, we met with a five-man delegation from the village and the coordinator from the local nongovernmental organization. The coordinator was familiar with the AJWS from other projects and thanked us profusely for coming to his country to assist and for "not bringing any Bibles. So many Americans who come to our country want to convert us. We want your help, but we don't want anyone telling us what to believe."

We all laughed. In none of the varieties of Judaism from which we hailed did we ever hear of, much less practice, proselytizing to non-Jews. We were not here to establish a Jewish foothold in Ghana. My prior Lubavitch missions were about connecting Jews to Judaism.

After we said goodbye to the delegation and the coordinator, we sat down on the floor of the living room for a group meeting. Aviva informed us that the AJWS had hired a local woman to cook strictly vegetarian meals for us in the kitchen in our home. Immediately, Adinah, a student at the Modern Orthodox Stern College with long, straight blond hair, interjected: "If a non-Jew is cooking for us, we need one of us to turn on the fire every morning so the food will be *bishol Yisroel* [considered cooked by a Jew], which is important for Jewish law."

Suddenly, Tamar, a recent graduate of the University of California, Santa Cruz, and community organizer with curly brown hair who was considering studying to be a rabbi, shot back: "It isn't fair to say just because a Jew turns a knob on a stove that the food cooked on the stove will be considered 'cooked by a Jew.' The fact is that a non-Jew is the one slaving away in the kitchen all day preparing it."

"Well," I said, "but that's what it says in Jewish law. All a Jew needs to do is turn on the stove."

"I'm just saying," Tamar said, as she took a sip of water from her green Nalgene bottle, "it's not right. And isn't the point of this whole program to do social justice and not just to follow Jewish law?"

Tamar's words were like a revelation to me. I had heard Orthodox Jews discuss the laws related to "cooked by a Jew" for years, but no one had ever said anything remotely like what she just said. Jewish law was always presented to me, and I always thought of it as a system of technical requirements that needed to be observed, like a checklist with boxes to be marked off. I never thought of the human impact of those requirements or of the possibility of directing the requirements in a way to ensure a more just outcome.

Her words made me think of the time in Singapore two years earlier when I was paid by a kosher certification company to drive to a tofu factory and push a button to turn on the oven in the factory so that the food would be considered "cooked by a Jew." My job took less than a minute, while the low-paid Indian migrant workers had to stay in the noisy and poorly ventilated factory all day to actually produce the tofu products. Why were the products considered "cooked by a Jew" when I had no part in their production, save for pushing a button?

The mood in the meeting was becoming tense. Aviva stepped in and announced that we would set up a rotation system for kitchen assistant, and that the assistant would both turn on the oven and actually help the cook prepare the day's food.

At the conclusion, Aviva told us that we would now be breaking up into pairs and doing an activity. The activity was to walk around the village and ask people questions about Ghanaian history. Just my luck, I was paired with Tamar, the most outspoken group member.

Tamar and I strolled around the village and spotted many scattered one-room shacks with mud-covered walls, some with tin and others with thatched roofs. We saw a row of small stores with Christian-themed names, such as the Lord Our Shepard Enterprise and God's Image Barbering. We also saw a large poster promoting condom use to prevent the spread of HIV. It depicted a vaguely phallic cylindrical drawing with the caption, "If it's not on, it's not in." We saw several women balancing large metal buckets of water on their heads, a man balancing a tall bundle of folded T-shirts on his head, and young children running around giggling. In the distance, several goats and chickens roamed freely.

We searched for a villager who spoke English. Although English is the official national language and public signs are written in it, many Ghanaians speak only various native languages. Everyone we met smiled and waved at us but spoke almost no English; they spoke Twi or Ewe (pronounced *Twee* and *EH-way*), regional African languages. Eventually, we found a man who spoke English. He turned out to be the headmaster of the village school.

When we explained to him that we wanted to know about the first president of Ghana, he was more than happy to educate us. "The first president was Kwame Nkrumah. He became president in 1957 when Ghana became independent from England. He was loved by his people."

Years later, I learned that Nkrumah had embodied anticolonialism and Pan-Africanism. He would often repeat, "The independence of Ghana is meaningless until it is linked to the total liberation of Africa." He challenged the paternalistic narrative that maintained that European colonialism was good for Africans and that Africans needed it to develop.

Although many Ghanaians I met expressed admiration and support for Nkrumah, I never felt from them any animosity as a result of America's alleged support for the overthrow of their beloved leader. This reminded me of the total lack of animosity felt toward me as an American when I visited Vietnam for a week on my way home from Singapore. It seems this kind of hatred is a luxury poor countries cannot afford.

The schoolmaster spoke with a strong West African accent, pronouncing and elongating each syllable, the linguistic equivalent of savoring every last morsel of marrow from a soup bone.

Without thinking about it, I started to mimic the accent of the headmaster. After saying goodbye to him, Tamar turned to me and said, "It's politically incorrect and offensive to mimic someone's accent."

I hadn't consciously thought about mimicking him. I just did it as a way to feel closer to him. I certainly meant no harm. But now I felt embarrassed to be called out and used a derogatory term to express my dismissal of her idea.

She responded, "You shouldn't say that, either. It makes fun of people who have a disability." My reeducation still had quite a way to go.

The next morning, we started on the building project. The building site didn't look like much. It was a large circle of overturned dirt surrounded by green grass and trees. The village supplied an experienced builder and a contingent of men and women who would help us with the many tasks involved.

We worked every day, Monday through Friday, from eight in the morning till noon. Past noon it was dangerously hot to work outside. Except for one volunteer in our group—who was more than six feet tall and had broad shoulders—none of us was especially well suited for manual labor. But we worked hard and we worked together and within a few weeks, it was possible to see the outline of the future library: a large structure with four rooms and many open spaces for windows.

I was especially proud of the countless buckets of sand I had schlepped on my head and the countless times I had swung a pickax while digging the hole. All this was done under the unremitting blaze of the African sun. It turned out this job was considerably more arduous than putting together our sukkah in Brooklyn.

We took many breaks while working on the building project to hydrate and catch our breath. As we worked, a small group of local kids would inevitably gather around the worksite, mesmerized by our presence. They pointed and shouted, "Oburoni, oburoni," the Twi word for foreigner. It literally means "Those who come from over the horizon" and is used colloquially to refer to white people.

These kids had never in their lives seen white people before in person. They inched toward us and reached out to touch our white skin, the way we as children would pet sheep at the zoo. The adult villagers shooed the kids away. But I didn't mind them petting me. I wondered whether this was how Black people in America felt when white people tried to feel their Afros.

Despite the language barrier, all of the members of my group got along wonderfully with all of the Ghanaians we worked with on the building project. This was no Tower of Babel. So it was disturbing, especially to the women in the group, when a young man from the village showed up to work one morning wearing a white T-shirt with large black letters proclaiming in English: "I screw on the first date." The women in our group found the shirt "sketchy," a term I had never heard before.

After much discussion in our house about whether we should confront the man about his shirt or just let it be, Yigal, who spoke passable Ewe, went to investigate. He returned with a smirk on his face. It turned out the man spoke no English and had no idea what his shirt said—and that it was donated by an American evangelical Christian charity.

The villagers were pleased that we cared enough to travel to Ghana to learn about their society and help out. They showed their gratitude by bringing us bushels of yellow bananas and armfuls of delicious mangos. For villagers who barely had enough to feed their families, this was real generosity. We felt guilty taking such gifts, but we accepted them, not wanting to offend.

Once as we were about to finish working, a group of men approached. One man was leading a scrawny-looking goat by a string. They said that they were going to slaughter the goat and give us the meat.

No one in our group was excited about this prospect. Not the vegans, not the kosher-only crew, not the health code enthusiasts. No one. But how does one decline a gift—and such a generous one, at that—without giving offence? Yigal thanked them for the gift and said that we wanted to share it with the village. The men agreed to eat the meat themselves, but not before getting Yigal to agree to drink a cup of *ak-*

peteshie, Ghanaian moonshine produced from distilled palm wine. He reported back to us later that it tasted to him like jet fuel.

Each evening after we finished eating the delicious dinners prepared for us—one of the cook's specialties was "red red," a traditional Ghanaian dish of slow-cooked black-eyed peas and tomatoes served with fried plantains—we had some downtime before we needed to crawl into our mosquito net–protected mattresses on the floor and go to sleep. At this time of night, the village was usually quiet, but on occasion the stillness would be broken by loud cries and the pounding of drums from nearby funeral ceremonies, which could go on for days.

Some of the women in the group used the evenings to write in their journals. I used evenings mostly to read and think. I thought about my engagement with Jewish rituals. I was willing to continue to do some of them but was desperate to remove the burden of obligation that, I felt, weighed so heavily on me. However, just as it is difficult to divert a long-standing stream from its accustomed path, it was difficult for me to stop performing the Jewish rituals I was accustomed to perform.

I had put on *tefillin* every day for ten years, in all weather and on five other continents. I brought my two pairs of *tefillin*, the one that follows the requirements of the medieval commentator Rashi (which is the most common form of *tefillin* for Jews around the world) and the one that follows the requirements of his grandson Rabbeinu Tam (which is used by Sephardim and Hasidim and only as a supplement to the Rashi *tefillin*).

I put on both sets of *tefillin* each morning before we went to work, pacing the porch of our home and gazing at the sleeping village. I am quite certain that *tefillin*, and especially Rabbeinu Tam's, had never before been donned in the village of Gbi Kpeme.

It was as foreign to me to be living in a house surrounded by young liberal Jewish men and women as it was to be living among Africans. The Ghanaians were not attuned to the subtle denominational differences between the other white Americans and me. My fellow volunteers, however, were acutely aware that as a bearded ultra-Orthodox man, I was out of place in a pluralistic Jewish program. Still, while they marveled at my ignorance of basic American pop culture—I didn't know a Red Hot Chili Pepper from a Dixie Chick—they were extremely kind and welcoming to me.

Although the group wasn't especially religiously observant, every Friday night after we had taken our freezing showers and put on the most presentable outfits we could scrounge up, we held services that consisted of a drum circle and communal singing, men and women together, of the highlights of the Friday night liturgy.

I had never prayed together with women before, so it was jarring at first, but the harmony of the different voices made it beautiful and stirring. After the service, one of us would recite the kiddush over wine—the only exception to the no-alcohol-on-the-trip rule. I resisted reciting the kiddush—although, given my background, I was an obvious candidate—lest someone in the group think I was a crypto-Lubavitch agent trying to missionize.

In an effort to get to know the people in Gbi Kpeme better, a group of us decided to attend the Sunday services at Oklahoma Faith Temple Church. The service took place in a large gazebo-like structure with a tin roof. The church was packed with many parishioners of all ages. My friends and I were the only white faces in the crowd.

The fear of churches that I had felt as a second-grader in Crown Heights—and even as a teenager in Moscow—was gone, replaced by a deep curiosity to see how others practiced their faith. The Ghanian church proved remarkable to me for being simultaneously so different and yet so similar to the prayer services I had grown up with.

The pastor preached in Ewe and translated his sermon into English for our benefit. Every time he said, "Jesus Christ, our Lord and Savior"—a phrase he managed to drop into almost every sentence—it sounded to my ultra-Orthodox ears like fingernails clawing on a chalkboard. And yet, when the sermon was over and the service resumed, the faithful sang and danced around the tent with great feeling. It was not unlike the way my yeshiva friends and I used to dance around the synagogue years ago on Friday nights to welcome the *Shekhinah*, the feminine aspect of God.

Our group didn't limit our learning to visiting churches. We also wanted to check out the village shaman. When Leah, an anthropology major at Yale, came down with a stomachache and nausea and was in need of some kind of intervention, we gleefully jumped at the opportunity it presented.

Our entire group trekked to the shaman's home-temple with its sky-blue-painted walls, beside which stood a cement altar spattered with dried sacrificial chicken blood. The shaman, in contrast to most of the men in the village, who wore Western-style clothing, greeted us wearing a black-and-white-striped dashiki.

A gray-haired man in his fifties, the shaman spoke no English. Nevertheless, he smiled and gestured to us that we should sit down on the chairs that were arranged in a circle in the courtyard beside his home. He asked in Ewe what concerned us. Yigal, serving as translator, explained that we were all Jews from America but that we wanted to see a shaman at work and that Leah was suffering from stomach pains. The shaman listened and then unrolled a blue-and-yellow woven rug and placed it on the floor. On top of the rug he placed several handfuls of small objects, including rocks, seashells, pieces of wood, leather, a large chicken bone, and three beaded necklaces with black stones.

Looking at the shaman and the rug, I was reminded of the biblical story of King Saul, who visited a witch doctor to speak to the dead, despite the repeated and emphatic biblical prohibitions against engaging in the occult. My excitement mounted. This was thrilling.

Thanks to popular media I'd experienced, I was expecting the shaman to play the drums, dance wildly, and enter some kind of trance state. Instead, he grasped two of the rocks and one of the seashells from the rug, closed his eyes, and recited several prayers beseeching the ancestors for Leah's recovery. He then opened his eyes and said that Leah's stomach troubles would be gone by the next morning.

In fact, Leah's troubles were not gone by the next morning. After another day passed with no relief, Yigal drove her three hours to the regional capital and had her examined at the hospital, where she was diagnosed with a stomach flu. She was told that it would clear up on its own by the end of the week.

We never went back to the shaman to report the failure of his prediction, but I wondered how he would have reacted if we had. Would he have shrugged and conceded that not all of his predictions come to fruition, or would he have blamed us for not believing sufficiently in the efficacy of his prayers, thus diminishing their potency and reliability?

Thinking back to Crown Heights, I wondered how many people didn't report back to their friends and families when the Rebbe's blessings failed to materialize. If the faithful only report back in cases where the prediction came true, this could certainly create a false impression that all the predictions were accurate.

Two weeks before our departure from Ghana, our group made a pilgrimage to the Cape Coast Castle, a fortress that was used by Europeans to house captured Africans who would then be shipped to the Americas as part of the transatlantic slave trade. The fortress was built in 1653 and had changed hands numerous times as the European powers fought among themselves for possession of this lucrative part of Africa.

On the day of our visit, the cloudless azure sky was radiant and the turquoise Gulf of Guinea that surrounds the castle and brushes up against its outer perimeter glistened. The violent disjuncture between the horrors associated with the castle and the natural beauty that envelops it grated. How could a hellish place like this be ringed by such splendor? Did this disjuncture compound the trauma of those captives doomed to languish here?

I was reminded of a passage from a Holocaust memoir by a labor camp inmate who described marching with his work battalion through a field on a magnificent summer day on their way back to their barracks. The field, bursting with verdant foliage, was indifferent to the angel of death lurking nearby.

After six weeks in Gbi Kpeme, our departure from Ghana loomed. The village decided to hold a formal farewell ceremony in our honor. At the designated time, several hundred villagers—men, women, and children—gathered in front of our house, along with a troop of musicians hauling blue-and-white *jembe* (massive rawhide-covered wood drums), a *shekere* (a gourd covered in a net of woven beads), and a *karignan* (a tubular bell). We fell in with them and were paraded through the village to the ceremony accompanied by enthusiastic singing.

The ceremony was held outdoors in a clearing on the edge of the village. The tribal chief of the village, draped in bright kente cloth, made a speech thanking us for all our contributions to the village and assuring us that the library would be completed by the villagers. He then took a bowl of wine and poured it on the ground as a libation to the ancestors.

The highlight of the ceremony occurred when the chief wrapped a blue-and-white sash around the head of Aviva, our group leader, and proclaimed her an honorary chief of the village tribe. The queen mother, the first lady of the village, dressed in a purple robe and two very long beaded necklaces, placed a blue sash around the necks of each group member. The sash was embroidered with orange letters that read, "Gbi Kpeme Thanks You."

At the end of the ceremony, the musicians took up their instruments again, and the crowd broke into a spirited dance. Some of our group members joined. I stood on the side and soaked it in. One lady in her seventies with a green-and-red kerchief around her head noticed me standing alone. She grabbed my hands and pulled me into the dance circle and twirled me around. I had never danced with a woman before in my life. As I clasped her firm wrinkled hands, I was preoccupied with a single thought: I look so foolish dancing with a woman in public.

"Is there a *kohen* in the house?" asked the *gabbai*, the synagogue leader, at Altshul, a liberal Jewish community-run prayer group in Park Slope, Brooklyn. The group balanced the traditional liturgy with gender egalitarianism. The prayer group didn't have a permanent location, so it would meet each week at the home of another member. The *gabbai* was looking for a *kohen*, a descendent of the priests of the ancient Jerusalem Temple, to honor with the first *aliya*, the first person to be called up to the Torah. By that time, five months had passed since my return from Ghana. In the interim, I had become close friends with Tamar, who had moved to Brooklyn and was working as a community organizer.

Tamar took me to protests organized by Jews for Racial and Economic Justice, a progressive group fighting for housing rights, employee unionization, and immigration reform. The organization also demonstrated against police brutality. She invited me to Friday night dinners and introduced me to Altshul.

Tamar once took me shopping for hip clothes at Urban Outfitters but told me not to purchase a train conductor hat, cute as she found it, fearing that "people might not get that you're wearing it ironically." She also tried to coach me to remove the grammatically incorrect Yiddishisms from my lexicon, such as, "I ate *by*," instead of, "I ate *at*." It was a bit too "My Fair Lubavitcher" for me, so I gave up the elocution lessons.

That morning at Altshul, Tamar was sitting next to me and, without asking, pointed at me and said, "He's a *kohen*." I was indeed a *kohen*, but I panicked. I was about to be called up to the Torah and have a woman read the Torah following my blessing. I was scared to death.

I thought back to what a Lubavitch rabbi had told me in high school about liberal Judaism. He said, "Like doctors playing golf, they're still doctors but they're not practicing medicine. So, too, liberal Jews are fully Jews but what they're practicing isn't Judaism." I was only starting to overcome this deep hostility to liberal forms of Judaism, and now I was to be at the ritual center of a liberal service—with a female reader standing just inches from me.

I also thought back to the first time I had ever seen women wearing yarmulkes and prayer shawls. It was a Shabbos morning and I was nine years old. I was praying with my father at the Lubavitch central synagogue at 770 Eastern Parkway when Moshe, a friend from school, asked me, "Wanna see something totally crazy?"

"For sure," I said.

I snuck away from my father and followed Moshe across the street to our school, Oholei Torah. We crept up the wide marble staircase to the second floor and peeked into the small sanctuary. What I saw made me doubt my own eyes. There, sitting in the pews where my classmates and I would pray the afternoon service every weekday, were fifteen elderly men and women sitting together, all clad in yarmulkes and prayer shawls.

What are these goyim doing in our yeshivah? Why are these goyim wearing yarmulkes and tallasim?

It was as if we had penetrated some mysterious barrier—like Harry Potter's arrival at Platform 9¾ at King's Cross Station for Hogwarts—and entered an alternate universe where up was down and down was up and none of the usual rules held true.

How could men and women pray sitting together, or women wear yarmulkes and prayer shawls, or a woman lead services? What were they doing in our school? Only years later did I learn that part of the agreement when the building, formerly the famous progressive Brooklyn Jewish Center, was sold to Lubavitch was that a liberal prayer service would be allowed to continue Saturday mornings for the handful of remaining members.

Now here I was, inside the very alternate universe I had stood gaping at nearly fifteen years before. I felt that time had collapsed and my younger self was staring incredulously at my older self. *What are you doing with these* meshugenas? My older self wanted to grab my younger self and hug him tightly and whisper that the Judaism these people were practicing was as authentic as the Judaism practiced in Lubavitch. I wanted to tell him that I no longer believe the horrible things I was told years earlier about egalitarian Judaism—and that neither should he.

They called out my Hebrew name and I went up to the Torah for my *aliyah*, as I had done so many times before. I grasped the fringes of my *tallis* (prayer shawl) and touched it to the spot where the reader would begin, dragged it down to the end of the portion to be read, and kissed the fringes. I recited the blessing with my *tallis* over my head and my eyes closed, in the Ashkenazi accent that was foreign to everyone in the room but was the only way I knew how.

As time passed and I thought over my trip to Ghana, I knew that I had gone there to help and learn about Africa. But a major outcome of my trip was the opportunity to explore up close the liberal Jewish lives of my fellow volunteers. Just as Uncle Jeff had introduced me to the unknown world of secular books and Rebecca had introduced me to academic inquiry and higher education, Tamar had introduced me to egalitarian and progressive Judaism.

Through Tamar and her circle of friends I encountered non-Orthodox Jews who were spiritually and intellectually engaged in Judaism, minus the superstition. They connected their practice of Judaism to social justice and repairing the world. I started to realize that Judaism didn't have to be an all-or-nothing proposition. It was possible to embrace and cherish the parts that spoke to me while discarding the parts that didn't.

I was starting to feel as if I could be a part of the liberal Jewish world. But despite sporting new blue jeans that I had bought with Uncle Jeff at Sam's Club, I still had a beard down to my chest. Everyone knew what my beard signified. I yearned to be able to go incognito and look the part I longed to play. But with a full beard, I still had the ability to slip back into the Lubavitch camp without drawing the attention of the neighbors and thus the ire of my mother. Trimming my beard would be a public declaration of desertion from the Rebbe's army. Could I live with that?

13

The Beard Crisis

"I hate my beard," I complained to Rebecca during one of our regular hour-long phone conversations between Brooklyn and Singapore. Rebecca was still a professor at the National University of Singapore, and I was two semesters shy of graduating from Brooklyn College with a bachelor's degree in psychology. It was 9 o'clock on a cold November night, and I was pacing the floor of Bubby Ruth's small kitchen. I kept warm by wearing a brown plaid shirt covered by a black fleece, both hand-me-downs from Uncle Jeff's wardrobe.

"What is it about your beard that makes you hate it?" Rebecca gently probed.

I thought for a minute. "I was always taught that Jewish law forbids men to shave or trim their beards, and that this prohibition is as binding as the prohibition against eating pork."

The prohibition against cutting the beard is based on a verse in Leviticus (19:27) that states, "Ye shall not round the corners of your heads [the sidelocks], neither shalt thou mar the corners of thy beard." Although historically some rabbis interpreted this verse to afford leeway so their followers could shave their beards, Hasidim in general and Lubavitch in particular rejected this approach. According to the third Lubavitcher Rebbe, the Tzemach Tzedek, the prohibition against shaving is based on the biblical law against men resembling women, and thus any means of removing the hair (even indirect ones, such as with the aid of chemical depilatories) is strictly forbidden.

I told Rebecca, “I was also taught that according to kabbalah the beard has thirteen parts, and these correspond to the thirteen attributes of God’s mercy and that a beard is a source of spiritual blessings. But I don’t believe that. I think it just marks me as an ultra-Orthodox Jew, even though I’m really not one anymore.”

When I finished my answer, Rebecca didn’t respond. I realized the call had disconnected. This happened so frequently to us that we used to joke that either the Singaporean government or Lubavitch headquarters was dropping our calls because they were too subversive. I redialed Rebecca. “They’re at it again, dropping our calls.”

Rebecca laughed.

“Where did I lose you?”

“I heard you say something about your beard marking you.”

“Oh, OK. I was saying that the beard just marks me as an ultra-Orthodox Jew even though I’m really not one anymore.”

“If you’re so dissatisfied with your beard, why do you still keep it? There must be something that keeps you from just shaving it off.”

“I guess. I know that shaving my beard would be considered scandalous in my community and all the yentas would be squawking about it. But I would be OK with that if I knew that I was going to marry a woman from outside and leave the community. But if I was going to end up marrying someone from inside, then I would need to grow it back and somehow pretend that I was sorry for shaving it off. I wish I knew which way my life would play out in order to know if I should shave or not.”

“The thing is, Zalman, your story will end up differently based on how you appear. In other words, people will respond differently to you if you have a long beard and they think you are Orthodox from how they will if you are clean-shaven and they realize you aren’t.”

Rebecca paused to catch her breath. “I think you would get a lot out of Borges’s short story ‘The Garden of Forking Paths,’” she continued. “Borges describes Ts’ui Pên’s intricate novel where a universe is imagined that contains all the contradictions of limitless unfolding possibilities. Every fork in the road of life leads to other forks in the road, to other options, and still others. But in the finite world we inhabit, it’s impossible to know all the different permutations in advance. We only come to know the options that result from the paths we choose—not the ones we decided not to take."

For weeks, I returned to Rebecca's words. They made sense. But my thoughts would inevitably fixate on the pain I would be causing my mother, in particular, if I did something so extreme and so public as to shave my beard. Even elephants show compassion for their parents and try to protect them from harm. *Was I less feeling than these hulking beasts?*

Walking around with my untrimmed reddish-brown beard brushing past my collarbones and my large black velvet yarmulke, I felt like an ornate synagogue adorned with marble pillars and fine stained glass—but devoid of worshippers. My insides did not match my outsides.

I thought about the story of the fifth Lubavitcher Rebbe, the Rebbe Rashab, who lived in the town of Lubavitch, in Russia. He had a follower who lived in St. Petersburg who would visit him on the high holidays. The follower used to wear a long black coat in Lubavitch, but in cosmopolitan St. Petersburg he wore a short, Western-style jacket. Eventually, the follower felt uncomfortable switching back and forth, so the next time he visited Lubavitch he wore the short jacket. When the Rebbe Rashab saw this, he commented, "I always thought that you were fooling Petersburg. Now I see that you were fooling Lubavitch!"

One Friday afternoon I tried to prepare my mother for the possibility that I might shave. Armed with what was, in my judgment, literary dynamite, I came into the kitchen holding a copy of Kahlil Gibran's 1923 book, *The Prophet.* My mother was sitting, chopping carrots and onions for chicken soup. Chop, chop, chop. I began, like a rabbi quoting the Talmud, with the following passage from Gibran:

> Your children are not your children. They are the sons and daughters of Life's longing for itself. . . .
>
> You may give them your love but not your thoughts, for they have their own thoughts.
>
> You may house their bodies but not their souls, for their souls dwell in the house of tomorrow, which you cannot visit, not even in your dreams.

How could she possibly counter the beauty and power of Gibran's words? She didn't look up from her cutting board or even stop cutting. Chop, chop, chop. Her only reply was, "Did he have any children?"

A quick Google search revealed the unfortunate news that the only progeny he left in this world were books of poetry and paintings. With that, Gibran was disqualified. So much for easing the blow of my imminent shaving.

My beard caused me constant pain. It wasn't just when I looked in the mirror or when I touched my face. I felt like I was living a lie. A few weeks after the Gibran debacle, when I could no longer bear it, alone in Bubby Ruth's house I took a sharp pair of scissors and walked into her small, creaky upstairs bathroom.

I trimmed the edges of my beard. My hands shook. I couldn't imagine going any further. I left the beard mostly intact, but for the first time since it grew in when I was a teenager, it looked neat. I trimmed the bottom so it looked rounded, rather than scraggly and uneven.

I returned the scissors and went to bed, terrified of the fallout that awaited me. My college classmates would see what I had done. Although only some of them were Orthodox, and even they didn't have beards, I worried that they would be critical of my decision to openly change my religious status. Plus, when I visited Crown Heights my face would betray that I had transgressed one of God's fundamental commands.

And I was a coward. I couldn't shave it all off. I felt like a surgeon who freezes under the pressure and takes out only part of the tumor, knowing he'll have to reopen the patient later and remove the rest, enduring the pressure and dangers all over again.

The next day I went to class at Brooklyn College, expecting to get a tongue lashing. But much to my surprise, not a single person noticed what I had done. I was shocked and relieved. A possible explanation came from my psychology class: People see what they expect to see rather than what is actually in front of their eyes.

The surgery had to be completed. I took up the scissors again a few days later and started chopping off huge chunks, like a forester trying to clear away the underbrush in a dense jungle. Snip, snip, snip. The small sink was filling up with trimmings. I hadn't realized just how much hair there was on my face. Even after chopping away for ten minutes, my face still had clumps of hair. It was not the polished look I had fantasized about.

I looked in the medicine cabinet and found the package of disposable razors and shaving cream I now remembered buying a few months earlier, kicking myself at the time for thinking I had the courage to use them. I had only seen people shave in the movies, but it seemed simple enough. It wasn't. By the time I finished shaving off the last patch of stubble, I had nicked myself so many times that my twenty-four-year-old face looked like a war zone.

Beneath the wreckage, I had also discovered a birthmark on my right cheek that had lain dormant for so long that I'd forgotten it was there. I felt like my body was floating up into the air now that the tonnage of my beard had been removed. I was dizzy with joy.

The mirror kept surprising me. I had to familiarize myself again and again with my own face. I looked younger. I had a jawline. I didn't look Lubavitch anymore. My beard had covered up more than a third of my face for a decade. I was a child before that. This was the first time I was seeing my own face as an adult. It took a while for it to stop seeming like a stranger's face.

My hand would continue grasping for my missing beard, surprised that there was nothing past my chin to hold on to. But my beard had been like a limb that was no longer getting oxygen, so it needed to be cut off or it would jeopardize the rest of my healthy body.

I wasn't the only one who didn't recognize me. On campus the next day my best friends walked right past me. When it dawned on them and they realized what I had done—when they overheard me talking to someone—they came running over, screaming:

"Oh my God! You shaved your beard!"

"Dude! What happened to your beard!"

"Whoa, Zalman!"

Most of my friends and acquaintances, even the Orthodox ones, were supportive. The only exception was Anna, an attractive Russian Jewish woman who was involved in Jewish cultural programs on campus. Anna said, "You shouldn't have shaved. You're changing who you were born to be."

I was furious at her. She wasn't even Orthodox. She didn't have to carry the burden of Orthodox Jewish law. And now she was lecturing me? The best response I could come up with was, "You shouldn't have left Russia. You're changing who you were born to be." She walked away. That was the last time we spoke.

Anna had rattled me, but I knew it was nothing compared with what lay in store for me from my mother. Since I was planning to go home for Shabbos in a few days, I decided I needed to tell her the news on the phone. I didn't want her exploding at me in person.

I called her on my cell as I paced outside of James Hall and watched my fellow college students rush to class. I got straight to the point. "Mommy, I need to tell you something."

"What happened?"

"I . . . I . . . shaved . . . my . . . beard," I fumbled.

"*Dammit jerk, why did you do that?*" she screamed. Then I heard a click, and the line went dead. My mother had hung up on me. I stood there in shock. She had never hung up on me before. No one had ever hung up on me before. How was I supposed to deal with this, and what did this mean for our Shabbos plans?

Several minutes went by. I heard my phone ring. It was my mother again. I hoped that maybe she had been able to get hold of her emotions and apologize for hanging up on me. "That's it, Zalman. I'm so angry with you I don't want to see you again. I want you to take your stuff out of the house on Sunday when I'm not home and I don't want you to come back. You want your own life—*mazal tov*, you've got it. Good luck with your new life." Click.

I stood in front of James Hall. Tears rolled down my cheeks. My body was shaking. I felt like a Lubavitch mitzvah tank, one of those converted Winnebagos, had just rolled over my chest. As I walked the mile and a half to Bubby Ruth's house, my mind raced.

I knew Mommy would be angry that I shaved my beard. But I didn't think she would try to disown me. Would she ever let me back home? Would she prevent me from contacting Tatty and my siblings? Now I hate, hate, hated Mommy. What kind of mother throws out her son because he decides to be a little less religious than her? I was not on drugs, and I didn't kill anyone. I just wanted to make decisions about my own life. Was that such a horrible thing to want? How could Mommy just turn on me and throw me out like a bag of garbage? I wish Mommy had never joined this fanatic community that caused her to throw out her own son just for shaving his beard. Mommy wanted me to stay Lubavitch so that somehow her sacrifice of becoming Lubavitch, giving up on a career as a psychologist and instead bearing and raising nine children, would be worth it. It was not my job to make Beth Robin Janus from a broken family in Queens feel as if she was now a real Lubavitcher, a true Lubavitch matriarch at the head of a tribe of upstanding Lubavitch children.

As the child of *baal teshuvah* parents I understood that my siblings and I represented the fulfillment of our parents' religious hopes and dreams. I understood that it must be extremely painful for my mother to hear that I had rejected the religious life that she envisioned for me and had worked tirelessly to inculcate. But still, what kind of parent throws her own child out of her house over a religious infraction? What kind of Lubavitcher does that?

Thousands of Lubavitchers around the world welcomed non-Orthodox Jews into their homes, and now my own mother—who was herself once welcomed into Lubavitch homes when she didn't observe Jewish law—threw me out just because I had shaved?

January and February were bitter cold that year, but they didn't compare with the frosty silence that set in between my mother and me. As I completed my last semester of college, I regularly talked to my father on the phone. He was pleasant and even-tempered, as usual. I knew that my father would have allowed me to come home but was unwilling to stand up to my mother and insist on it. I was thankful that my father was still talking to me but was deeply hurt that he didn't protect me from my mother's religious zeal. What kind of father allows his wife to kick their son out of their home? What kind of man allows his wife to walk all over him without a peep of protest?

I used these conversations with my father to gauge my mother's temperature. The signs weren't good. When the holiday of Purim arrived, it had been two months since I'd seen her, and I decided it had gone on too long. I called up my father and said I wanted to come over for the Purim meal. He said he would have to speak to my mother and suggested, "Since everyone puts on costumes on Purim, maybe you can put on a fake beard. That way it won't be so noticeable that you shaved." I think he was joking, but I also understood that my parents just wanted to cover over what had happened rather than deal with it.

A few days later, my father reported, "I mentioned to Mommy your idea of coming for Purim and she didn't say anything. She didn't accept it or reject it. I think you should come."

On the day of Purim, I arrived and was greeted warmly by my father and siblings. We stood in the dining room and talked for twenty minutes. My mother was in the kitchen preparing the holiday feast. No one said anything, but I felt as if there was an invisible line—one that separated the dining room from the kitchen—beyond which I shouldn't pass for my own sake. Eventually my father called out gently, "Mommy dear, we have a special visitor."

My mother emerged. In honor of the holiday, she was decked out in a pink wig and a colorful Mexican poncho. She took one look at me and said with a smirk, "I heard Zalman's voice, but I don't see him. Where's Zalman?"

"Very funny, Mommy. I'm right here," I said and kissed her on the cheek. She didn't flinch but accepted it with as much warmth as a cold marble statue would accept a kiss.

She looked me over again. "I really don't recognize you. I want to grab you and shake you out of this. This is not who you really are." As if I were an Etch A Sketch on which a child had scribbled a messy set of mistakes, I just needed a few good shakes.

Although my Purim visit broke the ice, it had hardly resolved anything. My mother told me, "I love you, but I don't know if I should let you keep on visiting. Every time I look at you, it hurts me. And I'm worried about the negative effect you could have on the younger children." I had shaved my beard four months after Yossi shaved his, and my mother blamed him for my transgression. Now she was nervous that our corruption would spread to our younger siblings.

She started to push the idea that Yossi and I should go with her to a rabbi who would "set us straight." Every time she used that phrase, I thought of conversion therapy for gay people and felt that both forms of "therapy" were equally doomed to fail and equally unethical. Still, I wanted to be welcomed in my childhood home, and she wanted this, so I agreed to go see Rabbi Minsky, my former middle school teacher.

On the appointed day, as we sat finishing our breakfast of bagels and cream cheese in the kitchen, my mother exclaimed, "Remember, Yossi and Zalman, not to say anything embarrassing or inappropriate when speaking to Rabbi Minsky." Yossi and I could discuss our "problems" with our Lubavitch upbringing as long as we didn't say anything heretical or scandalous. Gazing down at us from the walls of the kitchen were three 8 × 10 framed black-and-white pictures of the Rebbe.

When Yossi and I made a last attempt to wiggle out of this meeting, my mother, whose headscarf was slightly askew, revealing a few escaped strands of her brown hair that now showed signs of graying, raised both hands as if to push back with physical force any opposition. "Stop this *nareschkeit.* We need to go to Rabbi Minsky because," she said, tears flowing down her cheeks, her voice quivering, "you are not acting like proper Lubavitchers. I can't talk to you boys about this stuff. It's tearing at my heart. I already lost Shimmy to cancer, now you two . . ."

I was horrified by my mother comparing our religious evolution to Shimmy's death. I wanted to scream at the top of my lungs: *Mommy, we are still alive! We are standing right in front of you. Why can't you see that we are the same people you loved and nurtured all those years.* But I couldn't say a word. Fighting back tears, I kept my silence.

My mother blew her nose and wiped her eyes with a tissue. "I can't answer all your questions, but it's obvious that you boys are in serious trouble and need help. That's why we are going to Rabbi Minsky. End of discussion."

I suddenly felt a deep connection to my mother's father, Pops. His mother also schlepped him to a rabbi to straighten him out of his secular activities, instructing him not to mention in front of the rabbi that he danced with women, which he promptly did as soon as he got talking with the rabbi.

My mother, my father, Yossi, and I piled into our family's champagne-colored Chrysler minivan for the hour-and-a-half trek from Brooklyn to the Hasidic hamlet of Monsey, in Rockland County, New York.

No one said a word the whole trip. Rabbi Minsky met us at the door with a smile and ushered us through his silent house, past the rows of bookcases groaning under the weight of classical rabbinic texts and through his kitchen, with its requisite twin sinks for meat and dairy dishes, and onto the back porch, where a table and chairs were set up.

Rabbi Minsky sat at the head of the table, my mother and father sat on one side, and Yossi and I sat on the other. I was shocked to notice that Rabbi Minsky's brown beard had turned mostly grey. Was this transformation due to the passage of years or to the stress of multiple confrontations like this with his former students?

After brief pleasantries, Rabbi Minsky asked: "Tell me, what's on your minds?" My mother began, "We are here because Yossi and Zalman are out of control. They shaved their beards, they don't *daven* [pray] anymore, and who knows what else they're up to."

Rabbi Minsky stroked his beard for a moment and then said, "Every illness has a source that causes it. Sometimes it's viral, sometimes it's bacterial. In order to understand how to treat the illness, the doctor has to determine the cause. What do you think is the cause of these behaviors?"

"I know the cause," my mother said in triumph, like a schoolgirl who is convinced she knows the answer to the teacher's question. "It's those *goyishe* books the boys keep on reading."

Rabbi Minsky turned to Yossi and me and, in a supercilious tone, inquired, "Velcher bichelach laynts du [What little books are you reading]?"

I was shocked that he would be so dismissive of our reading without even knowing what it was. "The little books I'm reading are from Aristotle, Spinoza, and Karl Marx," I said coldly. "I'm attracted to how they make sense of their world through physical observation rather than supernatural explanations."

"Nu [So]?" Rabbi Minsky retorted.

"So the point is," I began, trying to hold back my hurt feelings, "I've read a lot and I've come to see things differently. Just because I was raised a certain way to believe in *Hashem* and his Torah doesn't mean that I always have to believe this way. It's a free country, and I'm free to believe and act as I see fit."

"You're right, Zalmy," said Rabbi Minsky, calling me by the same diminutive form of my name that he used when I was twelve. "It's a free country, and you're free to choose what to believe and how to act, but true freedom is when you master your base instincts and accept the *oyl malchus shamayim* [yoke of the Kingdom of Heaven]. This ability to master our base instincts is what separates us from animals. A dog feels the urge to relieve itself in the gutter, so he does. Is that the kind of freedom you want for yourself?"

I sat there speechless and stared at Rabbi Minsky. I was so mad I could have put my hand through a glass window. I could not believe his chutzpah to compare my thoughtful rejection of Orthodox Judaism, based on years of reading and reflection, to a dog shitting in the street.

And to imply that my rejection of my Lubavitch upbringing was all due to rampant base desires! This strategy of the pious to malign freethinkers as enthralled to lust is nothing new. Epicurus, the rationalist ancient Greek philosopher and the origin of the Hebrew term *apikorus* (heretic), was and is often wrongly portrayed as a proponent of hedonism just because he encouraged his students to focus on happiness and peace in this lifetime.

Rabbi Minsky saw I was stung, so he changed course: "Tell me, do you believe in God?"

"No."

"Do you put on *tefillin*?"

"Sometimes."

Suddenly Rabbi Minsky got excited. He felt that he had caught me in one of his mental traps he was famous for springing on his unsuspecting students. "Wait a minute," he said with obvious relish. "If you believe in God, it makes sense why you would put black leather boxes with leather straps on your arm and head—because God commanded you to do so. But if you don't believe in God, it's a crazy thing to do."

"I do it because I find putting on *tefillin* a meaningful way to connect with past generations of Jews who did it—not because I believe in God."

"How can you find it meaningful to do an absurd thing?"

"Rabbi," I shouted, "how dare you tell me what I can and can't find meaningful!"

I didn't tell Rabbi Minsky that part of my motivation to keep putting on *tefillin* was out of a sense of solidarity with Jews of the past who were mocked by non-Jews for wearing *tefillin*—especially those bearded Jews draped in prayer shawls and wearing *tefillin* surrounded by young, jeering German soldiers in the grainy black-and-white Holocaust photos. I felt as if these Jews were telling me: "Do it for us. Stick it to the Germans!"

Rabbi Minsky pressed me on my *tefillin* practice because it touched a profound disagreement between us. My decision to put on *tefillin* even though I didn't believe in God meant that Judaism was something that I controlled and not something that controlled me. I thought of Judaism as a cultural treasure to enrich my life, not a master that held me hostage. I embraced the formulation of Rabbi Mordecai Kaplan, the founder of the liberal Reconstructionist form of Judaism, that the past "should have the right to a vote, but not the right to veto, in the determination of what we have to do to achieve salvation." Ultimately, I got to decide which parts I did and did not accept from the Jewish tradition.

For Rabbi Minsky, this was unfathomable and unacceptable. He viewed Jewish law as a "yoke," as something that must be borne regardless of one's personal feelings—just as the yoked oxen in the field don't choose where or when to plough.

After an hour of impassioned volleys back and forth, Rabbi Minsky said, "It's a terrible thing to fool oneself. Let's be honest. This is about you guys trying to take the easy way out, throwing off the yoke of Torah."

These words enraged me. I started to tear up. "You think this is about making my life easier? For God's sake, my life would be a lot easier if I stayed with the Lubavitch program and did what I was told to do. I wouldn't have to wake up every morning and struggle to figure out who I am. I wouldn't have to get kicked out of my parents' home. And I wouldn't need to deal with the shame of having everyone I grew up with pitying me: '*Nebach*, he's a *meshugener*.' The life I chose isn't easier. It's much harder, but it's the only way I can live."

The salvos continued for another hour. The rest is a blur. It became obvious eventually that we were speaking different languages and that it was not possible to have a meaningful dialogue. My mother and Rabbi Minsky were trying to rewind history and force a different outcome. But such efforts were as futile, and as destructive, as trying to prevent a child's physical development by locking him up in a form-fitting iron suit.

One good thing to come out of the meeting was that Rabbi Minsky said my mother should allow us back in the house. But while we were at home, we were obliged to respect her religious sensibilities. We had to go to shul, wear a yarmulke, and not discuss our heretical ideas with anyone. Don't ask; don't tell.

When I was in yeshiva and a holiday break approached, I would feel a sadness descend upon me. Going home from yeshiva, I missed my buddies and longed to be back together with them. Once I returned to yeshiva, the sadness went away. But now, as I was graduating college and struggling with my religious identity, I started to feel completely enveloped by a sadness like a soaked blanket that clung to my body and pulled me down.

I felt terribly conflicted and uncertain—not about my belief in God or the Rebbe, but about whether I should leave Lubavitch, the only religious community and social circle I had ever known. Would I find another Jewish community where I would feel at home? Would I be forced to disconnect from my mother and my siblings? Would I be able to live as a person without a community, without a family? Maybe it was better to stay in Lubavitch even if I didn't believe any of it than to venture out and pay the price?

My mother fueled my anxiety and inner turmoil. She would constantly report to me that she met such and such friend of mine and he looked like a proper Lubavitcher. "I saw Dovid at the Hershkowitz's wedding last night. He has such a nice long beard and he's going to be a rabbi in Florida. What a mensch. I bet his mother is very proud of him."

Each time she made these comments I felt a barbed hook digging into my flesh. When I was visiting her one night after she came home from a bar mitzvah, she reported that she had just met the mother of my friend Aryeh, who had also stopped being Orthodox. "Aryeh's mother told me that she accepts Aryeh for who he is. 'He's my son. I must love him even if I completely disagree with the choices he makes.'" My mother looked me straight in the face and said, "Just so you know, I will never accept you the way you are."

My mother would often taunt me with, "Are you happy now? Do you feel like your life is perfect since you shaved your beard?" These were unfair questions. It was like asking someone in the middle of getting a wisdom tooth pulled, "Do you feel happy now?" I was in a lot of pain but needed to go through this process. I looked forward to being happier once I settled down in my new life.

But at the moment, the pain from separating from my Lubavitch life and the anxiety of having no clear path ahead seemed unbearable. I thought of killing myself. For me, the thought of suicide was like an escape hatch in a dark and gloomy tunnel. Once I knew of the existence of the escape hatch, it proved difficult not to fantasize about availing myself of it whenever the pain of existence overwhelmed me.

The unthinkable had become a constant thought. I felt like the Hebrew letter *aleph*, whose two arms are pulled in opposite directions. I also thought of *kaf hakela*, the punishment the kabbalah says awaits people after death. In this torment, the soul is violently thrown back and forth through various mystical realms. I felt as if that was what I was going through at that moment—being thrown between my mother's love and the life I knew I wanted to live. I couldn't give up either.

I was physically healthy, employed by a social services organization that helped others, and the proud holder of a bachelor's degree, but none of that seemed to matter. Being in extreme pain narrowed my focus the way that a throbbing ingrown toenail makes you forget about the rest of your body. I was aware of only the immediate pain tearing me apart. It played tricks on me. Trapped in an endless dark void without even a glimmer of light, suicide seemed like the only option to escape the pain.

I didn't believe in God or an afterlife, so I didn't fear being punished for checking out early. I just felt that by ending my life I would put an end to all the turmoil in my soul. I never hatched a complete plan, but I did fantasize about it a lot, weighing the benefits of one stratagem versus another.

I thought of suicide as a means of getting away from the pain and suffering of religious turmoil and from a mother who rejected me. I also thought of it as a way to get back at her. I thought if I killed myself, then she would regret not accepting me.

Ironically, it was also because of my mother that I felt I shouldn't go through with it. It would be too cruel to pile on another dead son after Shimmy's death had already torn off a chunk of her heart.

During one of my phone conversations with Rebecca, I mentioned my thoughts of suicide. Rebecca suggested that I see a therapist. Although I had just graduated with a bachelor of arts in psychology and was planning to become a clinical psychologist, for some reason it had never occurred to me to see a shrink for my own problems.

I arranged to see a therapist through a Jewish social services organization. They set me up with a Modern Orthodox therapist named Jonathan. In our initial session, Jonathan asked me many questions, including the standard, "Have you had suicidal thoughts in the last month?"

I hesitated for a moment, then answered truthfully, "Yes."

Jonathan looked up from his notepad and with perfect calm said, "We should talk about that." I was shocked that he didn't freak out or immediately call for the ambulance to whisk me off to a psych ward. We just sat in his office and talked.

Jonathan, a graduate of Yeshiva University, wore a small black leather yarmulke atop his well-coiffed pompadour hairstyle, which is known in Lubavitch as a "chup." He exuded an attitude of "I'm Orthodox because it works for me, but I'm not here to try to convince you to stay Orthodox. I'm here to help you feel at peace with whatever choices you make." When he smiled, which was often, a bulging vein appeared running down his forehead, which added an exclamation point to his kindness.

Over the following months, and eventually over the next three years of weekly therapy sessions, Jonathan helped me to understand that I could not control what my mother thought any more than she could control what I thought and that I should not wait for her to accept me. That it was probably a fantasy that she would one day acknowledge that she was wrong to treat me the way she did. Jonathan helped me see that I would need to feel OK by myself, without her acceptance.

As I started to get a handle on my thoughts of suicide and generally started to feel much more positive about my life, I felt that if I could find a life partner to build a family with, I wouldn't be dependent on my mother's approval. I would be able to feel good about my own life choices. But where would I find someone who wanted to marry a person with so much religious and family baggage?

14

From Shidduch Dating to eHarmony

Parallel to my efforts to broaden my intellectual horizons, my college years were spent trying to lose my virginity. Once in yeshiva, I sat up late into the night in the study hall telling a classmate that I dreamed of having a girlfriend so we could walk down the street holding hands; I didn't need anything more. But as I got older, I started to feel as if I actually did want more. Only I had absolutely no inkling of how to obtain it.

On my first day at Brooklyn College, as I ambled across the grassy quad in the middle of the campus, I immediately felt inundated by the diversity of women at the school: I saw Muslim women, mostly of South Asian descent, wearing colorful hijabs with cell phones tucked inside, near their ears. I saw Russian women in tight jeans. I saw Black women with Afros and headscarves. I even saw Orthodox Jewish women whose floor-sweeping skirts and form-fitting tops technically followed Jewish modesty rules but were still extremely fashionable—*and unlike the women at every other stage of my life, they spoke to guys like me.*

Yet I felt clueless as to how to flirt with women. I was talkative enough and managed to become close friends with a few of the women I met, but I had no idea how to signal that I was interested in something more. These women could have come from a different galaxy as far as I was concerned.

Given these limitations, my dating life was less than a complete success. Once I went out to dinner with a classmate on what I thought was a "date," only to find out she was already happily married. Another time I asked a female friend whether she wanted to take our relationship to the next level. She had invited me to her apartment and made an elaborate dinner for me that included gazpacho, baked acorn squash, and chicken marsala, so this seemed like a logical question. Her response: "I thought about it. You're a nice guy, and you're not on drugs. But no."

What was wrong with me, I wondered? Did these women see me as a Hasidic eunuch who was safe to be friends with because I had no sexual desire of my own? I was sick of hearing, "You're so sweet! You're not like other guys! You're so easy to talk to!" I wanted to be seen as attractive, and even virile.

I needed guidance. I asked a female friend, and she suggested that I stop acting the clown and focus my attention on a single woman instead of on all the women in the room. These were interesting suggestions but involved the total overhaul of my entire personality at the time. A male friend suggested that I act more like a "shark" and use pickup-artist techniques such as wearing ostentatious clothing ("peacocking") and what he called "kino escalation" (periodic casual touching during a conversation) to attract women. He swore that would do the trick. This sounded creepy, so I ignored him.

Besides not knowing how to flirt, I was also ignorant of mainstream American culture. On Valentine's Day right before the start of my Asian philosophy class, a petite Chilean classmate named America gave me a small red paper heart and whispered, "You're my Valentine." I immediately overestimated what this probably meant. I felt my ears turn beet red. I had joked with America a bit in previous classes, and I was certainly attracted to her, but I was surprised that she would just come out with such a declaration without any warning. But I figured, you don't ask pesky questions when a pretty woman makes a generous proposal.

Suddenly the more rational part of my brain wondered whether maybe, just maybe, saying that someone was your Valentine didn't mean what I thought. Maybe this was a gesture of friendship not necessarily tied to physical intimacy. As I pondered this unsettling thought and the professor lectured about the Bhagavad Gita and how Arjuna must fulfill his dharma, I noticed that America had turned to another guy in the class and handed him the same sort of heart she had bestowed on me. Worse still, she repeated the same enchanted phrase.

At this point, I considered that my doubts about America's intentions were well founded. When she repeated the entire process with a third classmate, I was sure of her intentions—or lack thereof—and sank back into my desk, disappointed but relieved that I hadn't accidentally let slip what I had initially imagined.

Another confusing experience occurred when I went out with a friend to see a documentary screening at a cinema. While standing in a line for tickets I met a wiry, funny, and fiercely intelligent student from Barnard, a nearby women's college. We immediately hit it off and had a great five-minute conversation. Right before we took our seats, she tore off a piece of paper from a notebook and handed me her phone number. My heart did a backflip. *A woman gave me her number and I hadn't even asked for it.* Things were really looking up.

I called her a few times and we talked. Then one day I called and she didn't pick up. I left a message. She didn't return my call. I called again. I left another message. I kept calling and leaving messages. Eventually a female friend let me in on the secret that when a woman stops returning your calls, it means she's not interested.

It's not that I had absolutely no experience with dating. I had been on a Lubavitch-style *shidduch* date that was arranged by a matchmaker. Since Lubavitchers believe love comes *after* marriage and is based on shared commitment to raising a large and pious family, and since absolutely no physical contact is allowed before marriage, dates usually consist of sitting awkwardly in a public area, such as a hotel lobby, for a few hours taking turns asking questions to determine whether the stranger sitting across from you would make a suitable lifelong companion. Lubavitch dates have just a hint of a KGB interrogation.

By the time I went on the arranged date, I was already in college, and the matchmaker, Rabbi Matusof, who had never met me and probably never met the woman, assured me that Devorah, my date, was a "*modernische maydel*" (modern girl). I was still nominally Lubavitch but was attending college—something largely unheard of at the time for unmarried Lubavitch men—so a modern woman sounded promising.

I didn't own a car and instead picked Devorah up in a taxi. I thought it was a good omen when she allowed me to pick her up at her home rather than insisting I follow the common practice of the man picking up the woman on an isolated street corner beyond the borders of the Lubavitch section of the neighborhood, lest a community member observe the pickup and gossip. This was the last good omen of the date.

As soon as Devorah sat down in the back seat of the taxi, I turned to her and tried to engage. "So, Devorah, I understand from Rabbi Matusof that you work in business. What kind?"

"I work for my father's import-export business."

"What do you do?"

"I keep inventory."

"Is it interesting?"

"No."

Silence prevailed in the back seat of the taxi that would have been the envy of a Trappist monk. I discerned that the date wasn't going well. We needed a different topic. If only our taxi would crash into the car in front of us and give us something exciting to talk about.

I asked Devorah, "Do you like books?"

"Nah, they're boring," she answered and laughed slightly, rocking her head backward.

"Do you watch movies?"

"Not much. I watched *Borat* last week."

Finally, something I could work with. "Did you like it?"

"No. Too *grub*" (crass).

These were not the answers I was hoping for. Worse still, I noticed that the whole time Devorah was in the car, instead of looking at me, her body was stiffly coiled and turned in the opposite direction, looking out the window. By the time we pulled up to the New York Marriott at the Brooklyn Bridge, where we were supposed to have our date in the lobby, Devorah finally turned toward me.

At that point, it was perfectly clear to us both that this date was dead. If we were so inclined, we could have recited the mourner's kaddish for it then and there. Instead, to save face, we walked inside and sat down at a table, ordered two bottles of water, and made small talk for an hour.

When I got back to my apartment, I was so frustrated that I couldn't sit. I paced furiously up and down the living room. I had lost a night I desperately needed to study for a psych test. I had endured all the stress of a date. And I had gotten all dressed up—I had even worn a tie, and I never wear a tie unless someone is getting married or being buried. The next morning I called the matchmaker to complain.

"Rabbi Matusof, Devorah has no interest in books, movies, or anything else secular. Why did you think she's modern?"

"She Rollerblades!"

It was not only rabbis who tried to play matchmaker. One bright summer morning, my Uncle Jeff got into the racket. Jeff decided to take on the role of the sagacious Jeeves to my bumbling fool of a Bertie Wooster as he endeavored to straighten out my dating life. It all started with a phone call.

"Zalman, I'm at Central Park waiting to get our tickets." Jeff and I were planning to see Shakespeare in the Park's *Romeo and Juliet* that night. "You have to come now."

"Why?"

"There's a gorgeous Swiss Jew, Elena, on line next to me, and she's perfect for you."

"Seriously?"

"Do you think I would joke about such things? She's fluent in Hebrew; she's talking about Nietzsche, Camus, and Sartre. She's cracking jokes left and right, and she's drop-dead gorgeous."

"You mean it?"

"Trust me. So listen: It's 10:30 now, and the box office doesn't open till noon, so she's stuck on line for another hour and a half. That's plenty of time for you to make it from Brooklyn."

"OK, I'm on my way."

"I'll keep talking to her—but hurry."

As I approached the open-air Delacorte Theater, I came to the huge snaking line of theatergoers camped out waiting for tickets, some since 4 A.M. I wound my way through the crowd until I found Jeff. Unlike Rabbi Matusof's about Devorah, Jeff's reporting about Elena was spot-on.

Elena's auburn hair cascaded in ringlets, and the lilting cadence of her Swiss-accented English was mesmerizing. We were immediately in a conversation that covered Freud, Judaism's attitude to pain, and Tennessee Williams. We were on a roll. Soon the line started to move and we exchanged email addresses.

I didn't see Elena at the show, so the next morning I sent her a 676 word missive with my assessment of the previous night's performers, along with some quotes from Tennessee Williams on loneliness (including my favorite one, "We're all of us sentenced to solitary confinement inside our own skins, for life!") and further thoughts on nineteenth-century Hebrew literature.

Over the next few weeks, we exchanged several long emails and eventually agreed to have dinner one Friday night. I took her to Kulushkat, a Mediterranean place near Park Slope, and enjoyed a plate of falafel and hummus. The dinner conversation was lively, until, toward the end of the evening, Elena blurted out: "You should know I'm too depressed now to date or get seriously involved with someone." I suppose the relationship was doomed from the start. After all, it had begun on the ticket line for *Romeo and Juliet.*

After two years in college, I eventually met Sam, short for Samantha, through a mutual friend. She had brown hair and a dry sense of humor. Our third date, on a cold January night, was at the Chocolate Room, where she introduced me to the delights of salted chocolate truffles with hot chilies. When we left, it was snowing outside. We made our way through the falling snow toward the subway, and without thinking, our gloves touched. We clasped hands.

When we arrived at the subway, right before I disappeared down the stairs into the station, Sam leaned over and kissed me on the lips. *It was the first time I ever kissed a woman.* It lasted only an instant. Still, I was shaking. My cheeks felt as if they were on fire. I tasted a metallic substance in my mouth. I was certain that I had the mark of Cain on my forehead and that everyone I passed on the subway platform knew what I had just done.

Over the next month and a half, Sam and I became very close. We decided it was time to be more physically intimate. We were sitting on the bed in Sam's Fort Greene studio apartment, an otherwise darkened room with a single bed light on. A Manchester United jersey hung on her wall, a relic of her junior year at Oxford, and a stack of French cookbooks sat on her counter. She was a wizard in the kitchen.

We were about to begin when she turned to me and asked, "Are you sure you really want to do this?" My mind flashed back to the countless admonishments I read in yeshiva against the terrible sin of "wastefully spilling seed." According to the Talmud (Niddah 13a), a person who wastes his seed is considered a murderer on account of the children that could have been born from that seed. The Zohar states that the wasting of seed is a sin more serious than all other sins in the Torah and is punished most severely.

I remembered the years I studied the *Tanya* and how it taught that it is necessary to use the mind to master physical urges. But I no longer believed in God, and those threats no longer held sway over me. I reached over and hugged Sam and whispered in her ear, "Yes, I'm sure." She stretched out her arm and shut off the light.

I went with Sam to the large AMC movie theater on 42nd Street to watch *The Namesake.* Sam had read the book. I had no idea what it was about. I watched teary-eyed as Gogol, the American-born son of parents who had emigrated from Calcutta and settled in Cambridge, Massachusetts, struggled against the cultural norms of his traditional family while still loving them deeply. When the film was over, I managed to make it to the hallway of the theater and then burst out crying. Sam put her arms around me and held me tightly.

Although Sam was a generous partner and a good person, I felt that she was not the person for me over the long term. I was twenty-five and dating for marriage, so I decided to break up with her. I went over to her apartment one night to deliver the news. I could hardly speak. Sam realized something was up.

"Zalman, what's wrong?" I couldn't say a word. "Spit it out. What's going on?" Not a word. My face turned red. "Are you breaking up with me?" I burst out crying. Sam turned stone-faced.

"I'm . . . really . . . sorry," I sputtered.

Sam left the room without giving a verbal response. I sat glued to the wooden chair. She retrieved the toothbrush and toothpaste I kept in her bathroom and flung them on the table in front of me. "Take them and get out," Sam ordered.

After Sam, I dated two other women. Although each of these relationships lasted only several months, they changed me. They helped me expand my wardrobe to include khaki pants and pink dress shirts and my music repertoire to include Dar Williams and Leonard Cohen. They introduced me to the comedy of Eddie Izzard and Garfunkel and Oates. They also helped give me a better perspective on what I was looking for in a partner, especially in terms of her religious status.

Sam was not Lubavitch but observed Orthodox Jewish law (although she was flexible on the sex-before-marriage bit). My second girlfriend was born Lubavitch but, like me, drifted away from Orthodox observance. My third had never been Orthodox but was still deeply Jewish. I came to realize that among Jews, the third kind made me the most comfortable.

Shortly after breaking up with number three, in September 2008, I entered the doctoral program in sociology at New York University (NYU). While in college I had planned to become a clinical psychologist. After graduating and spending a year at a social services organization, I realized that in addition to helping people, I was passionate about scholarship and conducting my own research. I also realized that I was especially interested in studying religious communities like the one I was raised in to enhance my understanding of their internal dynamics. After consulting several professors, I concluded that an advanced degree in sociology rather than psychology would be better suited to my academic interests.

As an undergrad at Brooklyn College, part of the City University of New York, a publicly funded institution, my tuition was relatively modest, and I was able to raise it by begging from my non-Orthodox relatives, as well as by dipping into my savings. At NYU, however, the situation was different. I was lucky enough to earn a fellowship that covered my tuition and provided me a modest stipend to live on.

Nonetheless, starting the doctoral program at NYU required a huge adjustment for me. For one thing, unlike Brooklyn College's picturesque campus with its quad, library with a bell tower, and numerous red brick mid-twentieth-century college-looking buildings, NYU, in strict terms, didn't have a campus at all. Its buildings were honeycombed throughout the entire lower Manhattan landscape, which meant that the city's sights and sounds become part of the university's culture.

In addition to my new physical environment, the intellectual climate was different and challenging. At Brooklyn College, I stood out due to my enthusiasm for learning and my willingness to read every text on the syllabus. My cohort at NYU consisted of erudite graduates of Harvard; Columbia; the University of California, Berkeley; and the University of Chicago. They all seemed to have read and memorized more scholarly tomes than I could name. Each course at NYU required that I read several books a week, while as an undergrad I might have read that many for an entire semester-long course. I felt as if I was being force-fed stacks of books. If I couldn't digest quickly enough, I would choke on the stuff.

As I struggled to adapt, the question of how to find my ideal partner weighed on me. Now that I was a grad student with even less free time, I resolved to take the plunge into online dating. I heard about eHarmony and gave it a try. I was a bit skeptical of the strong claims for the service's "patented Compatibility Matching System," but I filled out the lengthy profile anyway.

When I got to the question about religious status of potential partner, I paused. Before me was a list of all different religions—such as Christian and Jewish—as well as secular, atheist, and so on, and I had to choose which to check off as acceptable. Suddenly I was presented with a greater range of available religious identities than had ever occurred to me.

My first instinct was to proclaim that my partner did not have to be Jewish. I imagined marrying a lax Christian, moving to Montana, and buying a farm. I could picture our three blond-haired, blue-eyed sons named Gage, Garret, and Gavin, all clad in flannel shirts and denim overalls, helping out on the farm grooming horses and mending fences. I could almost smell the manure caked on my boots. For some reason, the idea of marrying a non-Jew and staying in New York City never crossed my mind.

After enjoying a few minutes of this reverie, I decided that, although in principle I was not committed to marrying a Jew, in practice it might make sense first to give the Jews a chance. After all, if my partner had a Jewish background, we would share many cultural associations and religious sensitivities that would prevent misunderstandings and hurt feelings down the road.

The other eHarmony question that gave me pause was: "Describe the last book that you read and enjoyed." I was horrified. How could I possibly gamble on a single book to capture the entirety of my literary interests? My solution was a two-pronged strategy: I chose one book on Jewish history—Pierre Birnbaum's *Geography of Hope*, which explores the relationship of several influential Western thinkers and their heritage—and the other a literary classic, Thoreau's *Walden*. This felt like the right balance of conformity and bravery.

After completing the entire questionnaire, all that remained was to upload a photo. I felt that none of my old pictures was suitable, so I recruited my friend Aaron to snap some new ones. Aaron was no Annie Leibovitz, but he had a sense of style, and with the 100 percent discount, his services were affordable.

We agreed that for the purpose at hand I should try to convey a stern look, no smiles, not even a hint. We were aiming for the highly dramatic and severe portraits that populate fashion magazines. I wore dark blue jeans and a dress shirt with a brown corduroy jacket. We experimented with several poses in a side room in the basement of the Brooklyn College library, but the winner had me seated on a couch, my feet crossed and resting on a second couch, my right index finger placed on my temple and my left hand holding a newspaper. I looked as natural as a mannequin in a window display. Once I had the shot, I uploaded it to my account. Then I waited for eHarmony to do its magic.

The eHarmony website takes the information users provide to create potential matches and then sends several matches to users each day. One of the matches I received on the first day was from Jenny, a religious studies graduate student. From her pictures I saw that she was tall and had high cheekbones and long, flowing brown hair.

Reading her profile, I noticed that in the question about the latest book read, she discussed *five* books, covering American history, Mormonism, comedy, and astrophysics. I realized right away that she was smart, had a sense of humor, and was wise enough to know that you couldn't limit your answer to a single book. I was intrigued and texted:

Me: I see you're a grad student. What do you study?
Jenny: I study the Talmud and ancient Judaism.
Me: Cool. I studied some Talmud in yeshiva a while back.
Jenny: You did? Where?
Me: A bunch of places. I can tell you about it in person.

We agreed to meet. It was the middle of February. I arranged for us to meet at Alice's Tea Cup on the Upper West Side of Manhattan, an elegant setting with teal- and maroon-colored walls and an assortment of fancy pastries. Luckily, at this moment in my life I was in between army trench coats.

I arrived at 4:40 for our 5 P.M. date—just to be safe. That's when I discovered that the restaurant was jammed, and it would be more than an hour before we could be seated. My mind raced. I wasn't familiar with that neighborhood. Damn. I had chosen it only because I knew about this one place. I had no backup plan. *How could I not have a backup? Why didn't I prepare for this?* I paced around the crowded area near the door. Ten minutes later, an attractive woman in a long, black winter coat entered.

She looked just like her photos on eHarmony. I approached.

"Jenny?"

"Zalman?"

We both smiled. I explained to her the logistic hiccup, and she must have sensed the terror in my voice because she calmly responded, "It's fine. It's Manhattan. We can just walk down the street and find another place."

What an idea. We wandered up Columbus Avenue for half a mile, eventually settling on Columbus Café, a neighborhood bakery that had a small seating area with crummy old chairs. We could get out of the cold and enjoy hot drinks and danish.

For the next two hours the conversation was eclectic and electric. Our discussion meandered seamlessly from philosophy to Judaism to literature and back to Judaism. The wall that stood between the Torah and these other authors for all those years for me in yeshiva was completely foreign to her. She told me about her biblical and Talmudic annotations of her volumes of Aristotle, Immanuel Kant, and John Stuart Mill. I was enthralled. We talked about our families. Jenny had two brothers.

"Wow," I said, sipping my Lipton tea. "My family is huge. I have three brothers and five sisters. When we travel, we don't visit. We invade."

"Wow," said Jenny. "That's a lot of birthday calls."

"I don't call them all on their birthdays."

"You don't?"

"You do?"

As we prepared to leave, it occurred to me that although Jenny mentioned that she was getting a doctorate in Talmud study, I had never asked her what her dissertation was on.

Standing outside the café I asked, "By the way, what are you writing about?"

Jenny looked at me, her long hair blowing in the wind. "I'm writing about ancient rabbinic attitudes toward non-Jews."

I recalled a book I had once skimmed by the legendary Jewish studies scholar Jacob Katz on relations between Jews and non-Jews, and I thought this would be a great opportunity to show Jenny that although I studied sociology, I'm not wholly ignorant of the academic study of Judaism.

"Is your dissertation related to Jacob Katz's *Exclusiveness and Tolerance*?" I asked, feeling pretty good about myself.

Jenny started waving her hands and shaking her head from side to side. "My dissertation has nothing to do with Katz. That book is on the

Middle Ages and Early Modernity. I work on antiquity. If you ask me, everything after the sixth century is a waste of time."

"Oh, I see."

That's kind of weird. She has really strong feelings about antiquity. But, wow, this person is amazing.

Shortly thereafter we said our goodbyes and went our separate ways.

Notwithstanding my Katz gaffe, I thought the date went well. It turned out Jenny thought so too. We ended up seeing each other a lot the next few months. We dined at vegan restaurants; we attended her liberal synagogue on Saturdays; and we took long walks in Riverside Park.

Although Jenny was not Orthodox, she was very religious in her own way. She prayed every morning wearing a *tallis* (prayer shawl) and *tefillin*. She made blessings on food before eating and abstained from eating nonkosher meat or chicken. At that point in my life, although I still couldn't bring myself to eat pork or ham, I no longer put on *tefillin* or prayed regularly.

At first I thought that our religious differences might be a stumbling block. But Jenny assured me that she was OK with it. "I don't need you to be religious for me. I can be religious for myself. I need you to be my partner, not my rabbi."

Although the idea of partners with significantly different observance levels was foreign to me—I always heard growing up that it was essential for both partners to maintain the same religious standards for a marriage to work—I realized that our marriage inevitably would be a sort of "mixed marriage," since I was raised Lubavitch and she was raised in a liberal Jewish family. We agreed to give the relationship a chance.

As time passed, I realized that although Jenny was very religious, she had none of the rigidity of Orthodoxy. She didn't use computers or phones on Shabbos but did watch television. I challenged her, "But you're just picking and choosing whatever rituals suit you." (The charge of "picking and choosing" was the ultimate insult in Orthodox circles.) To my surprise, she responded, "Of course I am. Everyone does. That's how religions work."

Jenny's commitment to Judaism was very deep but was rooted in meaning and joy. If it was not joyful or meaningful to her, she was not wedded to it. Jenny preserved Jewish ritual neither out of a sense of divine commandment nor out of allegiance to Jewish continuity, but because she believed it enriches life with structure, purpose, and thoughtfulness.

Around this time I had a phone conversation with Shraga, a close friend, about Jenny's observance level. As I paced the wooden floor of my apartment, he delivered a dire warning:

Shraga: Listen, Zalman. You're listening?
Me: Yes.
Shraga: OK, good. Maybe for now Jenny is willing to put up with your subpar observance level, but if you get married, she will demand that your observance matches hers.
Me: She wouldn't do that.
Shraga: Just hear me out, Zalman. What happens if she does? Then you will resent her, and the marriage will be in trouble. What happens if you already have a kid together? I'm telling you this for your own good.

I understood what Shraga was saying, but I did not share his concerns. I felt that any extra observances I would undertake because of Jenny, I would do willingly, with a full heart. And I was convinced that Jenny would never pressure me to do more than I was comfortable with.

Although Jenny never pressured me to act differently, she was horrified when I stayed home from synagogue on Yom Kippur to write a sociology paper and ate a full lunch. "You ate on Yom Kippur? Even secular Jews fast on Yom Kippur."

Yom Kippur was still a special day for me. I'm sure if I sat in the pews on that day listening to the haunting melodies of the service, I would have felt moved. But I didn't view it as the "Day of Atonement," and I didn't feel like I was required to be there. I had a paper to work on and was content to stay home and work on it. As for fasting, I didn't find it spiritually nourishing or invigorating. It just made me weak and sick, so I dropped it.

One night Jenny said, "My mother is having a birthday dinner in the city next week. Want to come?"

Immediately I answered, "Yeah."

"You sure? My extended family will be there."

"I'm sure."

The following week Jenny and I went to Osteria Morini, an Italian restaurant in SoHo, to meet her family. I was happy to meet them, but I wondered how they would respond to my ultra-Orthodox background. Would they press me for details about my current religious practices and beliefs? Would they ask me uncomfortable questions about why I had left?

As we entered the dimly lit restaurant, heavy with the scent of olive oil and oregano, Jenny a half-pace ahead of me, I saw a long table full of people, some waving in our direction. We walked over. A man in his sixties with salt-and-pepper hair and a striped button-down shirt, a Bloody Mary in hand, stood up: "Hi, I'm Ralph, Jenny's father."

Standing next to him was a woman about the same age with short brown hair and high cheekbones just like Jenny's. "Welcome. I'm Jenny's mother, Marilyn. We're so glad to meet you." Both had huge smiles plastered to their faces—the kind you couldn't peel off with a crowbar.

I introduced myself to the rest of the family. Our waiter arrived, and I ordered the eggplant parmesan. Jenny's family never ate nonkosher meat—at least, not while they were together, or, at the very least, not in front of Jenny's mother, whom, I had already learned, placed special value on the Jewish dietary laws.

By the time the eggplant parm arrived I felt completely comfortable with Jenny's family. Jenny's father told jokes; her Uncle Joel did an impression of their late Aunt Sybil; and her younger brother, Barry, discussed plans to open a microbrewery. No one ever asked about my religious status or upbringing. I felt totally embraced by Jenny's family.

The first encounter with Jenny's family led to many more. We visited her parents' house in New Jersey for barbeques, and we ate out at restaurants a lot. Once while we were dining out, I asked Jenny whether it would be OK for me to order a nonkosher steak in front of her mother. Jenny leaned over and whispered the question to her mother. The answer came back that I was free to order it.

When Barry, Jenny's younger brother, discovered what was afoot, he piped up. Barry hadn't followed Jewish ritual laws in years, but, at least at that point in his twenties, he would never eat nonkosher in front of his mother. "Hey, why can he order a steak but I can't?"

Without missing a beat, Jenny's mother responded: "I didn't pay *his* Jewish day school tuition for twelve years!"

All the warmth and understanding showered on me by Jenny's family made me dread even more the day, which couldn't be postponed forever, when Jenny met my own. I had mentioned Jenny to my parents on numerous occasions, but they hadn't said anything. They seemed to feel that this relationship would fizzle out after a few months like my previous non-Orthodox relationships. I tried to tell them that this one was different, that I thought Jenny might be "the one."

That year for Passover my family went to a hotel in Sanibel, Florida. Jenny was visiting her grandparents a few hours' drive away. My parents agreed for Jenny to come for a visit. Jenny pulled up in a rental car, and I took her to the hotel dining room, where my parents and most of my sisters and brothers were gathered. My heart pounded fiercely in my chest.

Although it was eighty-something degrees that day, my mother and my sisters wore modest long-sleeve blouses and long skirts. I was *schvitzing* just looking at them. My brothers and father got away with wearing short-sleeve white shirts with their dark pants. My mother was also wearing a *sheitel* (wig), with the hair cradling her neck and the top of her shoulders. My father completed his own ensemble with his black fedora.

As soon as Jenny and I entered the room, my mother took charge and introduced each family member like a general reviewing troops on parade. She stated each family member's full name, although our full names are seldom referenced, except when she is angry.

After reviewing the troops, she fell silent for the rest of the visit, as if she had already discharged her duties for the day. My father said nothing at all, as was his custom. Chaya, age twelve, walked over to Jenny and gave her a white bead bracelet she made that day in arts-and-crafts. Chaya intended to write out Jenny's name on the bracelet but apologized that she only had one "n," so it read "Jeny."

"You made this for *me*? That's so nice of you. It's beautiful. Thank you so much," Jenny cooed and slipped it on her wrist.

Then, Mendy, age thirteen, struck up a conversation with Jenny.

"So Zalman tells me you know *Gemara* [Talmud]. How many *mesechtas* [tractates] do you know?"

"Well," Jenny said, caught off guard by the directness of the question, "I've only read a handful of *mesechtas* cover to cover, but I've read chunks of many. What *mesechta* are you learning this year?"

"I'm learning *Mesechta Makos*, and we're talking about the laws of *aray miklat*" (the cities of refuge for accidental killers fleeing the relatives seeking blood vengeance for the victim).

"Oh! That's a hard one," Jenny quickly replied. "It gets so confusing. Is it accidental if the killer falls on the victim while he'd been climbing *up* the ladder, or only if he fell while he was climbing *down* the ladder? Who can keep track? And you're learning that at what, thirteen years old? Amazing."

He grinned widely, bouncing a little in his seat. He echoed some more confusing ins and outs of *Makos* as they chatted for a while about this obscure topic.

My parents, by contrast, had no words of substance to share with Jenny. Overall there weren't many smiles that day, a lot fewer than at my introduction to Jenny's family at the Italian restaurant.

As the months passed, I started to feel deeply connected to Jenny, but I still wasn't certain whether this was the woman I should marry.

My brother Yossi and I had been speaking for years about visiting Ireland. Although all our ancestors originated from Eastern Europe, we would joke that Ireland was "our motherland." Finally, we arranged to go in June. Each morning in Ireland, after downing a breakfast of toast smothered in baked beans, we went on excursions. We examined the Book of Kells, an ornate illuminated Latin Gospel manuscript dating from the ninth century housed at Trinity College Library, Dublin, and enjoyed the breathtaking view of the Three Sisters, the mountain peaks at the northwestern end of the Dingle Peninsula in County Kerry. Along the way, we toured many churches and castles that dotted the landscape, including Blarney Castle, where I relished the chance to kiss the Blarney Stone.

But whatever was on our itinerary, I made sure to get to an internet café so I could update Jenny and read her responses to my previous email. After just a week, I felt miserable being so far away from her. I cut my trip short and came back to New York. That's when I knew without a doubt that this was the life partner for me.

As my relationship with Jenny became more serious, it was disturbing that my parents hadn't said anything substantive about her. One day as I was driving with my father around Crown Heights to buy groceries, I said, "You know, I'm going to marry Jenny. What do you think?"

He responded, "Of course, I'd prefer if you would marry someone Orthodox, but I realize this is the best deal I'm going to get. Jenny is not Orthodox, but she is very religious." He paused and sighed. "I understand that Jenny is much more religious than you are now and that by being with her you're raising your observance level."

A relieved smile crept across my face. This wasn't the most enthusiastic reaction from a parent about a child's future wife, but it was the best I was going to get.

My father saw my smile and added, "I knew that you and Jenny were serious, so I called Rabbi Tipish on the *beis din* [rabbinic court] of Crown Heights to get his opinion of the match. You're not going to like what he said."

"What did he say?"

"He said that since Jenny is not Orthodox, her history with men is not assumed to be kosher. Therefore, she has the legal status of a '*sofek zonah*' [a 'possibly promiscuous' woman], and a person like that is prohibited from marrying a *kohen* such as yourself."

"That is really insane."

"Rabbi Tipish added that even if Jenny promised that she was never with a man, her testimony would be invalid because she has a strong incentive to lie—she wants to marry you."

From a liberal Jewish perspective, one could argue that such laws are outdated. They assume that premarital sex makes a person polluted and of a lower social status, thus unfit to marry a *kohen* who is viewed as possessing an elevated status. These laws are also fundamentally sexist. They only concern themselves with the sexual behavior of the bride, but not the groom. No one dared to hint at my premarital sexual behavior. But I had no interest in dignifying any critique of my marital choice with scholarly argument.

"This is all so insulting."

"I told you you weren't going to like it."

"Good thing I'm not Orthodox and don't feel bound by the legal opinions of such rabbis."

Unlike with my father, my mother and I didn't talk about Jenny at all. For my mother, Jenny was the coup de grâce to my religious life. Without a marriage sealing my fate as a nonbeliever, my soul might yet return to Lubavitch. But a marriage and children would make a permanent break with her vision of my life. She had joined Lubavitch out of devotion to its definition of family. To choose otherwise for my own family struck her as the deepest possible rejection.

In those days, I lived a fifteen-minute walk away from my parents, in Prospect Heights. My mother and I spoke on the phone only about once a month, and I visited the family home a few times a month. For a while, the don't ask, don't tell policy between my mother and me about Jenny worked well enough. But over time it bubbled up in me, and I had to push the issue. "What do you think of Jenny?" I asked over the phone.

Silence. A moment later: "Look, Zalman, Jenny is a lovely person, but if you marry her, you'll create a split in the family forever." The threat of losing even those infrequent visits and calls, the hugs and kisses of my siblings, and the giggles of my nieces and nephews hit me like a whack with a frying pan. But I shook it off and ran with the adrenaline.

"I'm not making any split. If you don't accept Jenny, you are the one making the split. Besides, I think as time goes by you'll get to know her better and you'll come to accept her."

"You're wrong."

"Today little Zalman kissed the *mezuzah* [the encased scroll attached to doorposts in a Jewish home]," read a mitzvah note sent to my kindergarten teacher.

"Today Zalman made a *brachah* [blessing] on a chocolate chip cookie."

"Today Zalman kept his yarmulke on all night."

My mother wrote notes for my teachers to report my religious actions while at home so I could claim my sticker and a proud smile from my preschool teacher the next day. She wrote those notes daily, diligently celebrating my every act of piety.

"Kiulu atem yigiyim b'torah yoymum valayla in bichinas oylum shelimata."

"That's wonderful Zalman! I'm so proud of you! You learned your whole bar mitzvah *maymer* [discourse] by heart in just five months. That's really a wonderful accomplishment."

"Zalman! It's your turn to make kiddush. Yossi—give him the cup! Shhhh! Go ahead, Zalman. Not by heart! Look in the *siddur* [prayer book]. Chana Sara—give him the *siddur*!" As I chant the blessings on Friday night, with the smell of the chicken soup wafting in from the kitchen and the warm challah bulging out from under its cover on the table in front of me, no one is more attentive than my mother.

For her, my impending engagement was a repudiation of my upbringing—crumpling up those mitzvah notes, forgetting my *maymer*, and spitting out the kiddush wine.

"You're wrong," she says.

For me, the mitzvah notes are tucked into my breast pocket; the *maymer* is lodged in my brain forever, whether I like it or not; and I still await my Shabbos dinner each week. But these days, Shabbos dinner is with Jenny. She chants the blessings in her strange accent, the one used in liberal Jewish communities, and chicken has given way to quinoa and zucchini.

I'm going to marry Jenny.

15

The Promised Land

"*L'Chaim! L'Chaim!*" Yudi Aaronowitz, my elementary school classmate, wished me at the Crown Heights party my mother arranged in honor of my engagement. Holding a shot glass of scotch in his hand, he smiled warmly and then added, "May you build a *binyan adei ad* [an everlasting edifice]." Yudi offered me the traditional Lubavitch blessing for a harmonious marriage, a union in which the Eternal One is invited to be present.

Jenny and I had become engaged three weeks earlier, in November 2009, in the fall of my second year as a graduate student at New York University. We'd planned an evening together and exchanged white gold rings with no diamond; Jenny was firmly opposed to diamond rings on moral, aesthetic, egalitarian, and financial grounds.

She didn't even want the engagement ring, but I felt that "regular Americans" gave rings. Plus, I liked the idea of having a tangible reminder of our love. Jenny went along. We chose biblical verses in Hebrew to have inscribed on each other's rings. The verse she chose for my ring, from *Song of Songs*, reads, "This is my beloved, this is my friend," and the verse I chose for Jenny's, from *The Book of Ruth*, reads, "Wherever you go, I will go."

Mommy was hardly sanguine about the match. She arranged the party to put a Lubavitch veneer on a match she did not approve of but could not prevent. After I got engaged, my father and siblings didn't say anything about Jenny but seemed willing to celebrate with me. The few of my yeshiva friends at the party seemed genuinely to share my joy looking forward to the wedding.

Since the engagement party took place at a synagogue in Crown Heights, it went without saying that there would be a *mechitzah* (partition) between the men's and women's sections, even though most of the guests were either Jenny's non-Orthodox family or our secular and non-Jewish friends.

Out of respect for my mother, Jenny wore a modest floor-length black skirt and pink blouse with a black jacket, and I wore a dark striped suit and a black Lubavitch fedora. My mother insisted that I recite a classic Hasidic discourse at the party, which is standard Lubavitch practice. I did so but went out of my way to deemphasize several points from the original text that I found sexist.

Two weeks after my engagement party I called home. "You gotta stop this Chaya Ronit stuff. Jenny can't stand it," I told my father.

From the time Jenny was introduced to my family, they had taken to calling her by her Hebrew name, Chaya Ronit, rather than her English name, which everyone else used. Her Hebrew name sounded very Jewish, and Chaya sounded especially Lubavitch. The Rebbe's wife's first name was Chaya, and many Lubavitch women were named after her, including my younger sister. Jenny understood all this and was upset by the subterfuge, because she felt that using this name was a way to pretend that she wasn't who she was: a decidedly *non*-Orthodox person called Jenny.

"Is Mommy available? I need to speak to her about the wedding invitation."

The problem was that Lubavitchers the world over use the exact wording of all four paragraphs of the Hebrew text of the wedding invitation from the Rebbe's marriage in 1929 in Warsaw, Poland. They even keep the time of the wedding as stated in the original—5 P.M.—and use an asterisk to note the actual time if it differs.

When she picked up the phone, I said, "Mommy, we're willing to use some of the Rebbe's invitation, but not all."

My mother didn't need to think about this one. She snapped, "This is not a menu where you pick and choose. Either you use the whole thing or none of it."

In fact, I had by now come to feel that Jenny's answer to my question about her Shabbos observance was wise: that we *can* and *should*—and, in fact, already *do*—choose the parts of Jewish law and the tradition that suit us and leave the rest. My mother, however, saw everything Jewish as an all-or-nothing proposition. To use part of the Rebbe's invitation would be a "slap in the face" to the Lubavitch guests rather than a sign of respect and accommodation.

I shot back, "Jenny spent *hours* working out the perfect language that incorporates the Rebbe's invitation in part but is also to our taste."

"Forget it," she said.

"We like the version that we came up with, so we're going to use it."

"In that case, I'm going to send my own invitations to the Lubavitch guests."

I was hurt that my mother was sending my guests her own invitations, but I was willing to put up with this indignity because at least it meant she would be coming to the wedding. Since the moment I informed her that Jenny and I were engaged, I was concerned that she might not show up at the wedding.

Yes, she threw an engagement party for us in Crown Heights, but she never explicitly stated that she would attend our wedding. Neither did she definitively state that she would not attend—but I had my concerns. Now that she was insisting on sending the hundred or so Lubavitch friends and neighbors her own invitations, I actually felt reasonably sure she would attend.

As the wedding preparations unfolded, it became clear that Jenny's parents were organizing and paying for most of the arrangements—the hall, the band, the caterer, the flowers, and the photographer and videographer. My mother was particularly concerned that the kosher level of the caterer be up to Lubavitch standards. She eventually paid fifteen hundred dollars so that the meat and chicken served would have specifically Lubavitch kosher certification.

Then there was the dancing. Lubavitch weddings include a tall *mechitzah* separating the men and women for both the meal and the dancing. We managed a deal for the dinner seating: We got away with no *mechitzah* and simply set up several men's tables and women's tables for the Lubavitch guests. But if we didn't have separate men's and women's sections for dancing, my parents and siblings would never get to dance at my wedding.

Every time I discussed this issue with my mother, she would say, "I understand this is not the standard of Jenny and her family but why not accept our higher standard of Jewish practice and make separate dancing areas for men and women?"

I tried to explain to her that I shared Jenny's standard and that neither of us considered her standard "higher" than ours. If anything, we viewed it as lower, since it was based on the misogynistic idea that women had to be sequestered and isolated to protect male virtue.

My mother and I weren't the first to have this conversation. David Ben-Gurion, the first prime minister of Israel, and the Chazon Ish, one of the leading ultra-Orthodox rabbis in Israel at the time, had the same discussion in 1952. Ben-Gurion asked the Chazon Ish how secular and religious Jews, with their conflicting viewpoints, should get along in the newly created state of Israel.

The Chazon Ish answered by quoting a passage from the Talmud (Sanhedrin 32b) that states that if two camels, one carrying a load and one without any load, meet at a narrow path and there is only room for one camel to pass at a time, the camel without the load must yield to the one with the load. He argued that, unlike Orthodox Jews who are carrying the full load of the Torah and its commandments, secular Israelis are like a camel without any burdens who should therefore yield to the religious requirements of their Orthodox coreligionists.

Like the Chazon Ish, my mother saw Jenny's and my Judaism as the camel without a load. She didn't see or even acknowledge the values of egalitarianism, community, and family that underlay our interest in mixed dancing. "You should accept our higher standard."

Jenny came up with a plan that was grudgingly accepted by all sides. We agreed to a three-way partition system: one large area for mixed dancing, one area for men, and one area for women. Like all classic compromises, no one was especially happy with this arrangement, but my mother and Jenny agreed to it. For my part, as with all these arrangement details, although my own personal preferences perfectly aligned with those of my wife-to-be, I felt that I could live with anything that the two of them could agree on. My sole interest was that both my mother and my bride show up at the wedding.

My mother wasn't finished. It's customary in both Lubavitch and liberal Jewish weddings to provide each guest with a *bentcher*—a small prayer booklet to use for the Grace after Meals, the cover of which is decorated with the bride and groom's names and usually some artwork, along with the date of the wedding. Guests then take these booklets home as mementos.

"Are you going to give out Lubavitch *bentchers*?"

We had ordered *bentchers* from a liberal Jewish artist who designed the cover with the Hebrew and English verses from our engagement rings forming a circle around our names.

"As far as I know, all *bentchers* have essentially the same wording."

"If they are not Lubavitch *bentchers* we'll need to bring our own Lubavitch *bentchers* to give to the Lubavitchers."

I'm not sure my mother even knew what she was fighting for. Was she worried that the devious liberal Jews would sneak something heretical into the blessings, such as, "Blessed are you our God Adonai, and Zeus who dwells on Olympus"? Once again, I felt humiliated, but I also felt that the more she was involved in planning the event, the lower the risk of her being a no-show.

It was three weeks before my wedding, and my mother still hadn't shown any signs of embracing Jenny. But one night, on the platform of the B train at the Broadway-Lafayette station, I met a *malach*, an angel. It was years since I believed in angels or, for that matter, in the God in whose service they are said to be employed. But the man I met on that platform was so wonderful, and so wondrous, that I couldn't help feeling that if angels did exist, they would all take the form of this Hasidic sexagenarian clad in a long, black kaftan and Homburg hat.

I suppose it's odd that I chatted up a Hasidic stranger. But for several years I had felt the need to approach Hasidic strangers on the train and speak to them in Yiddish. I'm not sure exactly why I did this. Maybe to prove to myself that my Yiddish still worked; I still knew the secret handshake. Maybe to see the startled reaction of the strangers when they realized that the guy standing in front of them in jeans and a T-shirt with a trimmed beard and no yarmulke was once one of them.

We started talking on the platform and after we boarded the train, we continued the conversation. Huddled together on the hard plastic bench as if we had known each other for years, I explained that I grew up Lubavitch and was now in graduate school.

"*Nu*, are you married?"

"I'm engaged and getting married in three weeks."

"Is she Jewish?"

"Yes, she's very Jewish, but she's not Orthodox."

He smiled broadly raising his cheeks and creating a crease above his mustache. "That's OK, as long as she's Jewish. The main thing is that she should be Jewish and you should raise up a proud Jewish family."

"My mother doesn't think so. She barely considers my fiancée Jewish."

My angel touched his hand to his mouth, as if to sooth a burned lip, and said, "God forbid to say that about another Jew. With God's help and time, hopefully your mother will see things differently."

We spoke for a few more minutes. Then suddenly the train stopped. He got out—and was gone. I sat there alone in the empty subway car as it screeched along the track toward Brooklyn wondering whether the whole thing had been a dream. But it wasn't.

My angel reminded me of the protagonist in Gabriel García Márquez's short story, "A Very Old Man with Enormous Wings," which describes how a village responds when the villagers discover a mysterious creature in their midst. My angel was even more mysterious than Márquez's creature. Not because of his appearance or speech—they were both what you'd expect of someone of his background. He was extraordinary because he was ultra-Orthodox and he didn't judge me. He affirmed me.

On July 25, 2010, our wedding day, I was amazed at how beautiful the venue looked. The Sheraton Parsippany Hotel's castle-like exterior added to the romantic feeling. Jenny's two personal requests for the wedding were that I gel my hair so the front wouldn't lie flat on my forehead and that I dance with her during the wedding. I didn't know how I would feel dancing in public with a woman—even my own newly wedded wife—so I told her we'd have to see how things went.

I gelled my hair up, knowing full well my mother was not going to like this. I went to check in on her in her dressing room. She took one look at me and said, "What happened? You stuck your finger in an outlet? You look like one of the Sopranos!"

I was surprised that she had heard of the Sopranos. I said, "Funny you mention the Sopranos. That show was shot in West Caldwell, right where Jenny's parents live."

"Great," she said to the makeup artist and hair stylist working on my sisters. "Now he's marrying into the Sopranos."

Following Jewish tradition, Jenny and I hadn't seen each other for three days prior to the wedding. Our first meeting would be at the *badekken*, the veiling and blessing ceremony, after Jenny was danced by her family and friends over to the dais, while I was with my family and friends in an adjoining room.

Jenny's parade to the *badekken* was boisterous and festive. As a musical accompaniment of my walk to meet her, I chose for the band to play the first Lubavitcher Rebbe's lugubrious melody, "Daled Bavos," which is traditionally played at this stage of Lubavitch weddings. The song's four stanzas were played at a slow tempo and in a minor key as I made my way to the veiling ceremony flanked by my father and father-in-law-to-be and surrounded by friends and family.

Why do Lubavitchers play that haunting tune at this pivotal moment in the marriage ceremony? Maybe it is to remind them of the destruction of the Temple and the fact that we live in an unredeemed world. Maybe it's to remind them that marriage has its own sad moments that must be confronted for the union to endure. Maybe because this melody was considered the most sacred piece of music in the Lubavitch repertoire, so it was deemed fitting for the most special day of a person's life. I couldn't imagine walking to my bride accompanied by any other tune.

When I was in high school in Chicago, I once came across a photo of Rabbi Lefkowitz standing under his wedding canopy, bawling. I asked him, "Why were you crying?"

"When you get married, you'll understand."

Sure enough, as I walked down the aisle, which was adorned with white rose petals, escorted by my mother and father, each holding a candle-lit lantern in one hand and supporting me with the other, I burst out crying. Throughout the ceremony, tears rolled freely down my cheeks.

Standing beneath the wedding canopy fashioned out of the *tallis* from Jenny's grandfather who had recently passed away, the rabbi invited designated friends to come up one at a time and recite the seven blessings of the marriage ceremony.

"Gladden the beloved companions as You gladdened Your creatures in the garden of Eden. Blessed are You, Adonai, who gladdens this couple."

"Blessed are You who causes the couple to rejoice, one with the other."

Outfitted in my new black suit and pale-blue paisley tie, with a white calla lily for a boutonnière, I could sense that Jenny wanted me to look at her, to share the moment of our wedding ceremony together, but I couldn't. In her immaculate white dress, with her hair in an elegant updo crowned with a silk white flower behind her ear, she was radiant, and I feared watching her would only make me cry more. Instead, I stared intently at the brown-and-gray carpet. I averted my gaze until the end of the ceremony, when the rabbi handed me a glass cup to break under my foot, symbolizing the incompleteness of all earthly joy in the millennia since the destruction of the Holy Temple in Jerusalem.

I'm still not sure exactly why I cried. Were they tears of joy for having landed such a beautiful and wonderful bride? Was it the bubbling up of the sheer exhaustion from all the months and months and months of planning every detail of the wedding? Was it the creeping irrational fear that *the God I no longer believe existed* would now take revenge on me by doing something terrible to Jenny or to our future children? Was it a combination of all these?

I made it through the ceremony; the tears dried up; and Jenny and I each turned to hug our family members who were beside the chuppah. The band played a lively tune, and our friends surrounded us to dance us off to a private room, where we would, according to Jewish tradition, have a few moments of quiet to ourselves before the reception.

Just as I could feel her eyes tugging at mine to look back at her during the ceremony, I could feel her hand subtly angling to grab mine to hold hands as we danced away from the chuppah. I couldn't fathom touching Jenny's hand in front of all my Lubavitch relatives and guests. I clapped more vigorously than ever and kept my head looking straight ahead and singing as if nothing more in the world was wanted of me. Mercifully, Jenny forgave me for both offenses.

And during the third dance of the wedding, after the completion of the main course of macadamia-encrusted breast of capon and chateaubriand in a port wine reduction, Jenny and I took to the center of the mixed dance floor, held hands, and swayed to the music. Like so much else on that day, notwithstanding all my fears, it felt exactly right.

Aside from my flood of tears and the awkward parade after the ceremony, the wedding proceeded surprisingly smoothly—as if it was the most natural thing in the world for Schneur Zalman Newfield to marry Jenny Risa Labendz. As if it was just another day in Parsippany, New Jersey. As if we hadn't just pulled off a monumental synthesis of Lubavitch and liberal Jewish traditions, the culmination of months of painstaking and heartbreaking negotiations the likes of which the United Nations had never seen. It is a marriage that echoes the union within me, between my family and my future, my origins and my ambitions, the communities that built me and the one I seek to build.

16

Home

The morning after our wedding, Jenny's parents hosted a lavish brunch at their home for family and out-of-town guests. My leg muscles were killing me from hours of dancing and jumping at the wedding. As I slowly made my way around the brunch, each step reminding me why I avoid exercise whenever possible, several friends of Jenny's mother commented to me that my mother looked very sad at the wedding. One of them even handed me her cell phone and showed me a picture she snapped of my mother walking down the aisle.

I told them that my mother was an emotional person. This was true. But the picture was unambiguous. The contortion of her face looked as if she was walking to a funeral. Which in a way, she was. She was grieving for the loss of the part of me, the Lubavitch part, with which she most closely identified. She was grieving for her dream of how my life would turn out.

Every parent has dreams about who their children will become. The more clearly defined those dreams are, and the more starkly the reality differs from those dreams, the more intense the grief. My mother's grief was great, and it pained me that I was the source of that grief. It also pained me that on the happiest day of my life, she didn't share my jubilation.

Jenny and I moved to Hoboken, New Jersey, right after our wedding, and from the first Shabbos in town we became regulars at the egalitarian United Synagogue of Hoboken. Right away I felt at home there. Some members come to synagogue in suits and ties; others wear jeans and T-shirts; and still others come in shorts. None are judged; all are welcome.

We go to shul every Shabbos morning, but unlike every other man and many of the women there, I don't wear a *tallis*, a prayer shawl, during services. Partly this is because I find wrapping myself in an extra layer of cloth to be claustrophobic, and partly this may be because I want to symbolize my independence from my surroundings. I'm here. I'm a part of it. But as an atheist, I'm not in agreement with the theological aspect of the service.

In group discussions with the other congregants, I'm open about the fact that I appreciate the sense of community offered by the shul and am moved by the familiar Hebrew liturgy and melodies, but I don't believe in God. My constant assertion that I don't believe in God may be a case of an ex-Hassid projecting onto fellow congregants an assumption that they do believe in God. Or a reflex directed at the rabbis and teachers of my childhood.

But for me it felt, and feels, important that my community know that I reject the idea that God created the world; that events follow a divine plan; and that I am obligated to fulfill all of Jewish ritual as dictated by Jewish law. To state the obvious, this is less shocking to my fellow congregants than it is to my family.

Instead, I embrace those aspects of Judaism that I find meaningful. They connect me to all the Jews in history who have performed these rituals and to all those Jews today throughout the world who continue to treasure them. They also connect me to my parents and siblings and all the fond memories I have of performing these rituals together.

The familiar cycle of Jewish holidays divides up the year into their particular seasons, even in my atheist life. When winter's frost arrives, I think of Chanukah and gathering around the menorah with my family and lighting the candles, spinning dreidels, and munching on latkes. When the weather warms up, I think of preparing for the Passover seder, and as the summer heat mounts, I think of the fast day of Tisha B'Av. When school starts up in the fall, I think of the High Holidays that are soon approaching.

I also find the rituals a useful tool to remind me of important life principles. Shabbos reminds me to detach from technology and make time for family. I now make sure to attend Yom Kippur services and appreciate the reminder to acknowledge past mistakes and commit to doing better in the future. Chanukah reminds me to struggle to bring light to the broken parts of the world. Passover reminds me to be grateful for my freedom and work to help others who are oppressed.

I know that my interpretations of religious observance are not the dominant historical perspective of traditional Judaism, and my take might not be that of most Jews who practice these rituals today. But as I trained to become a sociologist and spent many hours discussing these things with Jenny, I became increasingly comfortable with the ever-changing nature of the meaning of traditional practices and the variety of ways religion fits into the lives of individuals and communities.

Our shul's historic Romanesque Revival structure was originally built for the Star of Israel synagogue in 1915, an Orthodox congregation founded by the European immigrant Jews who lived in Hoboken when it was a vibrant port town. Over the years the synagogue shifted its denominational affiliation from Orthodoxy to liberal Judaism. Now close to three hundred families in the current synagogue community use the handsome building to safely pray, study, and socialize.

High above the ark in the sanctuary stand two carved and gilded Lions of Judah flanking a stained-glass window depicting the Tablets inscribed with the Ten Commandments. Beneath them, perched above the ark on a small platform, is an American eagle with wings outstretched in golden splendor. The lions represent Judaism, and the eagle represents the commitment to America on the part of the immigrants who founded the synagogue, as they, too, incorporated where they came from and where they'd arrived into their lives.

I imagine that at night, after the congregants go home and the lights are shut off, the lions and the eagle struggle for supremacy. The lions roar and strike with their strong claws, and the eagle swoops and dives, attacking the lions with his razor-sharp talons. Their combat mirrors the competing forces in my own soul: the ancient traditions of Judaism, rooted deep within me, and secular culture, constantly tugging at me from the outside.

The Chinese novelist Yu Hua describes how during the Cultural Revolution, Mao strongly promoted the short stories of Lu Xun, and they became the only stories students read in school. Because of this, Yu came to hate these stories. However, years later when Yu took up these same stories on his own initiative, he came to appreciate the artistry and style of their author. It was the same for me with Talmud and

Hasidic thought once I finally was able to approach them on my own terms.

After months of living with Jenny and eye-opening conversations about Talmud and Jewish studies, I found myself interested in learning about the perspectives on classical Jewish texts that I was not taught growing up, aspects that would be considered heretical in Lubavitch. I wanted to learn the texts from a more academic perspective, free of the doctrinaire interpretations of my youth. If we came across a passage that contained an argument that was unconvincing or a teaching we found objectionable, I wanted the liberty to say so.

Jenny and I arranged to study together a tractate of Talmud every Saturday afternoon. This study partnership lasted only a short time (happily interrupted by the needs of our newborn), but while it did, it was amazing to see how differently we were trained to approach the same texts. I was taught that these texts were a timeless expression of divine revelation and wisdom; she was taught that they were a historically mediated record of ideas and beliefs of individual human thinkers.

I continued thinking about these classical sources, as well as the canon of Hasidic texts, as I delighted in arranging my new bookshelves so that authors who would never have spoken to one another in real life are now neighbors. The Quran and Al-Ghazali's *The Incoherence of the Philosophers* share a shelf with Schneur Zalman of Liadi's *Tanya* and Saint Augustine's *The City of God.* The King James Bible and the Dao De Jing are an arm's length away from Lucretius's *On the Nature of Things* and Spinoza's *Theological-Political Treatise.* Just as these books mix freely on the shelf, I let the ideas contained in these books mingle in my head without forcing them into an artificial agreement or synthesis.

Spending time with Jenny's family in New Jersey felt easy and comfortable. We could dress as we pleased, say what we wanted, and be accepted on our own terms. Their Jewish practices were similar to ours, and we spent most holidays with them. I quickly realized the extent to which I had lucked out in the in-laws department. They were warm, kind, and funny. Jenny's father, Ralph, was often quiet, but he loved to tell jokes and reserved a special smirk and chuckle for his favorite risqué anecdotes.

In many ways, Ralph and my father were similar: quiet and committed to Judaism and to family. Marilyn, likewise, was in some ways like my mother: a natural hostess and a born conversationalist who regularly cooked lavish holiday meals and savored the aesthetic details of a finely set table.

But in other ways, Jenny's parents were worlds apart from my own. Ralph enjoyed Scotch, cigars, and a juicy steak. He wore snappy Italian suits, played golf, and talked real estate. He owned a $4,000 mahogany card table and tried to teach me to play blackjack on several occasions. Marilyn was a social butterfly who kept in touch with hundreds of friends, many dating back to elementary and high school. She spoke fluent Spanish and enjoyed her early-morning swim class at the local pool.

The entire Labendz family—aunts, uncles, cousins, nieces, and nephews—would gather at Jenny's parents' home to celebrate Jewish holidays. Each holiday began the same. Everyone stood around the granite island in the kitchen, where the trays of candles were arrayed. Each woman, from oldest to youngest, lit her candles, and then we would all recite together the Hebrew blessings out loud: "Blessed are You, Lord our God, King of the universe, who has sanctified us with His commandments and commanded us to kindle the Yom Tov light."

While struggling to keep the children a safe distance from the lit candles, we would recite the second blessing together: "Blessed are You, Lord our God, King of the universe, who has granted us life, sustained us, and enabled us to reach this occasion."

The candles and the blessings were the same as in Crown Heights, but so much else wasn't. West Caldwell had no fedoras or *kapotas.* Instead, the men wore khakis and colored dress shirts with sweaters or sports jackets. Some of the men didn't wear yarmulkes, and some of the women did.

Each year at the Passover seder, when we came to the ten plagues visited on the Egyptians, we poured out ten corresponding droplets of wine from our cups. In Crown Heights, I was taught that this was to commemorate the glory of the punishment of our enemies. At my first West Caldwell seder I learned that this practice symbolizes that our joy is diminished in the face of our enemies' suffering. The Haggadah the Labendz family used attributed this explanation to the fifteenth-century Jewish Portuguese statesman and scholar Don Isaac Abarbanel. Diminishing our joy in the face of our enemies' suffering was news to me.

Three months after our wedding, we were overjoyed that Jenny was pregnant. Ecstatic, I called my mother to tell her. She seemed rather cool. When I told her my plans to call several close relatives and share the news, she exploded: "Why would you do that? That's like calling to advertise that you had sex!" I was speechless. What a bizarre reaction.

It took me some time to remember that, although in Lubavitch women typically had a half-dozen or more children, sex and especially women's bodies were things that were covered up, that were unmentionable in polite society. I was reminded of the story of the Lubavitch female Torah teacher who instructed a group of neighborhood women: "Never mention anything to your girls about sex until they are engaged." When a woman in the class asked, "What should I say if my daughter asks me point blank about sex?" the teacher answered, "Deny, deny, deny!" As I thought more about my mother's response, I realized that although I was then twenty-nine, it was the first time in my life I ever heard my mother utter the word *sex*.

The delivery went well, and our first daughter, Liba Pearl, entered the world in July 2011. Her birth was the scariest and the most thrilling day of my life. She had brown hair and my green eyes. My parents and sisters came to visit us in the hospital. The baby was fast asleep in her bassinet, cozy under a blanket with her head protected by a tiny pink-and-blue hospital cap.

My mother gazed at the baby and said to me, "So now you're a Tatty!" I teared up. It was the highest compliment she had ever given me, an acknowledgment that I was a grownup. It was also an acknowledgment that, despite all that had transpired and the man I had become, I still had the right to the title "Tatty."

Living on our own, away from our parents, Jenny and I had to learn how to take care of a newborn. To say the least, we were completely unprepared. Jenny joked when we got home from the hospital, "I can't believe they just let us take this baby home." As the days and months passed, we eventually figured out how to sooth Liba's colicky cries, how to cautiously change diapers, and how to trim the nails of a newborn. I began as the baby nail cutter, but after one close call that ended with Liba and me in tears, Jenny assumed the role. As we gradually gained confidence in our ability to take care of Liba, we started to feel like a real family. Two years later, in June 2013, our second daughter, Maya Esther, arrived. Now our family was complete.

At home I struggled to figure out fatherhood. At school, I struggled to find my place as a graduate student at NYU. I was in awe of and intimidated by my professors. There was one who was a recognized authority on gender and women in employment. Another was a friend of the linguist and activist Noam Chomsky and was himself an influential Marxist political economist. Yet a third was an expert on Émile Durkheim and had the distinction of having studied with two of the twentieth century's most celebrated British scholars: the philosopher Isaiah Berlin and the anthropologist E. E. Evans-Pritchard.

I was also intimidated by the other students in my graduate school cohort. To me they seemed far more prepared for graduate school than I was. I didn't speak up in class for fear of sounding dumb. I started to think maybe this whole thing was a huge mistake. I worried I wasn't smart enough; that I couldn't read fast enough or write well enough.

In my first semester of graduate school, I took a course in classical social theory in which I studied Durkheim's *The Elementary Forms of the Religious Life.* Durkheim, a secular French Jew and loyal son of the Third Republic, as well as the descendant of eight generations of rabbis, argued that religion is at its core a social institution that contains rituals and group celebrations intended to reinvigorate the communal spirit. It followed that he did not see a distinction among various forms of collective ritual:

> What essential difference is there between an assembly of Christians celebrating the principal dates of the life of Christ, or of Jews remembering the exodus from Egypt or the promulgation of the Decalogue, and a reunion of citizens commemorating the promulgation of a new moral or legal system or some great event in the national life?

When I read this passage, my heart raced and my ears turned red. I wanted to punch a hole in his reasoning. I searched for gaps in his argument for weeks, turning it inside out and upside down in my head. But in the end, I agreed with him. Religion is a social institution just like any other social institution. Religion is not inherently reactionary or progressive; it is a tool that can be used for different purposes and in different ways.

The more I read about the history of religion, the more this became apparent. I saw it in the Catholic theologians and activists of Latin America who were fueled by liberation theology in the 1960s to promote progressive social change to address systemic poverty and injustice. And I saw it likewise in the elements within the Catholic Church at the very same time that opposed liberation theology and instead promoted reactionary politics. This cast a new light on the various branches of Judaism, some reactionary, some progressive.

When I studied the concept of the self proposed by George Herbert Mead, an early twentieth-century American sociologist, it resonated instantly with my thinking during those years, as my view of religion shifted and I became more steeped in academic approaches to religion. Mead argued that there is no singular essence that a person is born with; there is no immortal soul, as I had been taught in Lubavitch.

Rather, the self is an ever-changing product of countless interactions with the people around us. The more people we meet and the more we internalize their reactions to us, the more we develop a sense of who we are. This, to me, was liberating. It meant that it is impossible to say that I am, in my essence, a Jew. Or anyone or anything else, for that matter.

I wrote my dissertation on people who grew up as I did, raised in ultra-Orthodox communities but then, like me, left those communities. I interviewed seventy-four such individuals and focused on how they hold on to various—sometimes surprising—elements of their upbringing, both consciously and unconsciously.

My own traversing of the boundary between the Hasidic and broader society led me to a wonderland of academic learning, family life, synagogue involvement, and progressive Jewish activism. It turns out William Faulkner was right: "The past is never dead. It's not even past."

As in my wedding invitation, my life today includes my Lubavitch upbringing, sometimes verbatim, but often with deletions and insertions. I'm not writing my own symphony from scratch; I have reassembled and reinterpreted the themes I was brought up with. The Torah forbids the mingling of different species in agriculture. But when it comes to religious culture, there is no such thing as purity. Everything is a hybrid, a commingling of disparate elements.

Maises (stories) were everywhere in my upbringing. I listened to neighbors, teachers, camp counselors, and my father repeat Hasidic tales over and over. When I did Lubavitch outreach and worked at a summer camp, I told the *maises* myself. The stories in my life today are mostly different, listened to on National Public Radio and read in collections of short stories by Jorge Luis Borges, Shmuel Yosef Agnon, and Anton Chekhov; told in the context of college courses, social gatherings with men and women from diverse backgrounds, and dinners at nonkosher restaurants. But in my heart, it's all *maises*, and I'm sitting at a *farbren-*

gen with half-drunk cups of vodka and the smell of tomato and onion salad doused in oil. I'm always at home in storytelling.

Every Lubavitch child is taught to be a *pnimi*, a person who is truthful to himself and acts out of intrinsic motives. I heard this at *farbrengens* all the time, "Don't *shuckle* [sway religiously] just because someone else has walked into the room while you're *davening* [praying]. Don't be a faker." The Rebbe spoke against false modesty; being humble doesn't mean pretending that you have no *kishronos*, no talents or strengths. It means recognizing your talents and acknowledging that they're a gift from God and that one has an obligation to use them properly.

Ironically, for me being a true *pnimi*, being my most authentic self—George Herbert Mead be damned—meant breaking with Lubavitch. One of the *maises* I heard countless times was of the great eighteenth-century Hasidic master Zusha of Anipol. He would say, "When I go to Heaven, they're not going to ask me why I wasn't *Moshe Rabeinu* [the biblical Moses]. They're going to ask me why I wasn't Zusha."

For my part, they're not going to ask me why I wasn't Schneur Zalman of Liadi, the founder of Lubavitch. My hope is that they also have no reason to ask me why I wasn't Schneur Zalman of Crown Heights.

While in my heart, much of me has never left home, the rest of me has very much left home and, moreover, has moved to New Jersey to live a radically different life from that of my parents and siblings. This became especially apparent when we made visits to my family in Crown Heights, which, from the start of my marriage, I tried to do often, and all the more so when we had children. But those visits came with rules, just as Rabbi Minsky had instructed.

My mother insisted that if we came for Shabbos or holidays I wear my black fedora along with my *kapota*, the traditional long black woolen coat worn by married Lubavitch men. Jenny was required to wear long-sleeve blouses and long skirts and to cover her shoulder-length brown hair completely. For a while Jenny tried wearing hats, but repeatedly stuffing her ponytail inside the hat and never being able to take it off made it uncomfortable both physically and emotionally.

My mother was elated when—perhaps in a moment of weakness—Jenny consented to have a wig purchased for her in advance of my sister

Chana Sara's wedding. My mother bought her a $1,500 human hair wig, the kind worn by Lubavitch women. It was stunning; more than once family members did a double-take, thinking it was her natural hair.

But Jenny's discomfort persisted and deepened as time went on. We continued visiting, crossing over the Hudson River even as it came to feel all too symbolic of the chasm between me and my family. But it was not working.

Yossi heckled me every time I wore my *kapota* and fedora when visiting my family: "Is this a Purim costume? Are you trying to pretend you're still Lubavitch?" (When Yossi visited my parents, he put on a yarmulke, but that was the extent of his accommodation.)

I always responded the same way: "I know I'm not Lubavitch, and I have no interest in trying to convince anyone otherwise. I wear this getup to keep Mommy happy. It's the least I can do."

But after four years of marriage, these requirements became too burdensome. I needed to have a talk with my parents to demand that they discard them. I dreaded this conversation. It would mean abandoning the don't ask, don't tell policy instituted seven years earlier.

Would our relationship finally fall apart now, after all these years of assiduous effort, like an antique crystal vase riddled with small cracks and fissures that eventually crumbles into a heap of jagged shards, lacerating our hands as we tried in vain to mend it?

I arranged to meet with my parents at their house.

Before we sat down for the meeting, I grabbed a box of tissues and placed it near me on the dining room table. I prepared a checklist with the main points I hoped to say, if only I could get through them all without crying. I started the meeting by telling my parents, "I love you both dearly, and I intend no disrespect."

My mother laughed and jumped in: "Great! So don't disrespect us."

"Mommy, this will go a lot better if you let me finish what I have to say, and then you will have a turn to say whatever you want to say."

My mother nodded and said, "You're right. I'll let you talk."

"We simply cannot continue going the way we have been. Mommy, you always say that out of respect for you and Tatty we should dress according to your standards."

"Yes, you should."

"But respect goes both ways. Whether you agree with Jenny and me or not, you need to respect our way of life too."

"What? You want me *not* to wear a *sheitel* when I come to Hoboken?"

"No, you can wear whatever you want in Hoboken."

"What are you saying?"

"I'm saying we need to be able to come to visit you dressed in a way that reflects who we are." I took a deep breath and steadied my nerves to deliver the toughest line. "Otherwise, we will have to totally stop coming to visit." I risked everything because continuing with the status quo was not an option.

"You want to come to my house without wearing a yarmulke?"

"No, I'm willing to wear a yarmulke, but I'm not willing to wear a *kapota* and black hat. And Jenny . . ."

"Jenny wants to come wearing a miniskirt?"

"Jenny doesn't even own a miniskirt, but she can't stand covering her hair and wearing long-sleeve shirts in the summer."

"Well, that's what all the women in this community do. They manage."

"Yes, but she isn't a part of this community."

"But she's a part of this family."

"Exactly. This family—not this community. She never accepted Lubavitch standards of dress, and she never will. Nor should she be forced to just to visit her husband's family."

I didn't "fly off the handle," as my mother often admonished me against doing when I was a kid. I didn't raise my voice once, unusual for me during these kinds of conversations. My mother listened to everything I said. She was also more in control of her emotions than on previous occasions. It seemed as if we had both gotten better at this. Then she announced: "I need to think about all this." This was a good sign.

A few days later my mother called to say that she would put aside the dress restrictions, on a provisional basis. "We'll see how it goes. Obviously, remember to be respectful." I was overjoyed. Our relationship wasn't the *vase* but the *living plant* in the vase, capable of growth and adaptation in response to changing conditions.

The removal of the dress restrictions allowed us to visit Crown Heights with a full heart. Liba and Maya loved visiting Bubby and Zaidy (as they call my parents), the "*tantas*" (their five aunts), and all their uncles and cousins.

We decided to send our children to the local public school and provide them with a Jewish education at home. We teach them how to read and write Hebrew and how to celebrate Jewish holidays. We teach them to read the Bible in Hebrew and translate it into English. For her seventh birthday party, Liba held a *siyyum*—a celebration on the completion of learning the entire book of Genesis. Maya followed in Liba's footsteps and also made a *siyyum* on her seventh birthday.

We are teaching them to love Judaism but to do so undogmatically and to savor the "pretend," to accept the mystical and miraculous as stories, and to know that this is a religion developed by human beings with all their inherent flaws.

When our daughters were toddlers, Jenny wrote them her own children's books in rhyming couplets about each holiday, packed with information and critical analysis. Her Chanukah book doesn't mention the miracle of the oil lasting eight days, a story that originated hundreds of years after the historical events celebrated on Chanukah. Instead, it makes subtle reference to the Second Book of Maccabees and to Josephus's interpretation of the holiday as a celebration of the renewal of Jewish customs in the face of Greek repression. In her Purim book, just as the terrible news arrives of Haman's plan to destroy the Jews, the narrative is interrupted:

Now hold on just a minute, kids,
This story is pretend.
So don't be scared and just relax,
And listen to the end.

Still, her books are infused with Yiddishisms, Hebrew, and celebration. Her Rosh Hashanah book concludes:

Gut yuntif and gut yor! That's what we say in Yiddish.
Shannah tovah u'metukah! We say in Hebrew after kiddush!
The shofar blasts are loud and clear: We hope you have a sweet new year!

By the age of five or six, our children had learned to chant the Friday night kiddush and took turns doing so in our home. They read the Hebrew words from their prayer books with meticulous accuracy, but they know to make one change. Toward the end of the prayer, instead of saying that God chose us "mikol ha-amim [from among all the nations]," we say that God chose us "im kol ha-amim [along with all the other nations]."

It's a change that many progressive Jews make. The textual deviation is subtle and only takes a second; the untrained ear would certainly miss it. But we, as a family, reject the exclusivist doctrine of Jewish chosenness and affirm the brotherhood and sisterhood of all humanity. We explained the change to the children.

"See, if we say *mikol ha-amim*, it means we're more special than other religions," Jenny explained.

"Oh! That's not right!" six-year-old Liba replied.

"But," Jenny continued, "if we say *im kol ha-amim*, it means we're all special in our own way."

"Oh, good. We should say that," Liba affirmed.

We tried from the beginning to imbue the girls with our love of books. We read to them every night and, in addition to our apartment decor of wall-to-wall bookcases, we placed a large white bookcase full of children's books in their bedroom.

I don't know whether it's our encouragement or simple genetics, but they appear to be the little bibliophiles we both hoped they would be. By first grade, Liba was reading through chapter books voraciously, from Beverly Cleary and Judy Blume to the brand-new authors we discover in the public library. In preschool, Maya loved to pretend she could read just as well, pointing with her finger at the words she couldn't quite decipher yet while loudly and proudly making up stories that related to the pictures on the page.

Liba and Maya often get entangled in heated debates around the pressing questions in the life of children. Is blood gross or not? How *exactly* should the Hebrew letter *chet* be written? Where do people go when they die? Should we or should we not eat our boogers?

One night at bedtime, as one such argument wound down—at least for the moment—they put on their matching purple-with-white-polka dots footy pajamas and made themselves comfortable on my lap. My voice was tired from teaching all day, so Liba agreed to read out loud to Maya the Dr. Seuss book *I Can Read with My Eyes Shut!*

My eyes welled up, and I let the tears roll down my face.

Liba asked, "Why are you crying?"

I told her, "I'm so proud that you can read this book at age six when I couldn't read it until I was sixteen."

I didn't tell her, I couldn't, that she is growing up in an intellectually and socially freer environment than I could ever have imagined as a child and that her life would offer her countless opportunities to read, think, and experience the world in ways I can't even imagine today. I remembered the words by Kahlil Gibran that I had quoted to my mother, now at last resonant for me as a parent:

You may give them your love but not your thoughts
For they have their own thoughts.
You may house their bodies but not their souls
For their souls dwell in the house of tomorrow,
which you cannot visit, not even in your dreams.

I don't plan to dictate the kind of lifestyle my daughters should live or the kind of Judaism they should practice once they're adults. Nor do I imagine that I have the power to do so. I can only hope that they make their choices thoughtfully. And I hope that their own upbringing becomes a cherished part of their future lives.

I collect keepsakes. They remind me of my travels and my connection to the places I've been. From my Passover in Syzran I've saved a Matryoshka, a Russian nesting doll set decorated with portraits of the heads of state from Lenin to Yeltsin. From my year in yeshiva in Buenos Aires I've saved a crisp two-peso bill with a picture of Bartolomé Mitre, the fifth president of Argentina. From my summer in Beijing I've saved a glass globe that has a miniature painting on the inside depicting the Great Wall of China. From my summer in Ghana I've saved a hand-carved wooden elephant figurine. From my eight-year journey at NYU I have a doctoral diploma and a hard-bound copy of my dissertation. Not surprisingly, I've also saved some objects from Crown Heights. I have a stack of Rebbe dollars and a *Tanya* with a turquoise cover that the Rebbe placed in my hands.

I think about the mornings in yeshiva, barely awake, grappling with a Hasidic text, trying to comprehend the nature of God. I think about how I cried while singing and listening to Hasidic *nigunim* on Shabbos afternoons. I think about nights spent together with classmates at *farbrengens* in yeshiva, talking and thinking about how to improve and elevate our souls. I return to those memories all the time. They're part of me. I do not wish to part with them, nor could I.

When I was in yeshiva, I felt totally comfortable with my place in the world. Once I started leaving Lubavitch, I began to feel profoundly uncomfortable, as if I didn't belong anywhere, as if I was taking up space that someone, somewhere else, could put to better use. When I was in Lubavitch and still believed that I was a foot soldier of the Rebbe marching toward the messianic Redemption, it was obvious what my orders were, and the fact that I had orders meant there was a reason for my existence.

I envy the Lubavitchers their belief in God and the Rebbe. Believing in a higher power and an avenue for divine blessings helps them get through the difficult patches in life. I wish I still believed in God. When I couldn't find a job and we needed money to pay our rent and keep food on the table, it would have been helpful if I believed that God would see to it all working out. When Jenny was about to undergo the caesarian section that brought Maya into the world, it would have been helpful, as I stood trembling behind her, to have a God to pray to and lean on. When Jenny's father died suddenly in February 2018, it would have helped if I believed in God and the next world and the promise of resurrection of the dead. But I can't will myself to believe any more than I can will myself to fly.

Instead of all that, I have the freedom to think any thought, read any book, listen to any piece of music, wear any clothes, watch any film, visit any temple or shrine, and befriend and break bread with anyone from any walk of life. It is a freedom I cherish and cannot live without.

I think about my friends from yeshiva and the many ways our lives intersected. I think about Alter occasionally. Recently I looked at my wedding album and spotted a photo of Alter dancing enthusiastically at my wedding. I'm reminded of how grateful I felt that Alter traveled across the country to celebrate my special day with me. Although I haven't spoken to him in years, I still feel affection for him.

I hope he is happy as a colonel in the Rebbe's army in the Midwest raising six children while bringing the Lubavitch message to unaffiliated Jews. I wonder if he ever thinks about me and the many adventures we shared. Is Alter ashamed of his association with me? Does he regret having me act as one of the ceremonial witnesses at his wedding? Does he feel betrayed by my decision to leave Lubavitch? Is it possible for a

Lubavitch rabbi who spends his days persuading others to be more religiously observant to see me as anything other than a disappointment, a failure of some kind?

On October 19, 2022, I attended the Crown Heights bris of my nephew, the second child of my younger sister Esty. The ornamental Chair of Elijah, where the newborn will be placed during the circumcision, was stationed against the wall. Esty was gently rocking the newborn to prepare him for the ritual that would formally usher him into the covenant between the Jewish people and God.

All my sisters are exemplars of Lubavitch womanhood. Esty, like my other sisters, is on her way to creating her own Lubavitch family: Miriam is a mother of eight, and Chana Sara is a mother of five. My mother, in a fancy black dress with blue and silver embroidery, sees me and comes over to chat. My mother's walk is a little more deliberate and cautious than in the past. My own head of brown hair is laced with more gray strands than I care to acknowledge.

We hug and schmooze in the loving and comfortable way we did before I shaved my beard. Over the past several years we have settled into a harmonious relationship. Neither of us is as headstrong as we were when we squared off in heated religious arguments during my college years. We each know that the other one will not change their position. Of course, I wish my mother would come out and say that she accepts me for who I am, but I realize she will probably never do that. Still, this tacit acceptance is a great blessing.

The mohel, his *tallis* efficiently tucked into the *gartl* at his waist, walks into the room carrying his black leather case containing his surgical instruments. The bris is about to begin, so my mother walks to the adjoining room where the women have gathered. Now my brother Yossi and I are standing next to each other off to the side of the crowd of Lubavitch men who encircle the Chair of Elijah.

Yossi comments to me on a recent *New York Times* article reporting on the lack of secular education in Hasidic Brooklyn yeshivas, an issue in which he is deeply involved. "Maybe this publicity will shame the yeshivas into teaching some English!" Yossi and I are the only men at the bris with trimmed beards and no Lubavitch black hats. We are both outsiders to this scene, but we love our family and are deeply connected to them. The two of us are still close. We are both finding our way in the world outside Lubavitch and still comparing notes of our discoveries.

My new nephew is not only being brought into the Jewish covenant with God. Little Chaim Aharon is also being led into the ranks of the Lubavitch faithful. Another chapter of the Lubavitch saga has just begun. Another foot soldier in the Rebbe's army has just reported for duty. For my part, my heart is full of love for Chaim Aharon and all my Lubavitch relatives. I don't care in which ranks they choose to live their lives. I just hope that they all feel free to choose a life that is true to who they are.

Acknowledgments

Huckleberry Finn ends the tale of his adventures by observing, "If I'd a knowed what a trouble it was to make a book I wouldn't a tackled it." I must confess that these are not my sentiments. Although I struggled to produce this memoir for more than nine years, and although it went through many drafts, and at times I feared it might never see the light of day, it was a labor of love that I relished. But one doesn't go through such a protracted process without accruing tremendous debts of gratitude.

My first debt is to Rochelle Jewel Shapiro, my most valuable formal writing instructor. Her six-week online course at the University of California, Los Angeles, in the fall of 2016 gave me the opportunity to sketch out initial stories that became the skeletal frame of this memoir. I got to know this gentle soul, the mother of a close Hoboken friend, over the years, and she always advised me to "write where the blood is," to write about things that moved me, even if it scared me to do so.

Stacy Tores, whom I befriended in graduate school and is herself a gifted writer, provided years of emotional support and encouragement. She also read several of my early chapters and provided valuable feedback.

Amy Hong came into my life much later in my writing process but was also pivotal. For a time she served as my writing buddy, and we would check in with each other every few months to ensure that we were both making progress on our projects. She also read part of Chapter 3 and supported me as I figured out how to say the difficult things I needed to express.

In addition, I was lucky to have so many kind and generous readers. Alex Star read two drafts of my book and encouraged me to go beyond simply telling stories about my life. He encouraged me to share my reflections throughout the work, including my scholarly thoughts.

Mira Sucharov read an entire draft of my book and helped ensure the text was consistent and logical throughout. Tom Goff also gave extensive editorial guidance on an entire draft and encouraged me to describe the history of my travel destinations. Goldie Goldbloom provided generous feedback on the entire manuscript and inspired me to interrogate and share my feelings regarding painful experiences in my narrative.

The following friends and family read either chapters or the entire manuscript and provided thoughtful feedback and much needed encouragement: Alana Alpert, Sharon Avni, Lucia Edwards, Daniel Iv, Jeff Janus, Kathryn Janus, Ilana Kurshan, David Lehmann, Chaim Levine, Molly Makris, David Plotka, Eshbal Ratson, Sarah Redmond, Rachel Safman, Ken Schept, Naomi Seidman, Karen Seigel, Laura Seigel, and Lynda Tortorello.

I must mention Steven Lukes, who was a huge supporter of this project and urged me to finish the memoir and share it with the world.

Throughout the writing process I was obsessed with accuracy and gained much from consulting the following experts: Loren Berman, Benjamin Bryce, Vivek Chibber, Nathanial Deutsch, Gennady Estraikh, Ethel Fisher, Stephen Greenblatt, Marilyn Labendz, Kate Lingley, Mike Macarthy, Amaka Okechukwu, Glen Pine, Ronald Rothenberg, and Ly Hoang Minh Uyen. Of course, any errors of fact or interpretation are mine alone.

I am tremendously grateful to Sefaria.org and HebrewBooks.org for providing the public with access to a treasure trove of Jewish texts at no charge. While working on my memoir I used these websites to locate passages in the Talmud, the midrash, the Zohar, and Maimonides, as well as Hasidic sources.

I am also very grateful to Temple University Press, especially my editor, Ryan Mulligan, for his professionalism and dedication to this book, and to Susan Deeks for a masterful job copyediting the manuscript.

I thank David and Ethan Glaubiger for their astute legal advice. I also thank the Footsteps organization, which contributed funds to cover the costs of a professional editor for the manuscript, and Joshua Rosenthal, who helped defray the publishing costs.

Writing a memoir can be a very lonely experience. Fortunately, I am blessed with an extremely warm and loving family who anchored me throughout this process. Special thanks go to my father, Dr. Shlomo Newfield, for carefully reviewing an early draft of the manuscript, and to my brother Rabbi Yossi Newfield for graciously assisting me with locating numerous Lubavitch and other rabbinic sources.

I thank my daughters, Liba and Maya, for their keen interest in the progress of my memoir and for blessing our family with joy and light. And last, but surely not least, I thank my dear wife, Dr. Jenny Labendz. Her love and acceptance mean the world to me. I am deeply grateful to have her not only as my life partner but also as an intellectual companion, and I cherish our discussions. Her generous feedback on this work has made it immeasurably stronger, clearer, and more beautiful.

Notes on Sources

Introduction

For a comprehensive and thoughtful introduction to the Rebbe's biography, teachings, and public activities, see Ezra Glinter, *Menachem Mendel Schneerson: Becoming the Messiah* (Yale University Press, 2024).

For an analysis of how Lubavitch reconciled its messianic aspirations with the death of the Rebbe, see Yoram Bilu, *With Us More than Ever: Making the Absent Rebbe Present in Messianic Chabad* (Stanford University Press, 2020); Simon Dein, *Lubavitcher Messianism: What Really Happens When Prophecy Fails?* (Continuum, 2011).

For the Rebbe's discussion of the Talmud's mention that the name of the messiah is Menachem, "We have Menachem, which refers to the righteous Messiah," see *Torat Menachem: Hisvaduyos 5749* [The Torah of Menachem: Gatherings 5749] (Vaad Hanochos Hatmimim, 1989), p. 95.

Chapter 1

For the Lubavitcher Rebbe on the dangers of television, including his quote about "bringing inside the home the church," see M. M. Schneerson, *Likkutei Sichos*, vol. 18 (Kehot Publication Society, [1982] 2006), p. 460.

I was shocked to discover recently that the "Chinese" script on the stained-glass windows of 770 is not genuine Chinese but, in fact, chinoiserie, a Western imitation of the form. For more on chinoiserie, see Dawn Jacobson, *Chinoiserie* (Phaidon, 2001).

For the source of the Baal Shem Tov's vision of the messiah and his pronouncement that he will come once "the wellsprings of Hasidic thought" are spread around the world, see A. Kahane, *The Book of Hasidism*, 2d ed. (in Hebrew) (Warsaw, 1922), pp. 76–77.

For the quote "We can no longer ignore that voice within women," see Betty Friedan, *The Feminine Mystique* (Laurel, 1983), p. 32.

On race relations in Brooklyn, see Nathaniel Deutsch and Michael Casper, *A Fortress in Brooklyn: Race, Real Estate, and the Making of Hasidic Williamsburg* (Yale University Press, 2022); Brian Purnell, *Fighting Jim Crow in the County of Kings: The Congress of Racial Equality in Brooklyn* (University Press of Kentucky, 2013).

On Jewish and Black civil patrols in Crown Heights, see Amaka Okechukwu, "Watching and Seeing: Recovering Abolitionist Possibilities in Black Community Practices of Safety and Security," *Du Bois Review* 18, no. 1 (2021): pp. 153–180; Matthew Shaer, *Among Righteous Men: A Tale of Vigilantes and Vindication in Hasidic Crown Heights* (Wiley, 2011).

On the Rebbe's encouragement to Shrage to continue with the Maccabee patrols, see M. Seligson, "Rabbi Samuel Schrage: The Maccabee," *Crown Heights News*, December 18, 2010, https://crownheights.info/crown-heights-news/30851/rabbi-samuel-schrage-the-maccabee.

For the Rebbe's discussion of why it is against Jewish law to sell homes in Crown Heights to non-Jews, see *Toras Menachem*, vol. 56 (Kehot Publication Society, 2015), pp. 132–145.

For the Rebbe's discussion of buying shares in Chevra, see *Sichos Kodesh*, Shabbos Chanuka, 1971, vol. 1, pp. 360–362.

For an extensive list of Jewish surnames based on Yiddish words for particular lines of work and a discussion of Jewish occupations in Eastern Europe before the Holocaust, see Jeffrey Shandler, *Yiddish: Biography of a Language* (Oxford University Press, 2020), chap. 11.

Chapter 2

For reflections on the life of Rabbi Moshe Leib Rudshtein, including his attempts to make the Rebbe laugh, see *A Chassidisher Derher*, no. 105 (182), Iyar 5781/June 2021, pp. 42–51.

For a discussion of ancient Jewish and kabbalist sources that describe divinized humans in a way that parallels contemporary Lubavitch messianic claims about the Rebbe, see Shaul Magid, *Piety and Rebellion: Essays in Hasidism* (Academic Studies Press, 2019), chap. 8.

To view a clip of the anarchic and painful moments of the Rebbe's funeral procession in front of 770, see Rabino Shalom Ber Solomon, "Funeral of the Rebbe of Lubavitch 3 Tamuz 1994," video, YouTube, June 13, 2021, https://youtu.be/CuxAaM0EdP0.

Chapter 3

For an analysis of the development of the ritual of *tefillin* in the context of ancient Greco-Roman magical amulets, see Yehudah Cohn, *Tangled Up in Text: Tefillin and the Ancient World* (Brown Judaic Studies, 2008).

For a discussion of Larry Weeks's possession and reluctant sale shortly before his death of Houdini's film *The Grim Game*, see Joe Posnanski, *The Life and Afterlife of Harry Houdini* (Avid Reader Press, 2020).

Chapter 5

To view Rabbi Immanuel Schochet's video challenging Christian claims using the Christian Bible, see UserMB770, "Let the Christian Be a Christian and Let the Jew Be a Jew," video, YouTube, April 28, 2013, https://www.youtube.com/watch?v=EoTJK2DPwwY.

For a popular treatment of Heraclitus's dictum that things are always in flux, see Bertrand Russell, *The History of Western Philosophy* (George Allen and Unwin, 1947), chap. 4.

For the Rebbe's injunction limiting his followers' alcoholic intake to three shots per *farbrengen*, see *Toras Menachem*, vol. 36 (Lahak Hanochos), pp. 351–353.

For Adrienne Rich's quote, "There must be those among whom," see Adrienne Rich, *Collected Poems: 1950–2012* (W. W. Norton, 2016), p. 588.

For the Rebbe Rashab's view of the pleasures of the intellect, see Sholom Dov Ber Schneersohn, *Kuntres Umaayin*, translated by Zalman I. Posner (Kehot Publication Society, 1991), pp. 4–6.

For the Rebbe's distinction between Jewish and non-Jewish learning, see *Sichos Kodesh*, Shabbos Parshas Mikaytz, Shabbos Chanukah 5731, [1971] 1987, pp. 341–369.

For a nuanced discussion of classical rabbinic sources on the wisdom of non-Jews, see Jenny R. Labendz, *Socratic Torah: Non-Jews in Rabbinic Intellectual Culture* (Oxford University Press, 2013), chap. 6.

For the wording of the Rebbe's blessing to the first group of Miami yeshiva students, "May the Almighty bless you to be successful," see Yeshiva Gedolah Rabbinical Collage Miami, https://www.ygmiami.com.

For the Lubavitch maxim "A Jew neither wants nor is capable of being separated from Godliness," see M. M. Schneerson, *Hayom Yom* (Kehot Publication Society, [1943] 1990), p. 119.

For Maimonides's use of the legal concept of "captive child" to the children of Karaites, see *Mishneh Torah*, Hilchot Mamrim, chap. 3, sec. 3. For a discussion of the "captive child" concept in contemporary Lubavitch thought, see N. D. Dubov, *To Love a Fellow Jew: The Mitzvah of Ahavas Yisrael in Chasidic Thought* (Sichos in English, 1999), pp. 77–100.

For the Rebbe's statement comparing the spiritual risks involved in contemporary Jewish outreach with those faced by ancient priests in the Temple who prepared the ritual ashes of a red heifer, see M. M. Schneerson, *Likkutei Sichos*, vol. 4 (Kehot Publication Society, [1964] 2006), pp. 1056–1061.

For the Rebbe's views on how to reconcile ancient fossils with belief in a young Earth, see M. M. Schneerson, "Theories of Evolution," Chabad.org, 1961, https://www.chabad.org/article.asp?aid=60946. For Philip Henry Gosse's views on this subject, see *Omphalos: An Attempt to Untie the Geological Knot* (John Van Voorst, 1857).

For the Rebbe's statement "Every Jew could perform miracles if he connects his soul to God," see M. M. Schneerson, "The Rebbe Speaks to Hillel Students," Chabad.org, March 7, 1960, https://www.chabad.org/therebbe/article_cdo/aid/392177/jewish/The-Rebbe-Speaks-to-Hillel-Students.htm.

The argument made by Ben, the Jews for Jesus devotee, that the downfall of humanity was caused by a virgin, a tree, and a death and that so, too, was its redemption, is found in the writings of John Chrysostom, *De coemeterio et de cruce*, in *Patrologiae cursus completus, series graeca*, vol. 49 (Jacques-Paul Migne, 1862), pp. 393–398; David M. Friel, "Chrysostom's Homily on the Word Koimeterion and on the Cross: A Translation and Commentary," *Vigiliae Christianae: A Review of Early Christian Life and Languages* 76, no. 1 (2022): pp. 1–36.

Chapter 6

For an extensive catalogue of the Rebbe's statements opposing the teaching of secular studies to Lubavitch children, see M. M. Schneerson, "Purity of the Mind: Educating Children Only with Torah," *A Chassidisher Derher* 97, no. 174, Elul 5780 [2019], pp. 38–49, https://derher.org/wp-content/uploads/2020/10/97-elul-5780-8.pdf.

For Petrarch's thoughts about the love of books, "Books give delight to the very marrow of one's bones," see *Epistolae familiares*, iii, 18, quoted in Stephen Greenblatt, *The Swerve* (W. W. Norton, 2011), p. 119.

Chapter 7

For a discussion of the Russian Jewish population in the year 2002, see David Singer and Lawrence Grossman, eds., "World Jewish Population, 2002," *American Jewish Year Book 2002*, vol. 102 (American Jewish Committee, 2003), pp. 601–642.

For a discussion of the immigration of Russian Jews to America in the early twentieth century, see Hasia R. Diner, *A New Promised Land: A History of Jews in America* (Oxford University Press, 2002).

For a discussion of the number of Jews in the Russian army during World War I and the impact this participation had on them, see Yohanan Petrovsky-Shtern, *Jews in the Russian Army, 1827–1917: Drafted into Modernity* (Cambridge University Press, 2009).

For the Talmud's description of Rabbi Shimon Bar Yochai and his son Elazar scorching farmland with their eyes, see Shabbat 33b.

For a detailed analysis of how contemporary Lubavitch rabbis in Russia balance their religious beliefs with a Russian national sense of mission, including support for Vladimir Putin's invasion of Ukraine in February 2022, see Galina Zelenina, "Serving the Jews, Serving the Empire: Discursive Hierarchy and Messianic Temporality in Russian Chabad," in *New Trends in the Study of Haredi Culture and Society*, edited by David N. Myers and Nechumi Malovicki-Yaffe (Purdue University Press, 2024), pp. 29–57. For a discussion of the complex relationship between Putin and Russian Jews, and especially with Rabbi Berel Lazar, see Konstanty Gebert, "Putin's Jews," *Moment*, November–December 2015.

Chapter 8

For a history of Jews in Moisés Ville and other agricultural colonies in Argentina and the complex relationship with their non-Jewish neighbors, see Javier Sinay, *The Murders of Moisés Ville: The Rise and Fall of the Jerusalem of South America* (Restless Books, 2022).

On the reception of psychoanalysis in Argentina, see Mariano Ben Plotkin, *Freud in the Pampas* (Stanford University Press, 2002).

For a discussion of the books Mendoza took to South America, see Alberto Manguel, *Packing My Library: An Elegy in Ten Digressions* (Yale University Press, 2018), pp. 122–123. For a broader analysis of the impact that books had on Spanish American colonial culture, see Irving A. Leonard, *Books of the Brave: Being an Account of Books and of Men in the Spanish Conquest and Settlement of the Sixteenth-Century New World* (University of California Press, 1992).

Chapter 9

For an extensive analysis of the Jews in China, including those in Kaifeng, see Jonathan Goldstein, ed., *The Jews of China: Historical and Comparative Perspectives*, vol. 1 (Routledge, 1998).

For an analysis of the role of Christianity in China, including the many missionary efforts, see Daniel H. Bays, *A New History of Christianity in China* (Wiley-Blackwell, 2011).

For a discussion of the causes of the Boxer Rebellion, including the role that resentment against Christian missionaries in China played, see Joseph W. Esherick, *The Origins of the Boxer Uprising* (University of California Press, 1987).

For an analysis of capitalist elements within China's contemporary economy, particularly capitalist industrialization and workers' resistance to it, see Eli Friedman, *Insurgency Trap: Labor Politics in Postsocialist China* (ILR Press, 2014).

Chapter 10

For a discussion of the history of Jews in Singapore in the context of Jews in other parts of Asia, see Jonathan Goldstein, *Jewish Identities in East and Southeast Asia* (De Gruyter Oldenbourg, 2015), chap. 1.

Chapter 11

For the Zohar's statement that "God looked into the Torah and created the world," see Volume 2 (Shemot), Parshah Trauma, p. 161b.

For a fascinating wide-ranging scholarly exploration of the Jewish taboo against pig, see Jordan Rosenblum, *Forbidden: A 3,000-Year History of Jews and the Pig* (New York University Press, 2024).

For a mention of Wilhelm Rothschild's strange pork-related handshake prohibition, see Frederic Morton, *The Rothschilds: A Family Portrait* (Diversion Books, 2014), p. 217.

To view Bugiardini's painting, see Giuliano di Piero di Simone Bugiardini, *Madonna and Child Enthroned with Saints Mary Magdalene and John the Baptist*, ca. 1523, Metropolitan Museum of Art, New York, http://www.metmuseum.org/art/collection/search/435824.

For a discussion of Maimon's struggles to fully integrate into the broader society, see Solomon Maimon, *The Autobiography of Solomon Maimon: The Complete Translation*, edited by Yitzhak Y. Melamed and Abraham Socher (Princeton University Press, 2020).

For Yerushalmi's thoughts on Freud and the criticism of psychoanalysis as a "Jewish science," see Yosef Hayim Yerushalmi, *Freud's Moses: Judaism Terminable and Interminable* (Yale University Press, 1991).

For Rashi's statement quoting the Sifre that Esau hates Jacob, see Rashi's commentary on Genesis 33:4. It should be noted that Professor Menachem Kahana, a prominent rabbinics scholar, argues that the most accurate texts of the Sifre do not have the phrase "it is a law" with regard to Esau hates Jacob: see Menachem Kahana, *Sifre on Numbers: An Annotated Edition*, vol. 4 (Magnes, 2011), p. 474, n. 96. For a discussion of how various rabbinic authorities have interpreted the concept of Esau hates Jacob, including how Rabbi Moshe Feinstein used this concept in a ruling of his in the early 1970s, see Marty Lockshin, "'Esau Hates Jacob'—But Is Antisemitism a Halakha?" TheTorah.com, 2016, https://thetorah.com/article/esau-hates-jacob-but-is-antisemitism-a-halakha.

Chapter 12

For a discussion of the history and wide application among progressive Jews of the concept of *tikkun olam*, see Or Rose, Jo Ellen Green Kaiser, and Margie Klein, eds., *Righteous Indignation: A Jewish Call for Justice* (Jewish Lights Publishing, 2008).

For a discussion of Nkrumah and Pan-Africanism, see Jeffrey S. Ahlman, *Living with Nkrumahism: Nation, State, and Pan-Africanism in Ghana* (Ohio University Press, 2017).

For Nkrumah's quote about the need for total liberation of Africa, "The independence of Ghana is meaningless," see Eric Quaidoo, "The United States and the Overthrow of Kwame Nkrumah," master's thesis, Fort Hays State University, Hays, KS, 2010, p. 72.

For a discussion of American and British government dissatisfaction with Nkrumah and desire to see him replaced, see ibid.

For Nkrumah's statements accusing the "imperialist and neo-colonialists" of supporting his ouster from office, see ibid., pp. 71–74. For evidence of U.S. Central Intelligence Agency involvement with the coup against Nkrumah, see John Stockwell, *In Search of Enemies: A CIA Story* (W. W. Norton, 1978), p. 201, footnote.

Chapter 13

For the Gibran quote "Your children are not your children," see Kahlil Gibran, *The Prophet* (Alfred A. Knopf, [1923] 2008), p. 17.

For an extensive discussion of the Jewish legal requirement for men to maintain a full beard and for its mystical significance and association with divine blessings, see Moshe Nisan Wiener, *Hadras Ponim-Zokon* (in Hebrew) (self-published, 2006). For a discussion of the position of the Tzemach Tzedek on beards, see Moshe Nisan Wiener, *The Beard: Where Chassidim and Misnagdim Agree* (self-published, 2020).

For an extensive discussion of Epicurus's ideas and how they have been misrepresented for centuries, see Stephen Greenblatt, *The Swerve: How the World Became Modern* (W. W. Norton, 2012).

For Rabbi Mordecai Kaplan's thoughts on the role of the Jewish past in determining current Jewish practice, that the past "should have the right to a vote," see Mordecai Kaplan, *Judaism without Supernaturalism: The Only Alternative to Orthodoxy and Secularism* (Reconstructionist Press, 1958), pp. 28–29.

Chapter 14

For the Zohar's attitude toward the wasting of seed, see Vayeshev, p. 188a. For an extensive discussion of the sin of wasting seed in Jewish law and kabbalah, see David M. Feldman, *Birth Control in Jewish Law: Marital Relations, Contraception, and Abortion as Set Forth in the Classic Texts of Jewish Law* (Jason Aronson, 1998).

For the Jewish legal prohibition of a *kohen* marrying a "promiscuous women," see Maimonides, Mishneh Torah, Sefer Kedushah, Issurei Biah, chap. 18.

Chapter 15

For a fuller account of the exchange between Ben-Gurion and the Chazon Ish in 1952, see U. Regev, "The Famous Meeting Between Ben Gurion and the Hazon Ish," *Hiddush*, July 5, 2020, https://hiddush.org/article-23402-0-The_famous_meeting_between_Ben_Gurion_and_the_Hazon_Ish.aspx#footnotes.

Chapter 16

For the Chinese novelist Yu Hua's changing attitudes toward the stories of Lu Xun, see Yu Hua, *China in Ten Words* (Anchor, 2012).

The attribution of the "diminishing our joy in the face of our enemies suffering" explanation of the drops of wine at the seder to Don Isaac Abarbanel is without any foundation. This explanation appears to be a much more recent invention, possibly from the nineteenth century. For a history of the appearance and attribution of this interpretation of the custom, see Zvi Ron, "'Our Own Joy Is Lessened and Incomplete': The History of an Interpretation of Sixteen Drops of Wine at the Seder," *Hakirah, the Flatbush Journal of Jewish Law and Thought* 19 (2015): pp. 237–255.

For Durkheim's thoughts on religious rituals, including the quote that begins "What essential difference is there between an assembly of Christians," see Émile Durkheim, *The Elementary Forms of the Religious Life*, translated by Joseph Ward Swain (Free Press, 1965), pp. 474–475.

For a discussion of the development and evolution of liberation theology, see Christian Smith, *The Emergence of Liberation Theology: Radical Religion and Social Movement Theory* (University of Chicago Press, 1991); David Tombs, *Latin American Liberation Theology* (Brill, 2003).

For Mead's thoughts on the self, see George Herbert Mead, *Mind, Self, and Society*, edited by Charles W. Morris (University of Chicago Press, 2015), part 3.

For the Faulkner quote "The past is never dead," see William Faulkner, *Requiem for a Nun* (Vintage, [1950] 2011), p. 73.

For Josephus's explanation of why the holiday of Chanukah is called the "festival of lights" without any mention of the miracle of candles lasting eight days, see

Josephus, *Jewish Antiquities, Books 12–13,* translated by Ralph Marcus, Loeb Classical Library 365 (Harvard University Press, [1943] 1998), pp. 167–169.

For Jenny's verses for the holiday of Purim, "Now hold on just a minute, kids," see Jenny R. Labendz, "Purim Rhyme," unpublished ms., 2015, in my possession.

For Jenny's verses for the High Holidays, "*Gut yuntif and gut yor!* That's what we say in Yiddish," see Jenny R. Labendz, "The Rhyming Rosh Hashana Book," unpublished ms., 2015, in my possession.

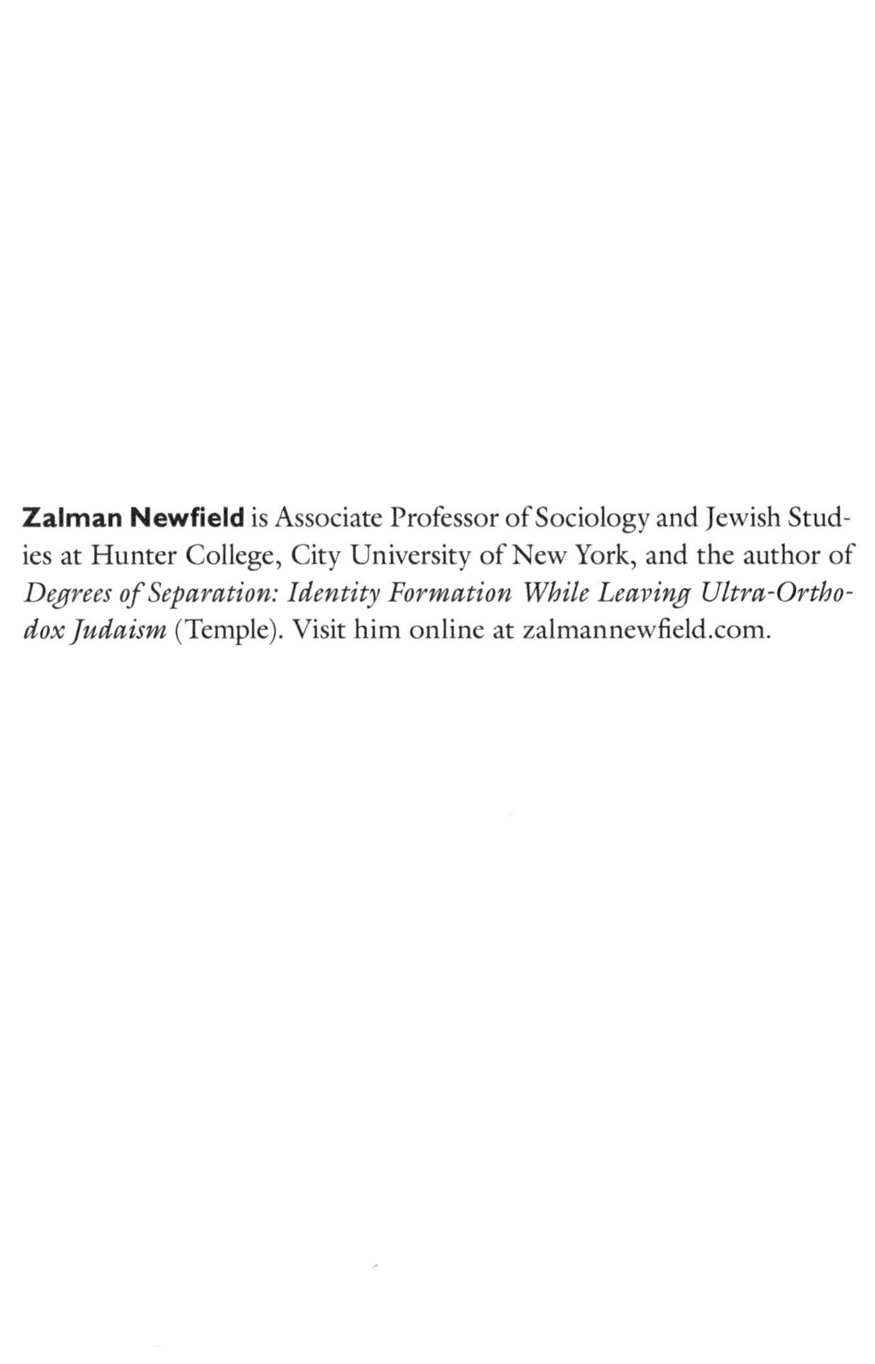

Zalman Newfield is Associate Professor of Sociology and Jewish Studies at Hunter College, City University of New York, and the author of *Degrees of Separation: Identity Formation While Leaving Ultra-Orthodox Judaism* (Temple). Visit him online at zalmannewfield.com.